Oz and the Musical

Oz and the Musical

Performing the American Fairy Tale

RYAN BUNCH

Oxford University Press is a department of the University of Oxford. It furthers
the University's objective of excellence in research, scholarship, and education
by publishing worldwide. Oxford is a registered trade mark of Oxford University
Press in the UK and certain other countries.

Published in the United States of America by Oxford University Press
198 Madison Avenue, New York, NY 10016, United States of America.

Library of Congress Cataloging-in-Publication Data
Names: Bunch, Ryan, author.
Title: Oz and the musical : performing the American fairy tale / Ryan Bunch.
Description: [1.] | New York, NY : Oxford University Press, 2023. |
Includes bibliographical references and index.
Identifiers: LCCN 2022027420 (print) | LCCN 2022027421 (ebook) |
ISBN 9780190843137 (hardback) | ISBN 9780190843144 (paperback) |
ISBN 9780190843168 (epub) | ISBN 9780190843151 | ISBN 9780190843182 |
ISBN 9780190843175
Subjects: LCSH: Musicals—United States—History and criticism. |
Musicals—Social aspects—United States. | Musicals—Political aspects—United States. |
Wizard of Oz (Motion picture : 1939) | Wiz (Motion picture) | Tietjens, Paul. Wizard of Oz. |
Schwartz, Stephen. Wicked. | Baum, L. Frank (Lyman Frank), 1856–1919. Wizard of Oz.
Classification: LCC ML2054 .B86 2022 (print) | LCC ML2054 (ebook) |
DDC 782.1/409—dc23/eng/20220705
LC record available at https://lccn.loc.gov/2022027420
LC ebook record available at https://lccn.loc.gov/2022027421

DOI: 10.1093/oso/9780190843137.001.0001

1 3 5 7 9 8 6 4 2

Paperback printed by Sheridan Books, Inc., United States of America
Hardback printed by Bridgeport National Bindery, Inc., United States of America

The publication of this book is supported in part by a grant from
the H. Earle Johnson Fund of the Society for American Music.

For Micah

Contents

Illustrations

Acknowledgments

It took a Munchkin village to help me write this book. I couldn't have done it without colleagues in academia, friends in the Oz fan community, people who agreed to be interviewed, and some innocent bystanders.

I'm forever grateful to my parents, Janet and Thelbert Bunch, for indulging my interests, for allowing me to join the International Wizard of Oz Club, and for traveling across the country to take me to its annual conventions. It was Mama who inadvertently started all of this on a summer day in our local public library when she spied the Oz books on a shelf and suggested I read them.

This book is in many ways an outgrowth of my master's thesis, which I completed twenty years ago as a musicology student at the University of Maryland under the direction of Luke Jensen with Jennifer DeLapp and Carolina Robertson serving on the committee. I'm thankful to them for getting me started.

Portions of this book were developed from two earlier publications: "Oz and the Musical: The American Musical and the Reinvention of the American Fairy Tale," *Studies in Musical Theatre* 9, no. 1 (2015): 53–96, and "Ease on down the Road: Black Routes and the Soul of the Wiz," in *Adapting "The Wizard of Oz": Musical Versions from Baum to MGM and Beyond*, edited by Danielle Birkett and Dominic McHugh (New York: Oxford University Press, 2018). I'm grateful to Intellect and Oxford University Press for allowing me to reuse these materials. I'm thankful also to Danielle Birkett, Dominic McHugh, Jonas Westover, Robert Gordon, and Olaf Jubin for helping me to bring those essays to publication.

Several people helped me with the research and acquisition of materials. Tim Hollis generously shared information, images, and recordings from the Land of Oz park. Sean Barrett, Jane Albright, Chris Robbins, and Cynthia Keller helped me track down additional information about the Land of Oz. Michael Feinstein alerted me to new information about *The Wiz*. Laura Lynn Broadhurst, Atticus Gannaway, and Michael Rosario helped me track down images of Margaret Hamilton/*Hamilton* parodies, and Dave Demoreski allowed me to reproduce his image in the epilogue. David Maxine granted permission to include two tracks from his CD *Vintage Recordings from the 1903 Broadway Musical THE WIZARD OF OZ* for the companion website and provided invaluable insights and updates from his research on *The Wizard of Oz* extravaganza.

I'm grateful for the assistance and expertise of the staff at libraries and archives where I conducted research, including the Billy Rose Theatre Division at the New York Public Library for the Performing Arts (especially Doug Reside), The Schomburg Center for Research in Black Culture, the Margaret Herrick Library of the Academy of Motion Picture Arts and Sciences (especially Louise Hilton), and the Lilly Library at Indiana University.

Friends and anonymous peer reviewers gave generously of their time and attention in commenting on my proposal and manuscript. Kathryn Edney and Raymond Knapp are among those who offered early support and feedback. Jessica Sternfeld, Kendra Preston Leonard, Kelly Kessler, and Kaleb Goldschmitt shared their experiences in book-writing before and during my work on this project. My husband Micah Mahjoubian has been infinitely encouraging and also read portions of the book.

Norman Hirschy is a wonderful wizard and the most patient editor on this side of the rainbow. Rachel Ruisard masterfully guided me through the publication process. Thanks to the design department at Oxford University Press for the wonderful execution of the book's cover. Thanks also to Kavitha Yuvaraj for guiding me through production.

Publication was supported by an AMS 75 PAYS subvention from the American Musicological Society and an H. Earle Johnson Publication Subvention Award from the Society for American Music.

Around the time I began in earnest to write this book, I also began working on a PhD in childhood studies at Rutgers University-Camden. Wisely or not, I chose to keep this project separate from my dissertation. My new friends, mentors, and colleagues have shaped this work. Meredith Bak has taught me much about the material cultures of childhood and how to play in the archive. Daniel Cook gave valuable feedback on an early partial draft of the last chapter during a course on play theory, and Lauren Silver guided me through the process of having my interview design vetted by an institutional review board. Other faculty and graduate students have given me their friendship, mentorship, and moral support in ways too varied to mention.

I'm thankful to have had the opportunity to develop and receive feedback on these materials by presenting them at conferences, including Song,

Stage and Screen, the International Association for the Study of Popular Music, Music and the Moving Image, the Society for American Music, the Children's Literature Association, Oz and the Cultural Imagination, OzCon International, and the Society for Cinema and Media Studies.

Many people shaped my outlook through our conversations or collaborations on Oz, musicals, and related topics. They include, among others, Jane Albright, Alyssa Auriema, Jacky Avilla, Samuel Baltimore, Lynn Beltz, Robin Bernstein, Tyler Bickford, Paula Bishop, Michael Booth, Daniel Blim, Suzanne Bratt, Scott Poulson-Bryant, George Burrows, Kate Capshaw, Renee Camus, Joel Chaston, Alisa Clapp-Itnyre, Elizabeth Craft, Sarah Crotzer, Christopher Culp, Sarah Culpeper, James Deaville, Eric Dienstfrey, David Diket, Jennifer Meyer Donovan, Cary Elza, La Donna Forsgren, Walter Frisch, Claudia Funder, Donatella Galella, Anna Wheeler Gentry, Philip Gentry, Paige Gray, Marah Gubar, Susan Hall, Elissa Harbert, Michael Patrick Hearn, Carrie Hedges, Jessica Hillman-McCord, Ryan Jay, Mary Celeste Kearney, Kenneth Kidd, Garrett Kilgore, Sandra Kilman, Peter Kunze, Paul Laird, Virginia Lamothe, James Leve, Aaron Manela, Matthew Lockitt, Mary Jo Lodge, Dina Massachi, Breanna McDaniel, Laura McDonald, Dee Michel, Gisele Mills, Mitchell Morris, Imani Mosley, Nathan Platte, Heather Reel, Donelle Ruwe, Janene Ryan, Adam Rush, Anne Searcy, Eric Shanower, Judith Sebesta, Robynn Stilwell, Dominic Symonds, Sarah Tomlinson, Tim Tucker, Jacqueline Warwick, Cecilia Watson, Sarah Whitfield, Stacy Wolf, Elizabeth Wollman, Graham Wood, Leanne Wood, Trudi Wright, and Ronald Zank. You're the best friends anybody ever had!

About the Companion Website

www.oup.com/us/OzandtheMusical

Oxford University Press has created a website featuring multimedia examples to accompany Oz and the Musical: Performing the American Fairy Tale. In addition to audio and video clips referenced in the text, the website includes sheet music for several songs. Examples available online are indicated in the text. These materials are available at www.oup.com/us/OzandtheMusical.

Introduction

The Fairy Tale, The Musical, and "America"

I was on a wooded path with some other kids at a church camp one summer when somebody started skipping and singing "We're Off to See the Wizard." Immediately, we all linked arms and joined in, singing and skipping together. Soon, still more kids, pretending to be Winged Monkeys, jumped out of the woods (or so I seem to recall) and started chasing us. Nobody said, "Let's play *The Wizard of Oz*" or explained what part of the story we were in. Everybody knew the script and, with some liberties, could join in as easily as if the whole thing had been rehearsed. Indeed, this performance has been, and continues to be, rehearsed as part of a shared American repertoire. The source was L. Frank Baum's book *The Wonderful Wizard of Oz* (1900), widely regarded as "the American fairy tale," but it was the MGM film adaptation of 1939—a musical—whose conventions made it possible for us to burst into song and dance in the ready repetition of a familiar story.[1]

There's a special relationship between Oz and musicals. Like many kids in the United States, I first encountered Oz not through Baum's books (he wrote fourteen before other authors continued the series), but in the MGM film musical, which was broadcast annually on network television. After discovering and devouring the Oz books one summer, I found out about the International Wizard of Oz Club, and by the time I was eleven, my parents were taking me to Oz conventions. Through the Oz Club, its journal *The Baum Bugle*, and a growing collection of nonfiction books about Oz, I learned that there was a highly successful stage musical based on *The Wizard of Oz*, in which Baum himself was involved, that was presented shortly after the publication of the book. In my teens, I became enamored of the songs in the film version of *The Wiz*, the classic Black musical retelling of the American fairy tale. After all this, I shouldn't have been surprised, years later, by the success of Broadway's *Wicked*, which has been running since 2003 and is an iconic twenty-first-century American musical.

Oz and the Musical. Ryan Bunch, Oxford University Press. © Oxford University Press 2023.
DOI: 10.1093/oso/9780190843137.003.0001

These stage and screen Oz musicals have surpassed the books in familiarity to US audiences. Many Americans' first experience of Oz is likely to be as a musical, and many people's primary experience of a musical might well be a version of *The Wizard of Oz*. The MGM film is so ingrained in the national consciousness that people may not even think of it as a musical, even as their participation in its mythology depends on the genre's conventions when they sing the songs, quote the lines, and break into the familiar choreography, as we did on that wooded path at camp. References to the relationship between Oz and musicals are easily come by in American culture. In Disney's *Oz The Great and Powerful* (2013, not a musical, and, notably, not one of the most successful Oz adaptations), the Wizard, arriving in Oz for the first time, asks if the Munchkins are able to fight. He's disappointed to learn that their primary talents are making beautiful clothing and singing. They promptly break into song to the Wizard's discomfort and Glinda's delight, reflecting gender stereotypes about those who love musicals and those who don't. As a teen Oz collector, I had a satirical t-shirt depicting a "Wanted" poster for Dorothy. The description: "Witch killer, Munchkin hater, sings at the drop of a hat."[2]

Reflecting on the relationship between Oz and musicals, I propose that Oz (the "American fairy tale") and musicals (the "American art form") reveal American identity as self-inventive performance invested in utopian ideals. Because of its familiarity, *The Wizard of Oz* is often deployed as an allegory to illustrate and explain a topic.[3] Here, I suggest that Oz and the genre of the musical illustrate each other, not arbitrarily, but based on their close relationship. With the childhood practice of make-believe as a guiding principle, Oz provides a set of fairy tale tropes for the American musical and its performances. In turn, the performance practices of the American musical—notably song and dance—script participation in the American fairy tale, ensuring that it thrives as embodied, participatory culture. These performances take place not only on stage and screen but also in backyard play, in formal and informal singalongs, and in school or community theater performances. In these performances, going to Oz and going to the theater are parallel journeys with departure, transformation, and return.[4] Along the way, the conventions of American musical theater enact social identities and relationships implying who is included or excluded in the performance of "America."

It's conventional wisdom that both Oz and musicals (at least musicals as cultivated on Broadway and in Hollywood), are characteristically American and utopian about "America."[5] Each took recognizable form at the beginning of the "American" twentieth century, and they reinforce each other's status as national institutions. While the American musical keeps Oz fresh in adaptation, Oz provides the musical theater with a national myth it can keep returning to in affirming its status as the American art form. The American pedigree of Oz musicals may be fiercely protected. When British composer Andrew Lloyd Webber produced a new stage revival of *The Wizard of Oz* in 2011, adding songs of his own, an American musical theater fan on the *Broadway World* message board decried such tampering with a "sacred" American musical: "there are some things you don't screw with in America. *The Wizard of Oz* is one."[6] Yet, for more than a century, people in "America" and beyond have been doing all kinds of things with *The Wizard of Oz*.

Oz and musicals express feelings of utopia and visions of social cohesion. Baum's Oz has been interpreted as an American utopia at least since literary critic Edward Wagenknecht published his 1929 essay *Utopia Americana*, noting the peaceful, generous, and ideal social conditions of Oz as well as such American touches in the Oz books such as their foregrounding of the magic of technology and the inclusion of such typically American characters as Dorothy, the Scarecrow, the Tin Man, and the Wizard, a recognizably American circus humbug.[7] Musicals, for their part, are utopian in their portrayal of a harmonious social landscape whose conflicts are resolved through song and marriage in what Raymond Knapp terms the *marriage trope*.[8] As film scholar Richard Dyer has famously argued, more than in any specific social organization, musicals are utopian because of the *feelings* of utopia they convey.[9] Similarly, performance theorist Jill Dolan describes live theater as constituting *utopian performatives* that bring about feelings of utopia rather than fixed social formations in their aspirational imaginings of another or better world.[10]

The idea of feeling utopia will be central to my argument about why musicals matter in the circulation of the American fairy tale. Oz musicals tell us something about the performance of an American dream. In each musical version, who Dorothy is and what her Kansas is like, and what Oz is like, tell us something about America as we find it and as we'd like it to be. Accordingly, the details of how Dorothy and her friends perform on the journey constitute lessons about how to act, or perform, like Americans. How home and Oz are reconciled in each musical implies some kind of feeling about the American utopia.

The American fairy tale becomes inherently participatory through the musical's conventions of song, dance, and acting. Oz's durability as a national mythology is often attributed to its universal themes such as the desire for home and the search for wisdom, compassion, and courage. But through the conventions of musical theater, we can more clearly see that the American fairy tale's power is not just in its themes and symbols but also in active participation, and not in homogenizing universals, but in plurality and difference. Musicals encourage their audiences to break into song and dance just like the characters on stage or screen, or at least to have the desire to. More obviously embodied than the act of reading, musical performances foreground how literature and fairy tales are already performed and participatory and how Oz and musicals are a repertoire for these performances.[11]

Who participates in the American fairy tale and its musicals implies who belongs in "America." In an art form created largely by immigrants, African Americans, and queer people for largely middle-class audiences, the story of an ordinary girl transported to a land of magic and beauty, where she makes friends and has more power than she did at home, echoes the American dream of social and geographic mobility. Yet in each of these performances of an American utopia there are notable exclusions—erasures of Black and Indigenous people, the white supremacy of minstrelsy, the heteronormative imperatives of theatrical love plots, and assumptions about certain types of bodies engaged in song, dance, and acting. Whether Oz and musicals can be sufficiently revised in inclusive performances of America while retaining their essential forms is a question I struggle with and to which I offer no definitive answers. While drawing on my personal connections with Oz and musicals, I recognize that many people have historically been left out of these performances.[12]

Humbugs, Witches, and American Theatrical Make-Believe

One year, I was at my grandmother's house when *The Wizard of Oz* was on TV. The familiar story unfolded. Maybe you know it. Dorothy, in Kansas, sings about a better life "Over the Rainbow," and with her dog, Toto, is carried by a tornado to the Land of Oz, where little people called Munchkins and the good witch Glinda greet her in song. They are celebrating because Dorothy's crashed house has landed on, and killed, the Wicked Witch of the East. Glinda gives Dorothy the Wicked Witch's magic ruby slippers and instructs her to follow the yellow brick road to the Emerald City, where the Wizard of Oz can send her home. Pursued by the Wicked Witch of the West, who wants her departed sister's shoes, Dorothy travels down the road, meeting new friends—the Scarecrow who wants a brain, the Tin Woodman who wants a heart, and the Cowardly Lion who wants courage. They join her to ask the Wizard to grant their wishes. On their arrival, the Wizard appears as an illusion—a gigantic head projected on a smoke screen. He agrees to grant their requests if they can bring him the broomstick of the Wicked Witch of the West, a task that requires her destruction by melting. When they return successful, the Wizard refuses to keep his promise, but Toto pulls back a green curtain, revealing that the Wizard is just an old circus man from Omaha, operating the theatrical machinery that creates the illusion of the great Wizard. The Scarecrow exclaims, "You humbug!"

Grandmother laughed out loud at this line. I vaguely understood that "humbug" meant something like "nonsense," but Grandmother, born in the first decade of the twentieth century, when *The Wonderful Wizard of Oz* was a new story and the fist musical stage version was touring America, seemed to recognize a more specific cultural reference in the word.

Oz and musicals have at their heart an American tradition of humbug. This practice is most famously exemplified by another circus man, P.T. Barnum, who was likely an inspiration for Baum's Wizard.[13] Barnum performed hoaxes on an American public grateful for the chance to be deceived. The transparency of his deceptions was a useful and pleasurable social education for nineteenth-century Americans, who could learn to recognize harmless hoaxes like those of Barnum as practice for protecting themselves against actual confidence men in the growing cities.[14] The humbug shows us that there is something of value to be gained by being fooled without *really* being fooled. In Baum's book, when the Scarecrow accuses The Wizard of being a humbug, the Wizard enthusiastically embraces the characterization. He takes pride in showing Dorothy and her friends how he accomplished his theatrical illusions using papier mâché, strings, and ventriloquism to appear to them in different forms. In language familiar to children, the Wizard confesses to Dorothy and her friends," "I have been making believe," equating theatrical performance with pretend play.[15] Like Barnum, the Wizard secures, rather than loses, his audience's confidence when his hoaxes are revealed. As in the movie, the indignation of Dorothy and her friends quickly subsides, and they continue to insist that he grant their wishes, so the Wizard gives Dorothy's three friends symbolic gifts of brains, heart, and courage. But readers come to understand that Dorothy's friends' actions, or performances, were already sufficient to demonstrate their character. Rather than literal transformations, the American fairy tale offers transformations of consciousness through awareness of performance.

It's not a cynical proposition, then, to say that musicals and fairy tales are themselves a certain kind of humbug. They inspire because of their obvious make-believe. Fairy tale scholar Maria Tatar suggests that *The Wonderful Wizard of Oz*, more than European fairy tales, winkingly acknowledges its own theatricality by including the character of the modern American humbug Wizard.[16] Like Dorothy's friends, many kids like to believe in fairy tales even though they know or soon discover that they are make-believe. Similarly, musicals are manifest performances that draw audiences in emotionally and make us feel like we're experiencing magic and spontaneous expression, even though the magic is explainable as a rehearsed performance.[17] The musical reveals and conceals its labor, like the curtain that conceals and reveals the Wizard's performance when Toto pulls it back in *The Wizard of Oz*. We're always aware of both sides of the curtain and its illusions.[18] As we'll see, singing in a musical allows characters or actors to reveal different versions of themselves that gesture toward the ways people must also perform different versions of themselves in American life.[19]

The significance of humbug and its helpfully duplicitous performances in the American musical theater is implied by the frequent appearance of larger-than-life showmen in the form. *The Music Man*'s Harold Hill, *Chicago*'s (1975) Billy Flynn, *Wicked*'s Wizard, and *Barnum* (1980) himself literally give us "the old song and dance," foregrounding the performance of American identity. This character—something of a ringleader, emcee, and carnival barker—can be traced not only to Barnum and his freak shows but also to the interlocuter of the minstrel show. He embodies sheer performative confidence and an ability to "sell" a performance, however make-believe or even exploitive.

Counterparts to the humbug Wizard are the diva witches, divine figures of the theater, appearing at critical moments to bestow theatrical solutions. Their imposing stature in musicals compels us to recognize their power. After the Wizard's humbug fails to send Dorothy home, the diva-witch appears, as if out of the machinery of the musical, to set things right. Like the *deus ex machina*, the "god out of the machine," in Greek drama, who appears at the last minute to resolve an apparently irresolvable plot point, the *diva* (literally goddess) comes out of the machinery of the musical to set things right when things have gone so wrong that only she can fix them. We might call this a *diva ex machina*. A prime example is Glinda's appearance at the end of the MGM film to reveal the power of the ruby slippers or her making it snow to save Dorothy and her friends from the soporific poppy field. Far from being artless, desperate devices, these appearances of the diva affirm the power of the theatrical enterprise and the role of the feminine performer who can change the world on stage with the power of her presence. Stepping in when the patriarch fails, she has magic that is theatrical and self-presentational, like the humbug Wizard's, but often more effective. Sometimes, the problem solved by the diva's arrival is simply her prior absence in an art form that belongs to her. The diva seems to be in charge of the whole show, pulling the levers of the theatrical machine, directing Dorothy on her journey, and, at times, bringing everything to a halt to center on her own performance. In Oz, Dorothy becomes a diva capable of her own theatrical magic when she learns that she already has the power to go home by clicking the heels of the magic shoes (a diva's accessory for sure) that she's had all along.

Divas and humbugs help establish the metatheatrical frame in which we might view the American fairy tale and the American musical. But it's Dorothy's journey to Oz and the musical performances she accomplishes there with the help of fellow performers that exemplify the performance of "America" in and out of the theater.

American Dreams and Gestures of the Musical Fairy Tale

The Wizard of Oz begins and ends in America. In-between is magic. A typical Oz musical follows a path from America to Oz and back, much as theater and fairy tales transport us from the mundane world and return us somehow different than before. As musical theater scholars have recognized, fairy tale musicals have been a mainstay of American family entertainment from the nineteenth century to contemporary Disney films.[20] However, I'm less interested in defining the fairy tale musical as a genre than in thinking about how a musical (potentially any musical) might *act* like a fairy tale. In musicalizations of *The Wizard of Oz*, Dorothy's longing for a better world cues the use of the musical's fairy-tale performance conventions in song and dance. In the ensuing journey to Oz, Dorothy and the audience learn something about how to perform in the American utopia.

On this journey, song and dance, what musical theater scholars Dominic Symonds and Millie Taylor call the *gestures* of musical theater, bring the

American fairy tale to life. These gestures are the embodied "acts of expressive commitment" that drive emotive and social transformation. Self-reflexive about performance, they also conform to Bertolt Brecht's concept of *gestus*, theatrical gestures that embody social relations and realities.[21] For me, song dances are analogous to the magic gestures and incantations of the fairy tale, as the root of *enchantment* or *incantation* suggests (Latin *incantare*, to sing). Song transforms singers by magnifying and externalizing desire and subjectivity. In Oz, these gestures figure an American dream of something better, a dream influentially expressed by Dorothy in the MGM film in "Over the Rainbow."[22]

The gestures of musical theater are, in themselves, what make the performances of Oz and musicals American. They are inherently political.[23] We can talk about how musicals, like any other texts, reflect their historical American contexts. But to consider how, for example, the very act of bursting into song can constitute a performance of being American is to get to a more fundamental argument about how the musical is American. For this reason, I focus as much on the performative acts as on correlations to the musicals' historical moments (e.g., *Wicked* can be understood in the context of the post-9/11 world). If song and dance are not exclusively American acts, they come in American inflections in these musicals, informed by American legacies of ethnicity, gender, class, age, and embodiment. The transformations made possible by these gestures are acts of self-invention, and, when done in an American musical, they constitute a distinctly American form of expression and performance. Over time, repetitions and adaptations construct "America" through intersecting and multivocal performances of what it is to be, or act, American. American innocence and guilt (or goodness and wickedness), helplessness and agency, are embodied in the possibilities and limits of song, dance, and theatrical or social acting.

Playing Dorothy is playing "American," and her musical gestures inform the American fairy tale. She's the dreamer of an American dream, and her feelings of being out of place in Kansas can be identified not only with individuals who are discontent, but also with those who are disenfranchised, marginalized, dispossessed, or displaced in America. The innocence of this icon of American childhood, especially when portrayed as White, implies the innocence of America and of the American musical.[24] Dorothy's blamelessness masks her potential role as colonizer as she upends the social order in Oz. At the same time, she represents the agency of immigrants and minorities, who must assert and claim their inclusion in the American dream, navigating their social choreographies in an America that infantilizes them and limits their social mobility. She's the protagonist of a repertoire of American scripts that can be followed, revised, or resisted by Americans performing their stakes in the American utopia.

In musicals, Dorothy is usually played by a teenager or young adult in the role of a young girl. As a result, her obvious theatricality reminds us that childhood itself is a performance and social construct. Its innocence can be questioned or remade in repeat performances with renewed implications for "America" and American childhood.[25] As an iteration of American girlhood, Judy Garland's teenage Dorothy is different from the younger heroine of Baum's book, while *The Wiz* strategically remakes the role for Black girls. Embodied in the transition between childhood and adulthood, Dorothy has prodigious agency, her maturing voice and body giving her access to the empowering affects and magnifying emotions of musical theater.

No other musical gesture more clearly points toward the longing for utopia and belonging than the "I want" song, which expresses the main character's motivating desire and of which the MGM film's "Over the Rainbow" is the quintessence. The fairy tale expression of deep desire in "Over the Rainbow" exhibits kinship with other classic "I want" songs, such as "I'm Wishing," and "Someday My Prince Will Come" (*Snow White and the Seven Dwarfs*, 1937), hinting at the form's affinity with children's lullabies and wishing songs. Embedded in the conventions of fairy tale as well as the American musical, "Over the Rainbow" represents an American dream of wish fulfillment that is expansive. Dorothy's longing for something better speaks to the utopian longings of immigrants, Black people, queer people, and others who invented the American musical. This utopian gesture originates at home where it is needed most. Kansas is nonmusical (and lacking in color) except for the "I want" song that envisions a better, and by the implication of song itself, more musical world. Whether it's Kansas in the MGM film or Harlem in the film version of *The Wiz*, home is a place where Dorothy is misunderstood or where she doesn't know how to fit into her family and community. The relative absence of song and color in the "real" America anticipates their abundance in its imagined counterpart, Oz.

"I want" songs and other gestures of the American musical are not only theatrical performances but also *performatives*, conjuring social realities and relations in their repetition.[26] Judy Garland singing "Over the Rainbow" in the MGM film or Stephanie Mills singing "Home" in *The Wiz* constitutes a performance in the sense of playing a role and singing a song, but it's also a performative in the sense of repeating and reinventing the performing subject and concepts like home, utopia, and America. Social performatives are always embodied performances, and embodied performances are always socially performative in the repetition and revision of Oz and musicals.

Oz: A Musical-Theatrical American Utopia

In answer to Dorothy's "I want" song, Oz is the world of the musical, where the ideals and contradictions of America can be acted out theatrically. As Dorothy travels through the Land of Oz, she and the audience learn to act American while joining up with people whose performances imply participation in the American community. These performances involve acting with an awareness of both sides of the Wizard's curtain to perform a humbug duality between dominant and subcultural American identities.

The world of the musical is a place where one has the right to break into song. This is established from the moment Dorothy arrives in Munchkinland. In the American musical and its fairy tale, singing is an act of multivalent possibilities. For anyone, the right to sing might be the American right to be loudly expressive in song and dance, but for the marginalized, the rupturing of normative expression by breaking into song might imply the right to be different. Song and dance are of course not exclusively American (nor is the musical), but in the American musical they have American consequences. Of crucial importance is the *differing* American forms these gestures come in. Dorothy in the MGM film or *The Wiz* sings and dances down the yellow brick road, but *how* she does it, and the particular steps and movements (skipping to Euro-American folk idioms in one, shuffling to soulful syncopation in the other), embodies different experiences and performances of being American. These gestures are adaptable from one musical to the next, but they can never be vacated of their historical specificities.

When Dorothy skip-dances down the yellow brick road in the MGM film, the dance choreographs friendship to the steps of an irrepressible optimism in an American dream. When she starts the journey in Munchkinland, lyrics in chanted repetition give explicit instructions ("Follow the Yellow Brick Road"), while the music provides the precise rhythm of the steps (companion website 0.1). Clicking one's heels to go home makes one kind of magic, but kicking up one's heels is magic of its own. The journey itself is musical. In contrast to a nonmusical play or movie, where dialogue might dictate the timing and movement, in a musical number, everything is set to the timing of song.[27]

In Oz, anything encountered on the journey has the potential to script musical performance. Traveling through Oz or a musical involves dancing with things on the roads traveled by Americans making do with what they have. Much as a coat rack may prompt Fred Astaire to dance with it, objects and environments in Oz become imbued with theatrical magic when encountered in performance.[28] A road says "travel." Shoes say "walk." Sparkly shoes say "walk in style," or "dance" (Do fancy shoes require dancing, or does dance require fancy shoes?). The ruby slippers add magical sparkle as Dorothy's feet move with confidence, almost of their own accord. Wands and broomsticks add magic to Glinda's "Come Out, Come Out, Wherever You Are," and especially Elphaba's "Defying Gravity." While cuing performances, these items script historically specific cultural meanings and social actions in what Robin Bernstein calls "dancing with things."[29] What the magic shoes say about mobility in dance—theatrical, personal, psychological, social—is different for Dorothy in *The Wiz*, in a critical way, given the history of Black displacement and migration, than it is for Dorothy in the MGM film.

At the end of the journey, Dorothy's friends learn about humbug when they discover the truth about the Wizard. Here they become more aware of their performances, arriving at an important realization for the ability to navigate American life on both sides of the curtain. The diva drops in (out of the machine) to send Dorothy home in what seems like an authentic final performance. But, ambivalently, the gestures that get Dorothy home vary. Sometimes, as in *The Wiz*, Dorothy gets home by singing about what she's learned before clicking her heels. In the MGM film, the commitment to music or performance in returning home is more ambivalent. Dorothy doesn't sing, but she clicks her heels (a kind of restricted dance) and repeats "There's no place like home" (a spoken, not sung, incantation that bears traces of musicality). There's some question about whether one can be "musical" or "theatrical" after the return home or must assimilate to prosaic reality.

But the music lingers on, even in the "real" world. In repeated performances, the musical and choreographic gestures of Oz come to represent song and dance themselves. Music students learn that the octave, a basic interval in music, sounds like the first two notes of "Over the Rainbow" (on the word *somewhere*). Similarly, dance instructors teach their students the common *pas de basque* with reference to the dance Dorothy and her friends do on the yellow brick road, a modification of the traditional step with feet kicking forward instead of pointing out.[30] When people recite lines together or sing songs from *The Wizard of Oz*, *The Wiz*, or *Wicked*, they perform a community in an act that matters as much as the text recited. These gestures bind social relations, community, and identity in their reiterative doing. They bring Oz home.

Whose Oz? Whose Musical? Whose America?

The humbug of fairy tales and musicals is related to a duality or multiplicity in the performance of American identity.[31] The separation of speech and song in a musical (or of narrative and musical number, or of walking and dancing), allows actors to transform into other versions of themselves in the moment of bursting into song.[32] This doubled theatrical performance elides with the doubled (or multiple) social performances of American minority groups, including many of the people who have contributed to the musical as the "American art form" and had to navigate performing "American" as well as something else. Bert Lahr's performance of the Cowardly Lion in the MGM film is an especially useful illustration. In "If I Were King of the Forest," Lahr alternates masculine and feminine singing and physical gestures in a send-up of operatic conventions. In parodying these conventions, he encodes ideas about class as well as gender and ethnicity, alternately twittering and singing with bravura. His Jewish identity is legible, to savvy audiences, in his New York accent and vaudevillian style of comedy ("If I Only Had de nehve!" [the nerve]). Jewishness and queerness elide in what performance theorist Henry Bial calls double-coding, where subcultural codes in mainstream media texts can be deciphered by people with inside knowledge and specific cultural literacies.[33] An important aspect of this performance is its demonstrated virtuosity, its evident skillfulness, which makes the performer visible in juxtaposition to the character, rather than being absorbed in it. Because of this revealed virtuosity, as Andrea Most argues, this kind of performance is an antiessentialist one, suggesting that identity is performed rather than fixed.[34] Implicitly, Lahr's performance argues for an inclusive, self-inventive American utopia through the artifice of song.

Lahr himself is recognizable through the makeup and costume in this performance, highlighting the layers of a performed identity. In Baum's *The Wonderful Wizard of Oz*, characters are written and illustrated in relatively straightforward style (Figure I.1, companion website 0.2). In the MGM film,

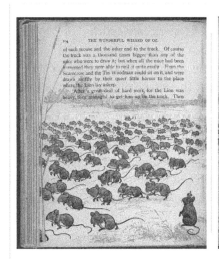
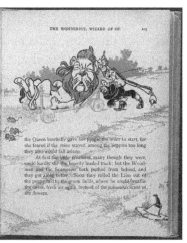

Figure I.1. *The Wonderful Wizard of Oz* by L. Frank Baum, illustrated by W. W. Denslow. George M. Hill Company, Chicago, IL: 1900.

Figure I.2. Bert Lahr as Zeke (left) and the Cowardly Lion (right) in MGM's *The Wizard of Oz* (dir. Victor Fleming), 1939.

the gestures of musical theater rupture a character's unity by drawing attention to the performing subject. Bert Lahr plays the Cowardly Lion, the farmhand Zeke, and himself (a star with a comedic personality familiar to contemporaneous audiences) all at the same time (Figure I.2, companion website 0.3). This playful performance, resembling kids' dress-up play in make-believe, reveals the complexities of American identity.

Oz musicals bear the traces of the histories of the groups who have collaborated on the American musical and used its gestures to stage utopian performances of belonging in America. The essentially collaborative nature of musicals widens the space for a "melting pot" of contributions by minority authors and audiences. The Cowardly Lion was developed by a number of collaborators, each influenced by prior theatrical depictions of the character and the established generic conventions of musical comedy, operetta, and fairy tales. Composer Harold Arlen and lyricist Yip Harburg, both also Jewish, had worked with Lahr before and tailored the words and music of the Lion's songs to his theatrical personality. Lahr himself drew on his vaudevillian training, adding gags of his own. To punch up the script during production, other lines were suggested by Jack Haley (the Tin Man and a fellow vaudevillian), and writer John Lee Mahin.[35] Because there is no single author of a musical or its characters, the performances are multivocal.

In considering those to whom, and for whom, these multivalent performances may speak, we should remember that kids are the primary audience for Baum's book and an important audience for the musicals. Oz musicals are, in the first place, performances of and about American childhood. Children have actively collaborated in the creation of both the fairy tale and the musical by being part of their intended audiences, by performing Dorothy and other roles in musical theater, and by being custodians of musical theater's legacy in school and community theaters.[36] Through these activities, they play a determining role in which adaptations become influential. Kids' performances—on stage, at home, or in the audience—aren't inferior versions of the professional ones. They are, from a certain perspective, the source, inspiring and influencing Oz and musicals through their example of make-believe play. In musicals, as in children's play, costumes and makeup prompt the act of bursting into song and the experimentation with different identities. The importance of the idea of childhood in the musical is suggested by the frequency with which it comes up as a matter of course in the scholarly literature.[37]

The double address of Oz and musicals to children and adults accomodates humbug performances of American identity. The conventional notion that family entertainment addresses children and adults on different levels is not to be taken too categorically. Audience responses are fluid, with children apprehending much of the "adult" material and the "child inside" the adult drawn to youthful aspects. Musicals offer models of how young people and adults might act in an American utopia through empowering performances. Children in musicals can belt with power rivaling that of adults, and adults can sing and play like children. Writers, composers, lyricists, producers, directors, choreographers, actors, singers, dancers, technicians, and audiences use the idea of childhood to navigate their own movement in American life.

Other groups of collaborators have played important roles in the creation of the American musical, and their contributions are felt in the adaptation of the American fairy tale as well. Jewish immigrants and their descendants, for example, found in the musical a venue for acting out their negotiations of American life between difference and assimilation through their particular doubled, self-inventive performances. Through the emotional effects of singing and dancing, they created a theatrical *assimilation effect*, as described by Andrea Most, drawing the audience into a utopian theatrical community that implicitly included America's immigrants and Others.[38] Oz musicals from the extravaganza to *The Wiz* and *Wicked* dramatize questions of inclusion in America. The ethnic stock characters and variety performers in the Oz extravaganza of the early twentieth century show the influence of immigrants and minority groups on the musical, even as, in this case, they were played by mostly Anglo-American actors. In the MGM film, ethnic performances are subtler, but still an important presence. Make-believe play with identity makes these performances possible.

Despite the role they played in the development of the American musical, African Americans have historically been marginalized on stage and screen. Black musicals were flourishing at the turn of the century, as *The Wizard of Oz* extravaganza was playing on Broadway and the form of the twentieth-century musical was emerging, but no Black actors or creatives could be involved in this show, which only acknowledged them through blackface minstrel tropes. People of color are altogether absent from MGM's version of the American fairy tale. It took a consciously Black production, *The Wiz* to claim the American fairy tale for Black people.

Indigenous Americans have been erased, acknowledged only superficially, or relegated to the mythical past in both the American musical and the American fairy tale.[39] While living in South Dakota in the throes of the Indian Wars, the assassination of Sitting Bull, and the massacre at Wounded Knee in the winter of 1890–91, Baum wrote editorials calling for the extermination of Native Americans. In *The Wonderful Wizard of Oz*, Dorothy's story is legible as a narrative of settler colonialism in which her "innocence" allows her to colonize Oz, overthrowing its government and killing its native magicians. Broadway, the street, was built over a Native trading route through Manhattan, and the musical has been paving a yellow brick road over Indigenous America ever since. *Oklahoma!* writes Native Americans out of its musicalization of Lynn Riggs's *Green Grow the Lilacs*, while in *Annie Get Your Gun* (1946) and *The Music Man* they are mimicked by White characters "playing Indian."[40] The only explicit depiction of Native Americans in Oz musicals that I can think of is a stereotyped specialty song about Sitting Bull in the extravaganza. In the musical *Wicked*, Fiyero retains no signs of his Indigeneity as portrayed in Gregory Maguire's novel.[41]

Oz and musicals have in common a privileging of feminine power and queer or antinormative aesthetics. *The Wizard of Oz* features a strong girl protagonist in a story where women and witches are stronger than men and humbugs, tracking with the power of divas in the theater. Baum's queer and feminist sensibilities, evident in his books and likely influenced by his mother-in-law, the prominent suffragist Matilda Gage, not only reinforce the queerness of the musical but also subvert its heteronormative forms.[42] Both musicals and popular fairy tales tend to repeat Cinderella stories in which the female protagonist heals and reconciles the community or the nation through her marriage to a leading man.[43] But musicals that faithfully adapt *The Wizard of Oz* construct their utopian community in the absence of marriage, instead finding individuals' performances of friendship to be adequate in the building of community. The musical gesture of four friends linking arms as they dance down the road emphasizes a solidarity in friendship formed by people with differences. Only the 1903 extravaganza and *Wicked* indulge in generic romantic plots, and even in these cases, the relationships are comical, incomplete, inconsequential, or potentially queer.[44]

The queerness of Oz and musicals is reinforced by their relationship to childhood. Children's literature often reads as queer because of its presumption of children's sexual innocence and its attendant muting of (hetero)sexuality.[45] This is especially true in Oz, where adult couples and romance are rare, and gender and its roles are unstable. Further, queer childhood is eternal in Oz, where no one ages, so that children, including Dorothy, who returns to live there in the books, never grow into heteronormative adulthood. The musical, with its enthusiasm for alternative forms of expression—singing, dancing, and big feelings in contrast to speaking, walking, and emotional restraint—is a suitably queer venue for the expression of perpetual childhood and the refusal of normative growth. The adolescent trope of longing for something and someplace better expressed in "I want" songs like "Over the Rainbow" is especially resonant as a queer myth.

In the "real" world, Oz and musicals resonate with an American mythology of queer identity. The theater has long been home to gender nonconformers, queer people, sex workers, cross-dressed performances, and unruly transformations.[46] Musicals have additional queer connotations, whether attributable to the camp aesthetic arising from the act of breaking into song, an attraction to divas, or simply the emergence of the form as a reflexive signifier of queerness.[47] Gender bending on the stage contributes to playful transgressions in the *Wizard of Oz* extravaganza of 1903, and the camp style of the MGM film bears the stamp of queer people working in Hollywood during the era of the Motion Picture Production Code. By the mid-twentieth century, Judy Garland became a queer icon, and *The Wizard of Oz* became, for some, a queer myth, with the journey to the Emerald City as an allegory for queer people leaving home for the urban places where they could join communities of other "musical" types.[48] As film historians Harry M. Benshoff and Sean Griffin note, MGM's Oz is "a land where difference and deviation from the norm *are* the norm.[49] Continuing in this tradition, *The Wiz* was a product largely of Black and queer authors and sensibilities, and *Wicked* extends the queer mythology in its allegories of difference and queering of musical theater conventions.[50]

In Oz, children, little people, people in wheelchairs, animals who can and can't speak or sing, scarecrows, tin men, and nonsinging humans decenter the normative, adult, human body. Humans and nonhuman animals performing together destabilize human–animal binaries, forcing reconsideration of intentionality, agency, and communication.[51] In Oz, animals can speak and sing, like the Lion, or not, like Toto, who influences the story in other ways—by barking, running away, and providing the motivation for Dorothy's leaving home. The range of expressive capabilities of actors in a musical, across lines of humanity, species, and thingness, has implications for how different subjects participate.

In general, the sung and danced gestures of the musical are proof of the ability to feel, implying who has personhood in America and its art form.[52] The thing-like Scarecrow and Tin Man can't feel physical pain, and are repeatedly torn apart and put back together, but the proof of their having brains and heart is in their ability to express feelings, often in song and dance. The evidence of feeling is especially important in *The Wiz*, where the Black concept of soul affirms the humanity of African Americans and their participation in the American dream. With these questions about body and performance, the journey on the yellow brick road becomes one in which physical mobility and vocal ability have consequences for social mobility in America.[53] At the same time, an inability to sing doesn't necessarily suggest an inability to participate.[54] MGM's Wizard may be more trustworthy because he doesn't literally indulge in the humbug's "old song and dance," and the Wicked Witch is powerful (if Wicked) without singing.

While some, like Dorothy's friends, are integrated into the community as they are, others are deemed incompatible with the American utopia. The nonsinging Wicked Witch of the West must be destroyed in the MGM film. In *Wicked*, Elphaba, with her vocal power and excess, is allowed to live, but she must leave the community. Even her performative superpower as a singer, which transforms her from a freak to a prodigy, produces something of an ableist overcoming narrative. Meanwhile, her sister, Nessarose, who uses a wheelchair, is the personification of disability as wickedness, irredeemable even after being "cured" by Elphaba.

Accidents and failures in performance have implications for the American utopia as well. On one level, these include forgotten lines, unconvincing effects, and performer injuries. But a successful recovery from an accident is evidence of performative virtuosity, and how Americans respond to these accidents is also a measure of their ability to act. The Wizard's humbug is ultimately insufficient to send Dorothy home, and his plan to take her back in a hot-air balloon fails when he accidentally leaves without her. In the wake of the Wizard's failure, Dorothy has to look to her own ability to act, and her actions matter too. In the MGM film, Dorothy insists that her killing of the Wicked Witch of the East is an accident. When she melts the Wicked Witch of the West, although the act itself is portrayed as somewhat inadvertent, she has in fact set out to kill the Witch following the Wizard's orders. This casts a bit of uncertainty on Dorothy's innocence, which also represents the "innocence" of America, where genocide and slavery are disavowed as accidents of the colonizer's destiny. There are accidents and "accidents" in the performance of America.

Oz and musicals simultaneously uphold and disrupt America's hierarchies and performances of race, class, and gender. A tension between the musical's middlebrow reputation and subcultural histories results in anxieties about femininity, homosexuality, the mixing of races and classes, childishness, and commercialism.[55] Arbiters of taste have sometimes rejected Oz musicals as commercial, indulgent, unsophisticated, and trivial. These are accusations often made against entertainment popular with children, families, girls, women, queer people, and non-White people. But the vitality of Oz and musicals, arising from the contributions of those who made the American art form, has kept American and global audiences enchanted as they imagine an American utopia that resonates across the limen separating home and Oz.

Utopian Performatives and the No-Place of Home/Oz

What has been learned in Oz transforms the possibilities of home, or "America." When we return from Oz, or by analogy, when we return from the theater, we bring a little bit of Oz back with us, and with it the hope of making home a little more like it. Utopia (literally "no place") is not Oz by itself, but the no-place where home and Oz meet. This is possible because of utopian performatives described by Dolan, which, in their very doing in the "good no place" of the theater, exceed the present time and space, allowing participants to communally feel another, better world that might come to be "if every moment of our lives were as emotionally voluminous, generous, aesthetically striking, and intersubjectively intense."[56]

Home and Oz are interdependent and recoverable in repeat performance. Sequels, adaptations, and home Oz play repeat the desire to return to Oz, while the gestures of the musical allow oscillations between Oz and home. Like Dorothy in the MGM film, we need look no farther for our hearts' desire than the backyard, where one can inhabit Kansas and Oz simultaneously by repeating the musical or singing "Over the Rainbow." Disrupting normative time and place, nostalgia (literally "homesickness") and utopia are fantasies of the past and future that help us navigate the present. The queer temporalities of childhood, musicals, and fairy tales rebel against linear time, moving backward, forward, and sideways in repetitions of the musical and the American fairy tale.[57] As suggested by Scott McMillin, when people break into song, they disrupt the linear time of the book, entering into a lyrical order of time, the time of music that is about the song rather than the progressive plot.[58] On a larger scale, musicals and theater are lyrical moments in life that take audiences out of regular time. We can return to those times and places by repeating the musical, in the same way or with a difference.

Consequently, experiences of the musical and the fairy tale are not strictly linear. As adaptation theorist Linda Hutcheon argues, audiences experience oscillations among different versions forward, backward, and sideways in time.[59] Oz and musicals performatively transform a story for which there is no original.[60] Even Baum's own "modern fairy tale" was a renewed performance of fairy tale tropes. There is no single authority, no genius author, and no single narrative for the American fairy tale. For many people, Baum's is not the definitive text but part of a more diverse and inclusive network or repertoire. To theater scholar La Donna Forsgren, who like many Black Americans grew up watching the film version of *The Wiz*, the MGM film seemed like "a rip-off," of *The Wiz*: "I was incredulous that Dorothy could be anything other than a black girl."[61] My White goddaughters also saw and liked *The Wiz* before they saw the MGM film. Examining the DVD cover of the MGM version on first viewing, one of them said, "Those don't look anything like the people in *The Wiz*!" Yet, fidelity to a familiar version often matters to audiences who are invested in it. In seventh grade, I gave an oral book report on *The Wizard of Oz*. When I got to the part about Dorothy throwing water on the Wicked Witch to get her magic shoes back (not to save the Scarecrow from fire as in the movie), a student in the audience vigorously objected, exclaiming "That's not how it happened!" It was only natural that the movie would serve as a text of equal authority to him. Known versions are reference points for new performances, new audiences, and the meanings made. Expectations have to be managed for audiences with different points of entry into the repertoire while at the same time expanding or changing the American fairy tale.

There's a distinction to be made between utopian "time out of time" and "timelessness," and this difference also matters when it comes to who belongs in the American utopia. It's a common claim that Oz in some pure form is universal and universally appealing. A musical version of Oz one doesn't care for allegedly lacks "timelessness." But the exclusion of a work from "timelessness" may involve exclusionary criteria. Critics of *The Wiz* partly dismissed it on the basis that its modern, Black style was a betrayal of the "timelessness" of the MGM film or Baum's book. In reference to various Oz musicals, I hear that one show's music is dated, or that another is too modern or "pop." These different engagements with Oz and musicals highlight the situatedness of their authorship, reception, and adaptation. Musicals are "unfinished show business," as described by musical theater scholar Bruce Kirle, always changing in the process of collaboration, repeat performance, and revival.[62] Even film musicals, which appear to have a set form, are unstable in reception, backyard reenactment, filmic remakes, and adaptation to the stage. Musicals, fairy tales, and utopia are never finished, and neither is America.[63]

And You Were There, and You, and You!

Like Dorothy, I grew up on a farm. At home, I was a misfit, privately queer, musical bookworm with a fondness for fantasy. During my adolescence, traveling to Oz conventions in the Chicago area (where Baum wrote *The Wonderful Wizard of Oz*), was akin to going to the Emerald City, a magical place where I could be among my people. These conventions replaced the broadcasts of the movie as my most important annual Oz event. The trips broadened my experience of America and brought me into contact with people who loved not only Oz but also musicals. My husband once described the Oz Club as "a weird mixture of stuffy academics, campy gay men and families."[64] No doubt, these are also core demographics for musical theater. Many late nights at Oz conventions were spent gathered around a piano, singing showtunes. Oz conventions also provided the opportunity for performances of rare or unusual material, such as Baum's musicals, *The Wogglebug* (1905) and *The Tik-Tok Man of Oz* (1913). Over the years, my involvement in Oz Club performances has included puppeteering, writing plays and songs, singing, acting, and especially providing clunky piano accompaniment. I even played the Wizard in an original musical (I was a very bad Wizard; no one was fooled by the magic tricks I tried to learn for the role). These are my own returns to Oz by way of music and theater.

Oz, musicals, and scholarly work have always gone together for me. I really became an Oz scholar when I was ten, poring over the pages of *The Baum Bugle*, the Oz Club's journal and one of my first models for serious writing about children's literature and popular culture. Concurrently with my early encounters with Oz, my fandom for musicals was nurtured through Disney films, children's television, and the film versions of *The Sound of Music* (1965) and *Annie* (1982), the latter of which was my first total musical obsession at age seven. I combined my interests in Oz and musicals as I majored in music in college, attended graduate school in musicology, and wrote a thesis on "Over the Rainbow" as a queer anthem. After working as a music director for school and community theater musicals and then as a singing teacher specializing in musical theater for young singers, I returned to academia as a musical theater scholar and eventually began pursuing a PhD in childhood studies. Songs from *The Wizard of Oz*, *The Wiz*, and *Wicked* are of course staples of the repertoire in these fields, so for me there's always Oz as long as there are musicals, and there are always musicals as long as there's Oz.

All of it has led to this book, which itself involves a little bit of humbug. Sometimes, maybe, I believe too confidently in the magic of Oz and theater despite their make-believe. Maybe I'm too hopeful that a fairy tale and an art form with some historically built-in exclusions can expand to include everybody. I write from the position of a White, middle-class, queer person who loves music, theater, and children's fantasy. Where I've attempted to center subjectivities beyond my own, such as those of non-White people, women, and transgender people, I've tried to highlight and heed the voices of those with authority to speak to those experiences. I've spoken with theater and entertainment professionals, musicians, musicologists, college students, and members of the LGBTQ, Jewish, and Black communities as well as members of the International Wizard of Oz Club and general fans of Oz and musicals. Their voices are woven through this book, especially in the later chapters.[65]

Richard Dyer describes musicals as combining the "historicity of narrative and the lyricism of numbers," and while the chapters of this book are presented in generally chronological order, they have lyrical consonances.[66] In each chapter I highlight certain musical or "lyrical" moments in the story that are revealing of American performance through the tropes of the fairy tale and gestures of the musical. These include the "I want" song, typified by "Over the Rainbow"; the revelation of Oz and its musical-theatrical world; the performance of community and the "American dream" on the yellow brick road or an analogous journey; the encounter with the Humbug; the appearance of the diva; and the return home.

Each of the first four chapters considers how a specific musical uses the gestures of musical theater to perform "America." The last chapter considers participatory performances at home, in the theater, and in the community. Baum's *The Wonderful Wizard of Oz* and the musical extravaganza adapted from it in 1902 establish the patterns of the American fairy tale and its humbug theatricality, with implications for American ideas about race, gender, and immigration at the beginning of the twentieth century. The influential MGM film of 1939 combines those theatrical conventions with practices of the Hollywood musical in a historical moment situated between depression and war. A more formally integrated musical exemplifying family entertainment in the era of the Motion Picture Production Code, it ostensibly promotes sentimental American values while covertly encoding the experiences of marginalized Americans in its musical-theatrical gestures and camp aesthetic. The stage and screen versions of *The Wiz* revise the predominantly White Oz repertoire to make an African American claim on the

American fairy tale, using soul music and Black performance traditions to celebrate Black life and bring the concepts of home and childhood into conversation with Black experiences of "America." *Wicked* allegorizes diversity and tolerance by making the Witch the heroine of the musical using expressive gestures to speak to a postfeminist politics of voice and social justice communicated in high-powered belting and a sophisticated pop-influenced score, all offered as a global commodity. Finally, participatory performances at home, in the school theater, and in other community settings enact utopia in the imperfect times and spaces of the here and now, making home and Oz aspects of each other.

Theatrical performances are ephemeral yet lasting. They live in the memory and return in repetition like refrains of a song. Embodied in the gestures of musical theater, memory engrains corporeal and national cultural meaning across time and place.[67] Like musicals and "America," this book is unfinished. It takes certain routes through a transforming landscape suggested by the differing representations of the yellow brick road—the spiraling road of the MGM film, the golden roller coaster that winds its way through the phantasmagorical city of the film version of *The Wiz*, and even the personified road of the yellow-tuxedoed guides in *The Wiz*'s Broadway production. The routes I take are only some of many that are possible. My readings are mine, and I can't tell you whether to believe them. As Glinda would insist, you'll have to find that out for yourself.

1

The Man behind the Curtain

L. Frank Baum's Theatrical Fairy Tale

> . . . said the Scarecrow in a grieved tone; "you're a humbug."
>
> "Exactly so!" declared the little man, rubbing his hands together as if it pleased him; "I am a humbug." . . .
>
> . . . Oz, left to himself, smiled to think of his success in giving the Scarecrow and the Tin Woodman and the Lion exactly what they thought they wanted. "How can I help being a humbug," he said, "when all these people make me do things that everybody knows can't be done?"
>
> L. Frank Baum, *The Wonderful Wizard of Oz* (1900)[1]

The Wizard is a lovable humbug, an artful salesman who gives his customers something to believe in, even if the thing is known to be pretend. Playing a role, he presents Dorothy's friends with talismans of brains, heart, and courage and takes pride in showing them how he accomplished his illusions, whereby he appeared to them in the forms of a giant head, a lovely lady, a strange beast, and a ball of fire. Why do Dorothy's friends put their faith in the Wizard's abilities to grant their requests even after he has shown them that he has only been putting on a show? Perhaps his virtuoso performances inspire their own, and ours too. His humbug performance guides the American philosophy of *The Wonderful Wizard of Oz* and the theatrical style of the first Oz musical, the extravaganza first mounted in Chicago in 1902.

The Wizard is a central figure in the relationship between Oz and musical theater. As a humbug, he invites us to participate in the song and dance of Oz's American performance. An American stock character in the tradition of P.T. Barnum, his obvious performances and deeds of make-believe are valuable models for acting in the world. Barnum's theatrical hoaxes, such as the famous Fiji mermaid, a monkey torso sewn to a fish tail, served a public good

Oz and the Musical. Ryan Bunch, Oxford University Press. © Oxford University Press 2023.
DOI: 10.1093/oso/9780190843137.003.0002

by training the American people to evaluate a trick and defend themselves against actual conmen.[2] Audiences delighted in trying to figure out how they were being fooled. Oz and musicals follow this tradition by inviting knowing participation in the performance of being American.

The Wonderful Wizard of Oz and the musical extravaganza that immediately followed it each rely in different ways on the humbug Wizard and his example of performance. These foundational entries in the repertoire of Oz and musicals at first might seem marginal—a book, which is not a musical; and a musical, which is not only no longer well-remembered but also not very much of what a musical looks like today. Yet, the book is both theatrical and musical in addition to being the basis of a repertoire of American musicals, and the musical extravaganza had a good deal of influence on Oz musicals to come. While the book treats midwestern Whiteness as the universal condition in its earnest American fairy tale, the musical extravaganza, an amalgam of popular theater forms, as a matter of course, brings the inherent immigrant and minority influences on theatrical culture to the fairy tale, offering a more diverse, if stereotyped, vision of America. Its musical and theatrical gestures acknowledged the American "melting pot" in performances and characterizations by mostly White actors drawing on minstrel and stock ethnic performance conventions. Its fluid performances of age, gender, and race speak to the context of the Progressive Era, and its self-conscious, up-to-date, and irreverent performances are characteristically American. Everybody's a Wizard in the extravaganza, offering a variation on the humbug's song and dance.

L. Frank Baum was himself a rather theatrical figure, often compared to both Barnum and the Wizard he included in his American fairy tale.[3] He began his career as an actor, playwright, and songwriter, combining these roles in an Irish melodrama, *The Maid of Arran* (1882), which toured New York state. After he left the acting profession, Baum's audacity in presenting himself as an expert in various occupations, including author, poultry breeder, sales guru, and filmmaker, was a kind of humbug typical of the age. He wrote the definitive book and journal on the commercial art of shop window decoration, instructing shop owners to draw customers in with colorful, sometimes electrified, theatrical displays with moving parts and animated figures.[4] As with Barnum's hoaxes, shoppers could marvel at these displays and try to figure out how they worked. It's natural that Baum would be influenced by the culture of humbug. Barnum's *Struggles and Triumphs* was one of the most popular autobiographies of the nineteenth century, and the culture of Baum's America was suffused with its philosophy.[5] Baum wrote, "Barnum was right when he declared that the American people like to be deceived. At least they make no effort to defend themselves."[6]

Humbug had an exploitive aspect, however, as evidenced by Barnum's profiting from the exhibition of Native Americans, Africans, and "freaks." While living in Chicago, Baum attended the 1893 World's Columbian Exposition, which included both the technologically utopian White City, which is said to have inspired the Emerald City, and the Midway Plaisance, where Native Americans, Africans, and other "primitives" were part of ethnological exhibits.[7] These two aspects of the fair represent the contradictions of the Progressive Era, with its utopian confidence in progress and technology and its discourses of scientific racism and eugenics.

The literary and theatrical cultures of Baum's time negotiated these contradictions amid emerging discourses about race, class, gender, and sexuality. Reform movements, often aimed at children, were motivated by a desire to assimilate new working-class immigrant populations. Meanwhile, the rise of sexology produced the species of the homosexual and other categories of sexual deviance in often racialized terms.[8] With feminism in its first wave, women were increasingly involved in public life, especially in philanthropy and issues related to family and childhood. The closing of the frontier, declared by Frederick Jackson Turner in 1893, and the accomplishment of Native American dispossession, containment, and massacre meant that American ideals of technology, progress, and social reform were in tension with the repercussions of settler colonialism, chattel slavery, and segregation. The "melting pot" ideology of American immigrant culture was popularized by Israel Zangwell's play *The Melting Pot* (1908), while W. E. B. Du Bois *The Souls of Black Folk*, with its influential theory of double-consciousness—the divided experience of being Black and American—was published in 1903, the same year *The Wizard of Oz* opened on Broadway. These are the contexts of the performances of American identity in *The Wonderful Wizard of Oz* and its first musical adaptation, a show that was very much of its time.

The American Fairy Tale: *The Wonderful Wizard of Oz*

Musicality and Theatricality in Oz

I first discovered the Oz books lined up in a row on a shelf in the kids' section of my local library. Although I'd always loved the movie, the version of

Oz I found in *The Wonderful Wizard of Oz* and its sequels became a distinct obsession for me. The book is a "modern" fairy tale, according to Baum, with distinctive American touches, including the humbug Wizard and a practical farmgirl as its heroine. Maybe the flatness of Dorothy's Kansas and the American topography of Baum's Oz reminded me of the landscape of my own Northeast Louisiana, a patchwork of cotton fields in the Mississippi River floodplain. As I enthusiastically made my way through Baum's fourteen Oz books, I took great pleasure in convincing myself that Oz was a real place. In make-believe play, the long curving driveway that wound through our large front yard was my yellow brick road. A work of fiction had worked its humbug spell on me. I had no choice, nor any desire, but to believe the unbelievable.

Perhaps I was responding in part to the books' fairy-tale qualities, which encourage repetition in imaginative play and performance. *The Wonderful Wizard of Oz* has lyrical, theatrical, and fairy tale conventions that make it stick in the imagination like a song and prime it for adaptation as a musical. Repeating episodes, such as those in which Dorothy meets the Scarecrow, Tin Man, and Lion in succession, each expressing a desire for a different symbolic piece of personhood, accommodate the repeating verses, choruses, and reprises in their musical counterparts on stage and screen. At the same time, the fairy tale is grounded in the sense of an American reality in its framing—the familiar, concrete setting of rural America where we find our heroine.

Dorothy is an ordinary American girl in the most ordinary of American places, Kansas. These are the perfect protagonist and starting place for an American fairy tale whose magic is the magic of the commonplace.[9] In producing a modern or American fairy tale, Baum may have been following the example of Hamlin Garland's "American" style, drawn from the plainness of the West.[10] He describes Dorothy's Kansas farm in stark detail, from the flat, gray prairie to the one-room house she lives in with Aunt Em and Uncle Henry. In contrast to the MGM film and many other adaptations of the story, very little happens in Kansas to establish Dorothy's character or suggest that she ever wants to go anywhere else. It's the MGM film and the musical convention of the "I want" song that later introduce the idea of elsewhere as a place to be desired. In the book, Dorothy shares her Aunt and Uncle's Middle American practicality. Once she finds herself in Oz, despite its color and beauty, she desires to return to Kansas and Aunt Em, simply because they are her home and her family. Her transportation to this magical land is nothing more or less magical than a Kansas cyclone.

On arrival in Oz, Dorothy encounters practical magic that is strange yet familiar in American life. The Munchkins, though invented by Baum, are a type familiar from fairy tale grotesquery and real-world theater.[11] In their curled-toe shoes and jingle-bell-rimmed hats, they are relatives to elves, dwarves, and other "little people" of European lore, but also owe something to the actual little people who were commonly employed in the American circus and variety entertainment. Among these was Charles Stratton, a little person employed by Barnum and better known by his stage name Tom Thumb. Because of their association with popular entertainment, these little people are culturally predetermined to sing and dance. The seeds of American performative magic are planted in the believable fusing of the wonderful and the everyday. Ordinary items such as those that children might use in make-believe are the basis of enchantment in Oz, where shoes have the silver sparkle of magic powers, Scarecrows talk, and a witch's writing slate gives magical advice. As props, these objects take on ever more enchanting qualities in the musicals, in which magic shoes script the special movement register of dance in the MGM film and the acquisition of a magic broomstick enables flight and powerful singing in *Wicked*'s "Defying Gravity."

As Dorothy and her friends travel through Oz, proving their abilities to play their roles in the American fairy tale, musical patterns structure the journey. Fairy tale rituals repeat lyrically in patterns often based on the magic number three—three Munchkins greet Dorothy, three friends join her, and three heel-clicks of the magic shoes take her home. As Dorothy meets her new friends one by one, each reveals that he seeks brains, heart, or courage. Their desires are repeated like a song along the journey. In just one example of a conversation that gets repeated throughout the book, when the Lion joins the party, the Scarecrow starts the refrain:

> "Have you brains? . . . I am going to the great Oz to ask him to give me
>   some," remarked the Scarecrow, "for my head is stuffed with straw."
> "And I am going to ask him to give me a heart," said the Woodman.
> "And I am going to ask him to send Toto and me back to Kansas,"
>   added Dorothy.
> "Do you think Oz could give me courage? Asked the cowardly Lion.
> "Just as easily as he could give me brains," said the Scarecrow.
> "Or give me a heart," said the Tin Woodman.
> "Or send me back to Kansas," said Dorothy.[12]

This repeating lyrical pattern easily translates to the iterations of song in "If I Only Had a Brain/A Heart/The Nerve" in the MGM film and the solo numbers that introduce each character in *The Wiz*. Meanwhile, The Scarecrow walks along singing to himself when he is happy, reminding us that singing while traveling is not something that only happens in musicals. Baum's description of the tinkling sound of Dorothy's silver shoes on the yellow brick road hints at a relationship between music and magic, anticipating the more overtly musical way Dorothy will dance down the road in the ruby slippers in the MGM film.

The characters' extraordinary embodiments anticipate the possibilities and limits of the body in the gestures of the musical. The Scarecrow and Tin Woodman don't eat or feel pain, but their performances of brains, heart, and courage ultimately prove their essential humanity. As in the musical, what they are able to do and feel emotionally is what matters. Animals like Toto and the Cowardly Lion, in the book and in the musical adaptations, demonstrate a range of communicative abilities from barking to speech to song, implying different ways of participating in the fairy tale or the musical. Despite an inability to speak, Toto's influence in the story is unmatched, as many of Dorothy's actions are motivated by her affection for him, especially in the MGM film.[13] It is Toto, too, who possesses the animal instinct to expose the Wizard behind the screen or curtain.[14]

The personal performances of Dorothy and her friends are ultimately affirmed by the models of performative magic conjured by the Wizard and the Witches. The Wizard, who initially appeared to Dorothy and her friends in different forms accomplished through circus tricks and illusions, assures her three companions that they have brains, heart, and courage. Indeed, along the way, the Scarecrow has thought up strategies to get them out of difficult situations, the Tin Woodman compassionately avoids stepping on insects, and the Lion pretends to be fierce in order to frighten adversaries. But it is the humbug Wizard who shows them how to have confidence in these performances. After taking them backstage of his throne room, the Wizard gives each a prosthetic—a bran mixture in the Scarecrow's sack head, a plush heart in the Tin Woodman's metal chest, and a dose of liquid courage for the Lion, but he insists that what they really lack is the performer's confidence, telling the Lion, "You have plenty of courage, I am sure. . . . All you need is confidence in yourself."[15] The ability of the humbug to believe his own flim-flam performance is the model for others to believe in theirs.

The limits of the Wizards' humbug performance become evident when he proposes to take Dorothy home in his circus balloon but accidentally leaves without her. Dorothy turns to Glinda, the Good Witch of the South, who, in a *diva ex machina*, reveals the power of the shoes. Even this magic turns out to be a power Dorothy has had all along. Dorothy only has to perform as directed, working the spell by clicking her heels three times. It's notable, however, that even Glinda and the other Witches rely on instruments and performance to work their magic. The Wicked Witch of the East's power apparently came from the silver shoes. The Wicked Witch of the West's main instrument is a Golden Cap that controls the Winged Monkeys, and it can only be used three times to summon them. Dorothy finds herself able to use these instruments when she has possession of them. Even Glinda does not use her own magic to send Dorothy home, but simply advises her to use the shoes by clicking the heels three times and commanding them to take her "home to Aunt Em."

Home, Oz, and Utopia

If the return home involves a transformation of reality resulting from what's learned on the journey, it's worthwhile to consider how Oz and home measure up to utopia and how the conventions of the musical embody the possibilities and limits of this ideal. Any consideration of Oz as an American utopia has to confront its implications for gender, sexuality, race, colonization, and personhood, which then also become salient in musical adaptations.

Many scholars have hailed *The Wonderful Wizard of Oz* as a feminist fairy tale with powerful women and a strong American girl protagonist.[16] Witches hold the power in Oz, while men, like the humbug Wizard, are ineffectual. Oz is ruled in later books by Ozma, a teenage girl, and Glinda remains the preeminent magician. In the context of the Progressive Era, these characters may reflect the growing role of women in the public sphere through philanthropy and reform movements, even as they relied on their authority as leaders of the home and private sphere to do this work. The feminist utopics of Oz are often attributed to the influence of Matilda Gage, a prominent suffragist who was Baum's mother-in-law.[17] Gage wrote about the relationship between the oppression of women and the persecution of witches, real or imagined, and Baum's depiction of witches as capable of being good or wicked may have been influenced by her views.[18] In any case, the prominent roles for women in the American fairy tale makes them a good fit for the centering of the diva and her power in the American musical.

Oz is a queer utopia with fluid gender roles, an emphasis on queer friendships among eccentric characters, and a lack of the marriage plots characteristic of musicals and many popular fairy tales in the European tradition. Baum believed romance to be of no interest or relevance to child readers.[19] As children's literature scholar Tison Pugh has argued, the presumption of children's sexual innocence paradoxically makes children's literature queer.[20] The Oz books, in addition, are polymorphous in their treatment of gender. The second Oz book, *The Marvelous Land of Oz* (1904) introduces Tip, a boy who is ultimately revealed as the enchanted, long-lost Princess Ozma. In later books, no one ages or dies in Oz, so that children retain their queer innocence indefinitely, avoiding the upward growth into heteronormativity described by queer theorist Kathryn Bond Stockton.[21] The replacement of heteronormative romance with a story about friendships transcending gender, species, and personhood means that a musical based on Oz need not incorporate the typical marriage pattern to do its work of symbolically consummating an American utopia.

Dorothy's innocence, which stands in for the innocence of America, is ensured by her ordinary White girlhood. Baum assures us that Dorothy's destruction of the Wicked Witch of the East could only be an accident, as "Dorothy was an innocent, harmless little girl . . . and she had never killed anything in all her life."[22] Her innocence assures her moral authority. On their meeting, the Wizard pronounces, "I am Oz, the great and terrible." Dorothy responds with "I am Dorothy, the small and meek," a speech act that simultaneously subjugates herself before him and makes a claim for her worthiness to receive his help on the basis of her powerlessness.[23] Dorothy's presumption of equality and innocence allows her to be a social actor as she liberates the Ozians from their oppressors and helps her friends find their performative confidence.

Dorothy's arrival in Oz, though, is not as innocent as it might seem, nor is the circulation of the musical in "America." The Good Witch of the North reveals to Dorothy that Oz "has never been civilized," accounting for the persistence of magic in its realm. Oz is ripe for liberation, or conquest, or colonization, depending on how you look at it, by an American newcomer. As the publisher of a South Dakota newspaper, Baum wrote two editorials advocating the genocide of Native Americans as conflicts between Lakota Sioux and White settlers culminated in the infamous Wounded Knee Massacre in the winter of 1890–1891.[24] This massacre was motivated by White settlers' fear of Native magic, the utopian ritual of the Ghost Dance, which the Lakota believed would rid the Black Hills of White invaders. Arguing that Native Americans, noble savages of a nostalgic, mythical past, had been corrupted and provoked to an irrational barbarism by contact with White settlers, Baum found it best for the preservation of "civilization" for them to be exterminated.

> The proud spirit of the original owners of these vast prairies inherited through centuries of fierce and bloody wars for their possession, lingered last in the bosom of Sitting Bull. With his fall the nobility of the Redskin is extinguished, and what few are left are a pack of whining curs who lick the hand that smites them. The Whites, by law of conquest, by justice of civilization, are masters of the American continent, and the best safety of the frontier settlements will be secured by the total annihilation of the few remaining Indians.[25]

These remarks invoke the constantly repeated trope of the inevitable disappearance of Native Americans, repeated in musicals like *Oklahoma!* and *Annie Get Your* Gun, where they are either erased in adaptation from the source material or portrayed as relics of the past, reduced to objects of entertainment and imitation.[26] Recurring references in Baum's fairy tale to "civilization" and to the Munchkins, Winkies, and Winged Monkeys as slaves of the Wicked Witches echo the discourses of Baum's America at a time when the frontier had been declared closed and the Civil War had ended slavery only to replace it with Jim Crow. Dorothy's White innocence masks her potential role as colonizer as she liberates the indigenous Munchkins and Winkies from the native witches who are characterized as having enslaved them.

The Wizard's humbug performance permits him to allege his innocence as well. When found out, he declares, "I'm really a very good man; but I'm a very bad Wizard, I must admit."[27] Small of stature like Dorothy and the Munchkins, his somewhat childlike or child-friendly character represents the blamelessness of the nation and its humbugs. This image belies his methods. The Emerald City is a spectacular hoax devised to dazzle and control the people. Residents and visitors must wear green spectacles, which are locked on so that they can't be removed because the city is only green when viewed through green glass (a common material for faux emeralds). For his own purposes, the Wizard sends Dorothy and her friends into danger to kill the Wicked Witch but then can't keep his promise to them. Despite it all, the people of Oz mourn his departure. These authoritarian aspects of the Wizard are explored more fully in *Wicked*, where they prompt comparison to contemporary politics. The transparency of the Wizard's performances is also more openly acknowledged in the musical extravaganza, which dramatically foregrounds the conscious performance of American life.

The Possibilities of Extravaganza: The American Fairy Tale Goes to the Theater

Given his devotion to the theater, it seems inevitable that Baum would seek to turn Oz into a stage production. With composer Paul Tietjens, he approached producer Fred R. Hamlin, who shared the script with director Julian Mitchell. Mitchell saw in the material the "possibilities for extravaganza," and with writer Glen McDonough, he refashioned the script to suit his vision.[28] The show opened in Chicago in 1902 and on Broadway in 1903 followed by national tours.

My first encounter with the extravaganza was probably through the Oz Club's journal, *The Baum Bugle*, when I was about ten or eleven. In photographs, I thought the characters looked odd, the costumes and makeup crude. What was this weird, mysterious show? Because the extravaganza is such a thing of its time, taking no single stable form, and, for good reasons, seldom performed today, it's necessary to reimagine and recreate it from an archive of scripts, photographs, programs, recordings, sheet music, and advertisements. One way to speculate about historical performances is to playfully recreate them through the archive of material culture.[29] By doing this, we can get some sense of how people may have experienced the show, while recognizing that we are always looking through the lens of the present. Because the show went through so many changes, those who saw *The Wizard of Oz* in the theater would have different experiences at different performances in different times and places. In particular, the Chicago production of 1902 differed significantly in its third act from the version that appeared on Broadway and on tour beginning in 1903. A 1903 script submitted for copyright, whose basic structure was retained through the Broadway and touring versions, is our main source of the action of the musical.[30] In 2010, with a group of friends from the Oz Club, I attended a rare revival of the show by the Canton Comic Opera. Necessary changes to meet modern standards of performance and content, rather than inauthentic, were in keeping with the show's historical tendency to change form for different audiences and performers.

Perhaps many would experience the show only through recordings, sheet music, and media stories. Published sheet music was sold at retail and sometimes published as newspaper supplements alongside lyrics, theater reviews, and feature stories. Sound recordings were issued by popular singers of the day.[31] Audiences of all ages could sing songs from the show at home and likely recreated performances of the show in home theatricals. At the centennial Oz convention in 2000, we reenacted this activity. With photocopies of the original sheet music we gathered around the piano, where I somewhat clumsily played through the music while everyone sang along, much as early twentieth-century consumers might have done at the parlor piano. Singing these songs from sheet music at home or listening to recordings would necessarily involve performances of race, gender, and class. Hearing original wax-cylinder recordings of the extravaganza songs at another Oz convention in my youth, I learned about "coon songs" and the racial and ethnic stereotypes typical of turn of the century theater.

In the extravaganza, the performance of "America" is an elaborate act of unabashed performance. In the book, characters are unaware of their performances of brains, heart, and courage before they meet the Wizard. In the musical extravaganza, they seem fully aware of putting on a show, acknowledging their performances of identity and "America" at the turn of the century. So whatever other kind of American utopia Oz might be, this first musical adaptation is above all a theatrical one. It abandoned the narrative unity of the book to stage a carnival of performance, in which the ritual of going to the theater stood in for the home-away-home pattern of the fairy tale.[32] The musicalization of Baum's book according to the theatrical conventions of the time inherently transformed the American fairy tale. While the book naturalizes a White American fairyland, the extravaganza is a carnivalesque immigrant "melting pot" synonymous with theatrical culture, though performed by mostly Anglo-American writers and actors in caricatured ethnic and gendered stock characters. Dorothy's desire to go home is eclipsed by the pleasure of indulgent performances reflecting a land of immigrants, colonizers, formerly enslaved people, and Indigenous people. The portrayal of American racial diversity in the extravaganza is in contrast not only to Baum's book but also to the MGM film.

What's an extravaganza? Even people in the time of the Oz extravaganza struggled to understand what it was. They struggled even more to understand what *The Wizard of Oz*, in particular, was as an instantiation of the genre.[33] Like its forerunners in the late nineteenth century, the Oz extravaganza combined a variety of forms of popular American entertainment. As one of the last of the extravaganzas, *The Wizard of Oz* was both a throwback to earlier shows and possibly more of a hodgepodge than ever. Its treatment of the fairy tale is in the traditions of pantomime and burlesque, which parodied familiar stories, adding topical jokes, cross-dressing, and chorus girls in tights. The general spirit resembled what we might now call the "fractured fairy tale." The script was serviceably zany, with obligatory romantic and political subplots added to Baum's story. The humor relied on puns and cross-talk inherited from the minstrel show and vaudeville, and its large choruses, extravagant sets, and spectacular transformation scenes were favorably compared to the visually opulent productions of David Belasco.[34] The show's textual instability exemplifies the "unfinished show business" of musical theater.[35] Songs were performance vehicles more than storytelling devices, showcasing the specialties of the performers and often serving as diversions rather than advancing or even commenting on the plot. Some songs by Baum and Tietjens were retained, but most were by other songwriters and were regularly switched out over time to suit changing actors and audiences. Dorothy was played by Anna Laughlin, a young woman in the role of a child, but the true stars of this Oz were Fred Stone and David Montgomery, a vaudeville comedy team who, as the Scarecrow and Tin Woodman, engaged in circus acrobatics, comedic cross-talk, specialty songs, and vestigial minstrel tropes that were key to the show's popularity (Figures 1.1 and 1.2).[36]

The Wizard of Oz was a family musical. Its melding of theatrical genres, its marketing, and its critical reception evidence a desire to appeal to mixed audiences of children and adults. Fairy tale theater, pantomime, vaudeville, minstrelsy, and the circus, all of which are represented in *The Wizard of Oz*, were entertainments for "children of all ages" in the nineteenth and early twentieth centuries, combining child-friendly elements with more "mature" material.[37] *The Wizard of Oz* was the first show to play the new Majestic Theater located on Columbus Circle, some distance from the heart of the Broadway theater district and its more adult fare. It was praised for being clean and family friendly.[38] At special matinees for children, Fred Stone, the show's star, greeted kids in the lobby in his Scarecrow costume and drew his signed caricature for them.[39] At the same time, the show retained

Figure 1.1. Anna Laughlin as Dorothy from the musical extravaganza *The Wizard of Oz*, 1902. Billy Rose Theatre Collection, New York Public Library for the Performing Arts.

some feminine sexual spectacle, especially in the chorus, and the marketing emphasized that the show was not *just* for kids. One advertisement (Figure 1.3) promoted the beauty of the chorus girls alongside the juvenile appeal of the pantomime animals.[40] The *New York Telegram* for January 21, 1903, declared *Oz* "an entertainment that will please children of all ages, from six to ninety-six."[41] Similar to efforts to make theater more family-friendly with the founding of vaudeville by Tony Pastor in the late nineteenth century, *The Wizard of Oz* may have helped define what a family musical of its time might look like by the way it addressed both children and adults in its audience.

Figure 1.2. Fred Stone and David Montgomery as the Scarecrow and Tin Woodman from the musical extravaganza *The Wizard of Oz*, 1902. Billy Rose Theatre Collection, New York Public Library for the Performing Arts.

The extravaganza imagines the parameters of participation in America, its musicals, and its fairy tales at a time when immigration was at a high point and the modern form of the musical was developing. The show's ethnic numbers included coon songs and songs in Irish, Scotch, Italian, and Dutch performances, whose conventions both transgressed and reinforced lines of color, class, and age.[42] At this time, theater presented an opportunity for immigrants and others to participate in, and shape, American culture. Jewish, Irish, Italian, German ("Dutch"), and other immigrant groups used musical theater to encode their minority identities while negotiating whether and how to assimilate in America.[43] Identity was performed as fluid, as one performer might change ethnic styles multiple times in the course of the show. However, even as Black musicals were flourishing on Broadway at the turn of the century, Black actors would not appear in a "White" show like *The Wizard of Oz*.[44] Instead, stereotyped performances of Black and ethnic stock characters by White actors ultimately served to reinforce White supremacy, especially in the performance of blackface minstrel tropes. Consequently, thing-like characters, such as the Scarecrow and Tin Woodman, in racialized performances, provoke questions about who possesses personhood in the American fairy tale.

Figure 1.3. Advertisement for the musical extravaganza *The Wizard of Oz*, 1902. Billy Rose Theatre Division, New York Public Library for the Performing Arts.

The style of the show invited participation in the conscious performance of American identity, playing to the audience while indulging in carnival-esque inversions and fluid performances. Characters appear in and out of disguise, adding to the playfulness around the performance of identity as the plot diverges farther and farther from the familiar story. These irreverent touches intentionally break the spell of the fairy tale and acknowledge it as performance.

The legacy of the extravaganza for Oz, musicals, and American culture is significant. Despite being ridiculed by New York critics as incoherent and unsophisticated, *The Wizard of Oz* was a big success, leaving its mark on the repertoires of both Oz and musicals.[45] After playing in New York for two seasons, it went on popular tours across the country. It was still being produced by local and regional theaters as late as the 1920s, and it remained in the minds of the MGM filmmakers, who borrowed some of its ideas, including the transformation scene in which the Good Witch breaks the spell of the poppies with a fall of snow, a detail not in Baum's book. The show also gave Dorothy her last name, Gale, a likely pun on the storm that blew her to Oz. Its success led to the production of Victor Herbert's *Babes in Toyland* by the same production team in the same theater in the following season, resulting in a "moment" for the children's musical and affirming the Majestic's reputation as "the much-needed women's and children's playhouse."[46]

The extravaganza offers a more urban, zesty, and irreverent performance of the American fairy tale than the book, both because of its collaborators, who were urban theatrical types, and because of the conventions of musical theater of the time. Differences between the book and the extravaganza are further attributable to the need for a live theatrical performance to more committedly address an audience of copresent adults and children. As a result, the American fairy tale unfolded on the stage according to its own designs.

Staging the American Fairy Tale

The extravaganza begins, as many Oz musicals do, in Kansas, but briefly, because what matters most in this show is that we get to the more theatrical land of Oz as quickly as possible. There is no "I Want" song for Dorothy in this musical. A wordless tableau on the Kansas farm, set to a musical prelude, portrayed farmhands, Dorothy, and her cow, Imogene, played by an actor in pantomime costume. There is no Toto. This scene is interrupted by a tornado, created with novel light projections and other effects. This display of American humbug was about its own accomplishment as theater, using the best technology of the time.

We are transported to Oz, an inherently theatrical version of America. It's several minutes before Dorothy appears on stage again, because first we have to be introduced to a motley cast of characters representing American and musical theater types. First there are the Munchkins (here played by chorus members of typical height) dancing around a maypole in celebration of Dorothy's house having killed and freed them from the Wicked Witch of the East. Like all the other characters, they speak in contemporary theatrical language full of patter and puns. Next we are introduced to Cynthia Cynch, a comic Ophelia-like "lady lunatic" who is searching for her enchanted lost love Niccolo, who plays the piccolo (and eventually turns out to be the Tin Woodman). She sings "Niccolo's Piccolo," which introduces the tune that, upon hearing, will make Niccolo remember who he is and return to her. The Good Witch of the North, named Locusta, finally arrives, not in a pink bubble, as in the more familiar MGM film, but rather unceremoniously. A member of the Sorcerer's Union, she informs the Munchkins that Dorothy's house has killed the Wicked Witch of the East, freeing them from her bondage. Sir Dashemoff Daily, the poet laureate of Oz played in travesty by a woman, arrives to announce that Pastoria, the rightful ruler of Oz, has returned to reclaim the throne from the Wizard. Pastoria himself then arrives in the garb of a streetcar motorman, a job he has been holding down while exiled in Topeka. He and his girlfriend Tryxie Tryfle, a waitress, have been blown back to Oz in the same storm that brought Dorothy. Showing their essentially theatrical characters, Tryxie sings "When the Circus Comes to Town," and Pastoria presumptively sells tickets to his coronation. If all of this is hard to follow, the main point is that there is a lot of conventional musical-theatrical fun going on.

Finally, Dorothy wanders onto the scene to be caught up in the theatrical enterprise. Setting a long-lived precedent of adolescents or young women playing Dorothy, Anna Laughlin played dress-up in a short skirt and bonnet ("round-eyed" in "baby frocks," according to one critic), heightening the impression of her precocity and attractiveness as a young performer.[47] Her mixture of childishness and maturity conforms to a theatrical tradition of women playing little girls, with a mixture of adult sexual availability and exaggerated innocence, a combination that allows her to become the love interest of Dashemoff.[48] Promotional photographs show her looking coy yet alluring, returning the viewer's gaze while playfully offering a bite of her apple or nibbling on the ribbon of her bonnet (Figure 1.1). In addition, her costume is suggestive of a milkmaid, a figure historically and conventionally portrayed as sexualized.[49] Critics described her voice as high, slight, and raspy, a sound perhaps associated with a conventional performance of infantile girlishness. One reviewer described her as "a small person with a voice of the emery-paper calibre" that "would ignite any match." Chicago critic Amy Leslie advised that she should learn a more mature style of singing before the strain ruined her voice.[50] Laughlin seemed to have the voice of a little girl in a young woman's body—the opposite of Garland in the MGM film, who was a teenager with a mature voice. In either case, the performativity of girlhood is highlighted.

With theatricality and diversionary entertainment the main purposes of the show, the stakes of Dorothy's journey through Oz and return home are generally low compared to other musicals or the book. Conforming to theatrical convention, Dorothy immediately catches the heart of Dashemoff Daily, played in the original production by actress Bessie Wynn.[51] Wynn was entirely legible as a woman in the role—critics praised her beauty and shapeliness in revealing tights, which was a point of such roles—so that a queer subtext is available when she sings "Love Is Love," to express infatuation with Dorothy. There is no Wicked Witch of the West in this version of Oz to raise the stakes for Dorothy's adventure, and although Dorothy gets into some trouble with Pastoria, he doesn't pose nearly the same threat.

As things proceed, Oz is at times barely distinguishable from turn-of-the-century America. References to popular entertainment approach metacommentary on American comedic and theatrical conventions. Pastoria reveals that his full name is Tony Pastoria, an apparent pun on Tony Pastor, the founder of vaudeville. Tryxie laments that she and Pastoria were whisked away from Kansas just as Barnum's circus was coming to town and she sings a solo in tribute to the American circuses that were training grounds for many performers, including the starring comedy duo of Montgomery and Stone. ("When the Circus Comes to Town"). Jokes about Theodore Roosevelt and other public figures acknowledge contemporary politics while inviting the audience into the performance through humor. The Scarecrow speculates that, as a man of straw, he might be related to Secretary of State John Hay, and when he meets the Wizard, he specifically asks for a Mark Hanna brain, referring to the Ohio senator who was regarded as the brains behind William McKinley's political success (another man behind the curtain). While the Wizard represents humbug as a general American practice, jokes about particular figures could prompt audiences to make specific connections between humbug and contemporary politics. These topical references set this version apart from the book and the MGM film, which tend to portray Oz as more distinct from the "real" America. It's in keeping, though, with the more referential humor of *The Wiz* and *Wicked*.

In contrast to their earnest treatment in the book, the extravaganza treats magical objects comically. Instead of magic shoes, Locusta the Good Witch gives Dorothy a magic ring, which will protect her and grant all of two (not even three!) wishes. Locusta then has to dash off because she has business with the Sorcerers Union, leaving Dorothy to her own devices in the use of the ring. This becomes a bit of a joke, as Dorothy wastes both wishes right away—first by wishing that she knew the melody to some song lyrics she finds and then by idly wishing the Scarecrow were alive. She can't use it to wish herself home, because it only works within the borders of Oz.

The most potent kind of magic in this American fairyland is performance, which brings the characters to life. During the action described up to this point, the Scarecrow has been carried onstage and hung up on his pole by some Munchkins. Stone took great pride in his ability to remain perfectly still until it was time for him to come alive to the audience's astonishment.[52] After Dorothy helps him down and agrees to take him with her to see the Wizard for a brain, she asks him if he can walk, and he remarks, "No, I'll take steps to learn" (get it?). With a little practice, the Scarecrow progresses from immobility to clumsy walking to bouncing around the stage in the manner that was a specialty of the acrobatic Stone. In a pattern that will repeat in other musicals, the Scarecrow and Dorothy's other new friends struggle in the use of their bodies in their first few moments as they begin learning the gestures of the musical. In this version, the Scarecrow sings a modest song, "Alas for the Man without Brains," by Baum and Tietjens, including an instrumental dance section that no doubt allowed Stone to feature his dancing and physical comedy skills.

Theatrical conventions and musical gestures motivate the party's progress as Dorothy and the Scarecrow encounter the Tin Woodman rusted on the road. They oil him up and he apologizes for being socially "rusty." Like the Scarecrow, he demonstrates virtuosity in song and dance as he joins Dorothy on the trip. The song the three friends sing at this point highlights a difference between this musical and subsequent ones. Instead of a song about group performance and shared objectives like MGM's "We're Off to See the Wizard" or The Wiz's "Ease on Down the Road," they sing one of this show's hit songs, "When You Love, Love, Love" (companion website 1.1). In a walking tempo it serves both as a song about the Tin Woodman's desire for a heart and as the song to which the three companions march down the road. It reflexively references the clichés and conventions of popular song and the importance of romantic sentiment in popular theater.

Oh, love's the thing that poets sing / Their sweetest lays regarding / And some say nay to love's gay sway / Which wounds when not rewarding . . .

When you love, love, love / In mad delirium, / When to love, love, love / That's quite sincere you come. / There is nothing so divine / There is nothing half so fine, / As the gladness Of your madness / When you love, love, love.

The song evokes basic forms of popular music of the time, the verse's 6/8 meter implying something like a waltz, and the chorus a march. Appropriate to this version of Oz, the song's ultimate significance is in simply being a rather conventional song, one that could be sold separately in sheet music and recordings. Yet, it's also a parody of its type. In the last verse, the heart turns "quite stony," as one finds their former lover "is seeking alimony."

Meanwhile, the pantomime animals, the Cowardly Lion and Imogene the Cow, put the comedy into musical comedy in their nonsinging, nonspeaking roles (Figure 1.3). The Lion never becomes part of the core group with Dorothy, the Scarecrow, and Tin Woodman, but he steals the scene when he preens comically while posing for Pastoria, who "shoots" him with a camera. He then becomes part of Pastoria and Tryxie's team, helping them to pose as circus performers as they plot to take back the throne of Oz. Imogene's running gag is that she's always trying to eat the straw-stuffed Scarecrow. This comedic role for animals, and for the Lion in particular lives on in Bert Lahr's performance in the MGM film.

The transformation scene that capped these performances in the act one finale was the spectacular highlight of the show.[53] On their way to the Emerald City, Dorothy and her friends wander into the poisonous poppy field, where they encounter Pastoria and Tryxie, in their circus disguises and accompanied by the Cowardly Lion, on their way to reclaim the throne from the Wizard. The Poppies are played by chorus girls with flower hats, whose faces are hidden until they look up. While they sing the "Poppy Song," Dorothy and the other human and animal characters fall victim to their soporific effects. The Good Witch, Locusta, sends a snowstorm to wilt the Poppies. Through stage effects, the scene changes to winter and Dorothy wakes up as the first act comes to a close. Such transformation scenes were a fascination to audiences, who marveled at the technology and stagecraft.

The great American humbug himself appears in act two, which takes place in the Emerald City where he sings, dances, and hosts performances by others. This Wizard is a more cynical version of the humbug than the book's. His magic act is a standard trick: an assistant steps into a large basket, which is filled with acid, pierced through with swords, and opened to reveal that he has safely disappeared. Audiences would likely recognize this as a familiar and explicable magic trick. Although in the plot of the show the Wizard is deposed when it's revealed that the basket has a false bottom, it's likely no betrayal of any magicians' secret to the audience. The Wizard's real magic is ethnic transformation. Played by different actors in the course of the Chicago, New York, and touring productions, his ethnic specialty changed from Irish to "Dutch" and back to Irish as he sang songs with such titles as "Mr. Dooly" and "Budweiser Is a Friend of Mine."[54] After his basket trick, the Wizard passes a hat, but no one gives, because they have no money till payday. So the Wizard sings "On a Pay Night Evening" while chorus girls dance with pickaxes. Appearing in different guises from one song or bit to the next (Figure 1.4), he is a precedent for the chameleon transformations of the Wizard in the MGM film and *The Wiz*.

As the various characters arrive in the Emerald City for their differing reasons, the Wizard's palace becomes a theater for their song, dance, and comedy diversions. Cynthia, believing the Wizard to be her enchanted lost

Figure 1.4. John Slavin as the Wizard in the musical extravaganza *The Wizard of Oz*, 1902. Billy Rose Theatre Division, New York Public Library for the Performing Arts.

Niccolo, serenades him with "'Twas Enough to Make a Perfect Lady Mad." Dorothy, the Scarecrow, and the Tin Woodman anticipate that the Wizard will grant their wishes, singing "When We Get What's a-Comin' to Us," a kind of collective "I want" song with a similar placement to MGM's "If I Were King of the Forest." After giving the Scarecrow and Tin Woodman brains and heart, the Wizard celebrates his own genius by putting on a show, presiding over a "Ball of All Nations," a long divertissement in which members of the cast perform a variety of national and ethnic specialty numbers (Figure 1.5),

Figure 1.5. Advertising poster depicting the "Ball of All Nations" and Poppy Chorus in the musical extravaganza *The Wizard of Oz*, 1903. Library of Congress, Prints and Photographs Division.

positioning national identity as a performance while ambiguously celebrating or ridiculing Americans of different national and ethnic origins. It
included such numbers as Stone's Italian specialty "Goodbye Fedora," and
Laughlin's coon song "Under a Panama." Tryxie Tryfle sings one of the show's
big hits, "Sammy," when she infiltrates the Wizard's palace in her circus disguise (companion website 1.2).[55] During the song, the actress would serenade
an unsuspecting male audience member seated in what came to be known as
the "Sammy" box. Both the song and the stunt, acknowledging the performance by acknowledging the audience, were hugely popular. Montgomery
and Stone's comedic duets in this portion of act two showcased their performing personae. In "Hurrah for Baffin's Bay" and "Football," for example,
the Scarecrow and Tin Woodman dressed up as sailors and football players.
In these routines, they were recognizable as themselves, as characters, and as
the comedy team Montgomery and Stone.[56]

In this spiraling carnival of pluralistic American performances, the story
as we know it is abandoned by the end of the second of three acts. Act two
ends with Pastoria successfully wresting the throne from the Wizard, culminating in a large production number with the chorus singing "The Wizard Is
No Longer King," while Dorothy tries to defend him on the authority of her
plain American sincerity, singing, "I am just a simple girl from the Prairie."
Because the Wizard grants the Scarecrow and Tin Woodman their brains
and heart on first meeting, the role of the Wicked Witch of the West is elimi-
nated. Instead, having aligned themselves with the Wizard, Dorothy and her
friends become enemies of Pastoria's new regime. The third act consists of
specialty performances and interpolated songs as they flee in disguise from
Pastoria's army. Here, one of Fred Stone's hit songs was a solo, "The Traveler
and the Pie," which he sang while evading arrest. This was followed by the
Scarecrow, the Tin Woodman, and Dorothy singing additional comedic
numbers and minstrel-derived coon songs. The show ends abruptly in a con-
trived happy ending typical of comic opera. The trio are apprehended, and
Dorothy, sentenced to execution by beheading, calls on the Good Witch just
before the blade falls. In a *diva ex machina*, the Good Witch in turn calls on
Glenda [*sic*], who never appears on stage but is apparently more powerful,
to create another cyclone. Pastoria declares that Oz can't deal with any more
cyclones and in frustration sets everyone free. The curtain falls. If Dorothy
returns to Kansas, it's not shown, and according to Oz scholar David Maxine,
in Broadway performances of the show, Dorothy stayed in Oz.[57] It's only the

fun of Oz that matters in this show (there are, in fact, several jokes ridiculing Kansas). More important than Dorothy's return home has been the transformative journey of theater.

Performing "America" in the Extravaganza

The star turns of Montgomery, Stone, and Laughlin as the Scarecrow, Tin Woodman, and Dorothy highlight the performances of race, gender, and "America" at the turn of the century. Montgomery and Stone brought vestigial minstrel, circus, and pantomime elements to their performances of the Scarecrow and Tin Woodman. The two had been performing in a British pantomime when they were hired for *The Wizard of Oz*, but they began their collaboration years earlier as a blackface minstrel act, drawing on Montgomery's experience as an end man in Haverly's Minstrels and incorporating coon songs and minstrel tropes in their vaudeville routines. Stone specialized in virtuosic, loose-limbed eccentric dancing influenced by blackface minstrelsy, African American dance, and his background as a juvenile circus acrobat. As noted by musicologist Jonas Westover, Montgomery considered blackface minstrelsy good comedic and physical training: "In the old days everyone was a good blackface minstrel, and then made his mark as a funmaker of one sort or another in whiteface." By "whiteface," he meant that performers continued to perform minstrel tropes without the blackface makeup.[58]

Stone's pale makeup for the Scarecrow, which he designed himself, made this idea of whiteface literal, preserving the practice of minstrelsy while giving it cover to pass as innocent, racially vacated clowning. He painted his entire face with whitish flesh-colored makeup so that it became a blank canvas for painting on the Scarecrow's features without being limited by the positions of his own eyes, nose and mouth. Audiences were so fascinated with this makeup that Stone would apply it sitting next to the window of his dressing room for the benefit of a gathering audience on the street.[59] This whiteface makeup simultaneously suggested and denied the racial nature of the characterization, recalling blackface while whitewashing it and displaying what Robin Bernstein calls black-and-whiteness, in which the minstrel performer's makeup holds "blackness and whiteness both in distinction and in tender contact," acting out the "promise and threat of racial flip-flops."[60] Oversized white gloves and Stone's eccentric dancing completed the minstrel-clown performance, and he was frequently and favorably compared to the legendary pantomime actor George L. Fox, who had achieved fame in the late nineteenth century playing Humpty Dumpty in white clown makeup. These comparisons aligned with the press's characterizations of Montgomery and Stone as performers embodying youthfulness in their antics and physicality, much like Fox, and, at the same time, much like the infantilized characters of blackface minstrel shows.[61]

Writing in in the Black newspaper the *Indianapolis Freeman* in 1904, Black theater critic Sylvester Russell, recognizing the musical's racially ambiguous appropriations, proposed a Black-cast production. He wrote, "the characters played by Montgomery and Stone are idiotic themes disguising their countenance with false faces and paints. Curious stage people—neither white nor black."[62] *The Wizard of Oz* had two road companies at the time. Describing Montgomery and Stone as White mediocrities, Russell proposed a third company starring Black minstrels Bert Williams and George Walker, who, having "had to plough through all the common prejudices of America" had achieved greater, earlier success than Montgomery and Stone. He added, "Mr. Williams could play Mr. Stone's part as it has never been played before (so could Bob Cole) and Mr. Walker could play Mr. Montgomery's part—but with plenty of clown grease on his face." The impossibility of this casting highlights the color line that blackface and whiteface both served to maintain. White actors could cork up in blackface as a means of tacitly reinforcing their own Whiteness, but blackness remained positioned as immutable.[63] Despite the flourishing of Black musical theater on Broadway at this time, Oz musicals would remain largely White affairs until *The Wiz* arrived on Broadway seventy years later.[64] Bernstein notes that because of Stone's influence on the character, minstrelsy "fundamentally structured the deepest logics of Oz after 1902," not only on stage, but also in subsequent Oz books.[65] With Stone's Scarecrow as the prototype, the legacies of minstrelsy potentially live on vestigially in Ray Bolger's Scarecrow in the MGM film, which he modeled on his eccentric dancing idol Stone, and in *The Wiz*'s Scarecrow, played by dancing actors Hinton Battle and Michael Jackson, who can be seen as reappropriating the character's minstrel tropes in authoritative performances of Blackness.[66]

Along with their racial complexity, Montgomery and Stone were queerly protean in their performances and quick changes of costume and identity.

Their unstable performing identities defied normative behavior and embodiment. As a male comedy duo, they can be seen in a tradition of comedy teams who read queerly because of their close relationship and the intimate situations in which they find themselves.[67] In their popular duet "Hurrah for Baffin's Bay," sung during act two in the Emerald City, their antics included climbing into cramped quarters in a small boat while singing a pun-filled account of a nautical expedition ("We'll tie the ship, whatever else betide") (companion website 1.3). The homoerotic connotations that historically attach to images of seamen adds to the queer potential of the performance. Similarly, in "Football," which at times substituted for "Baffin's Bay," they acted out the bodily violence of the contact sport in physical comedy that got them into compromising positions with each other and the football. Promotional photos of Montgomery and Stone show them in close contact, embracing or engaging in physical play—the Tin Man playfully reverses roles to oil the Scarecrow, and the Scarecrow pours liquid down the Tin Woodman's throat using his hat for a funnel. Such queer performances emerge as historically and situationally available in the antinormative cultures of the popular theater. In Oz musicals, the intimate homosocial comedy relationship carries through from the extravaganza to the "friends of Dorothy" in the MGM film and *The Wiz* to the relationship between Elphaba and Glinda in *Wicked*.

Somewhere between human and racially thing-like in their performances, the extravaganza's characters implicitly posed questions about who counted as a feeling, acting subject in American society.[68] Implying her White innocence, critics described Laughlin as "pretty as a doll and dressed exactly like one" and remarked on "her small face, with its always doll-like smile, her small figure, which twists its way into odd dances, and her small voice, which wavers through a half-dozen songs."[69] The observation that her "small body twists its way into odd dances" suggests how her Whiteness allowed her to participate in the show's minstrel tropes. Fred Stone's Scarecrow was "boneless as an india-rubber doll."[70] He had what Bernstein calls tossability, a characteristic of Black dolls that scripts their lack of sentience and invites their abuse.[71] In addition to walking on his ankles and the slapstick business from which he seemed bounce back unharmed, in one of the show's famous special effects, the Scarecrow was rescued from a prison by being cut apart, passed through the bars one limb at a time, and sewn back together before the audience's eyes.[72] For his part, Montgomery's Tin Man was described as a "toy soldier," with robotic movements. The delicateness of Dorothy and the inability of the Scarecrow and Tin Man as vestigial minstrel characters to be harmed conform to the convention that White people are to be protected while no amount of harm to a character racialized as other than White is of consequence.

A striking racial performance in the minstrel tradition is Stone's "Indian" specialty song, "Sitting Bull," which was added to the Ball of All Nations in 1904 (companion website 1.4). It tells the story of a lazy Indian who "would do no work" and "sat around the camp so much / They called him Sitting Bull." He was a "well red man" who became a barber, and once your hair was cut, "you'd never need it cut again."[73] In this number, Stone's black-and-whiteface was a blank canvas on which the tropes of redface could also be projected.[74] After a minor, percussive verse vaguely suggestive of "native" drumming, the chorus evokes what might be heard as a circus march. In a "Green Corn Dance" accompanied by chorus girls as Indian maidens, Stone performed an especially strenuous eccentric dance presumably combining the appropriated Black movement of the style with stereotypes of "Indian" choreography. The combination of exotic Black and Indigenous stereotypes, juxtaposed with insinuations of a circus act, recalls Barnum and his racial exhibitions. Sitting Bull, the Lakota leader, subject of Baum's genocidal editorials, was himself exhibited in Buffalo Bill Cody's *Wild West Show*, while his cabin was displayed at the World's Columbian Exposition of 1893 along with exhibits of living Native Americans. The practice of "playing Indian" among White children and adults, and which ultimately affirms White supremacy in the ability to grow out of or take off the primitive costume, here elides with theatrical traditions of the Native American as a stock character and spectacular fiction.[75]

Further demonstrating the supremacy of White actors over their Black and Indigenous characterizations, act three was popular for the placement of coon songs. Montgomery and Stone's "Cockney coon song," "That's Where She Sits All Day," a parody of British performers of blackface minstrel songs, was a big hit. Dorothy would often sing a coon song of her own. Her standard number was "The Sweetest Girl in Dixie," the type of song, in the tradition of Stephen Foster's "Oh! Susana," a minstrel man would sing about missing his sweetheart down South. In "I'll Be Your Honey in the Spring Time," which appeared in the Chicago production, she sings, in strong dialect, that she'll be a man's "honey" when he buys her a ring, while a characteristic short-long syncopation against steady accompaniment evokes the sound of ragtime and cakewalk (companion website 1.5). To imagine Laughlin singing this song in her reportedly babyish voice is to recognize the viciousness of the stereotype of an infantile Black character. Professional minstrelsy had been almost exclusively performed by adult men before the Civil War, but by the late nineteenth century, the association of minstrelsy with childhood gave it claims to innocence allowing its continuation in school and community performances. As Lynne Vallone has noted, White girls' amateur minstrel performances used the juxtaposition of ridiculed Blackness to reaffirm middle-class White girls' class and racial status.[76] Laughlin's performance here can be seen in this light. She was trained in the buck and wing, a dance she did in "I'll Be Your Honey in the Springtime," which was a synthesis of Irish and African tapping and clogging traditions, usually associated with male performers.[77] Thus, her performance compounds her age transvestism with crossings of the boundaries of race and gender but ultimately maintains the race line as she keeps her presumptive core of White innocence.

Each Oz musical teaches Dorothy and the audience something a little bit different about how to act American. In the extravaganza, it's the conscious performance, in and of itself, of an American character (or more accurately, characterization) with consciousness of racial, gender, and other social codes. As we've seen, these performances are complicated in the ways in which they include and exclude Americans in the performance of the American fairy tale.

Founding a Musical-Theatrical Repertoire

As it grew into a national phenomenon, Oz continued to be influenced by theatrical conventions and the memory of the extravaganza. Baum attempted to theatricalize his other Oz books through less successful stage and silent film adaptations. The books themselves, as children's literature scholar Joel Chaston notes, are carnivalesque in their theatrical influence and the intention that they would also become musicals.[78] *The Marvelous Land of Oz* (1904) was dedicated to Montgomery and Stone, who were illustrated in their roles as the Scarecrow and Tin Woodman on the dedication page and endpapers (Figure 1.6).[79] The story features the characters prominently in the hope that Montgomery and Stone would reprise their roles in the second

Figure 1.6. Dedication to Montgomery and Stone, *The Marvelous Land of Oz* by L. Frank Baum, illustrated by John R. Neill, 1904.

Oz musical (they declined). Dialogue included comedic cross-talk, backstory referencing the extravaganza's Pastoria, and an army of women in skirts, who could be portrayed by chorus girls in the eventual stage production. The musical adapted from this book, *The Wogglebug* (1905), was not as successful as *The Wizard of Oz*, however, nor was *The Tik-Tok Man of Oz* (1913), based on the third Oz book, *Ozma of Oz* (1907). Neither advanced to Broadway.

The extravaganza helped ensure the popularity of *The Wonderful Wizard of Oz* while standing as the first entry in the repertoire of musicals that expanded its mythology. The earnest quality of the book and the carnival theatrical artifice of the extravaganza are competing influences in subsequent musicals based on Oz, in part because of the tensions between cohesion and carnival, realism and artifice, are already inherent in musicals. The interplay of artifice and sincerity in the American musical also informs the multivalent performances of the MGM film, whose influence on both Oz and musicals is inestimable.

2

My Own Backyard

MGM's *The Wizard of Oz*

The Wizard of Oz has always been a movie I've seen. I can remember being
about four or five years old during the era of the annual television broadcasts
and being excited to see it again. Watching it every year was an almost religious ritual for me, as it was for many American children. It was my first encounter with Oz and one of my first musicals. The place the movie acquired
in American life through television is unmatched by previous versions of Oz
or other musicals. Around the time I was finishing high school and going
to college I became aware that the film was considered a gay classic. This
is probably also when I learned about camp, which gave me a new way of
appreciating the movie at a time when I was cultivating a sense of myself as a
gay person. This film, a symbol of middle America, adorning collector plates
and kitschy memorabilia lining the walls of my bedroom, had a whole new,
somewhat subversive, reason to be a feature of my identity. The changing significance of *The Wizard of Oz* in my individual case points to the multiple
ways Americans have engaged with this musical film. MGM's *Wizard of Oz*
is the most famous Oz adaptation, more widely seen than the book has been
read, and surely the most influential musical.

The MGM film adds to the utopian features of the American fairy tale
those specific to the conventions of the classical Hollywood musical. It exemplifies Richard Dyer's description of the film musical as utopian entertainment, as its characters ecstatically burst into song in musical and Technicolor
fantasy environments. In contrast with the extravaganza, it marks an early
entry in the emerging concept of the "integrated" musical further cultivated
on Broadway and in Hollywood in the 1940s, with songs meant to be driven
by plot and character.[1] In "Over the Rainbow," it introduces a quintessential
"I want" song, and in its technical wizardry, it presents film itself as the psychological dream factory with Oz as literally one of its dreams. Its performative excess and camp aesthetic, a specialty of the MGM film musical, appeal

Oz and the Musical. Ryan Bunch, Oxford University Press. © Oxford University Press 2023.
DOI: 10.1093/oso/9780190843137.003.0003

to middle American and subcultural audiences, all of whom see themselves in the film.

The film's conformity to the emerging model of the integrated musical reflects its apparent alliance with a nostalgic, sentimental ideal of America in the era of the Great Depression, the Motion Picture Production Code, and World War II, which began in Europe while the film was playing in theaters in 1939. As musical theater scholar Bradley Rogers notes, the ideology of "integration" of song and story in musicals is an attempted defense against the rupturing of normative identity produced by the act of bursting into song, but the musical in fact thrives on this "radical act of disintegration."[2] More cohesive than the extravaganza, the MGM film's relative musical integration superficially affirms sentimental, innocent, White American childhood as proof of the goodness of America and its utopia. At the same time, its musical and theatrical gestures, in their disruption of spoken and pedestrian norms, encode queer, Jewish, and other subcultural performances of the people working in classical-era Hollywood. These gestures—singing "Over the Rainbow," dancing on the yellow brick road—became part of an American vocabulary, available for repetition and revision. Its songs are the standards against which the songs in other shows can be understood in their functions and expressions of American performance. Its wholesome image papers over the darker themes and aspects of its American moment, in contrast to the irreverence of the extravaganza, ultimately necessitating responses in the Black joy of *The Wiz* and the ambivalence of *Wicked*.

Like the extravaganza, the MGM film is a family musical addressing both kids and adults in its time and place. In the era of the Motion Picture Production Code, films were made to the specifications of those who feared the ill effects of popular media on children. This is a fundamental respect in which the presence of children in the audience influenced the making of MGM's musical version of Oz. The film reflects a conservatism that the Code required in filmic representations of America. Much as theater had become more "innocent" family entertainment after Tony Pastor's vaudeville, as reflected in the Oz extravaganza, Hollywood was "innocent" American family entertainment after the Code. Of course, no media text is innocent when it comes to the representation of America. The many people who collaborated on *The Wizard of Oz* brought different experiences and perspectives to the film, including those that were outside the mainstream.

Anxieties the filmmakers faced about how to appeal to both kids and adults affected what kind of musical *The Wizard of Oz* became. MGM hoped to duplicate Disney's success with *Snow White and the Seven Dwarfs* (1937), but everyone was very concerned that adult audiences would not accept a live-action fantasy with actors in costume.[3] Possibly following the example of the extravaganza's burlesque treatment of the fairy tale, early screenplay drafts relied heavily on irreverent musical comedy. Various tentative scripts included a prince and princess in the mold of Jeannette McDonald and Nelson Eddy, a comedic Wicked Witch who worked in an office building with a frosted glass door on which her services of "Cruelties, Tortures and all kinds of Devilments" were listed, and a Lion who was in actuality an enchanted prince.[4] The final screenplay shares with *Snow White* a careful integration of song and story, somewhat aligning it with the Disney film's reliance on operetta, a form associated at the time with nostalgia, fantasy, and family audiences.[5] For a good additional measure of nostalgia, some marketing materials characterized the film almost as an adaptation of the extravaganza, which was still remembered as a popular piece of family theater.[6] In sum, the film consciously deployed the pleasures of music, lyrics, dance, and participation in its musicalization of the American fairy tale for an audience of all ages.

The dual address to children and adults creates a camp interplay of innocence in subversion in this iteration of the musical American fairy tale.[7] Dorothy's adult male friends in Oz, recognizable as actors and as the farmhands from Kansas, maintain a "realistic core," as described by Raymond Knapp, while seeming to indulge in dress-up play with Dorothy, anticipating and possibly inspiring kids' home Oz play after watching the movie.[8] Singing and dancing are integral to these playful performances, amplifying the camp ambivalence and dual address, and tacitly calling into question the innocence of the film, the audience, and the project of the American fairy tale. In contrast to the extravaganza, however, these performances are balanced by a sentimentality that was key to the film's long-lived success.

The film's dual address to children and adults may also account for Oz becoming a literal dream in the movie. This was the most (in)famous change from the book.[9] While this may have been a "bad faith" choice[10] to make the film's fantasy setting more acceptable to adult audiences, it had certain advantages. In a dream world, playful theatricality could be indulged without violating the cinematic realism established in Kansas. Oz is saturated in Technicolor to show off its extravagant sets, whimsical costumes, plastic flora, painted backgrounds, and most of all Dorothy's sparkling shoes, changed from the book's silver to the more colorful ruby slippers. As a journey into the "dream factory" of Hollywood, *The Wizard of Oz* is reflexive about film itself, a kind of surreal backstage musical in which Oz is a show put on by Dorothy's psyche within an art form theorized as dream work.[11]

Understood in this way, the entire film is a metatheatrical gesture, a performative presentation not just of Oz, the genre of the musical, and "America," but also of Hollywood humbug and what it could do. Overt technological spectacle let audiences in on the art of filmmaking as much as the song and dance aesthetics encouraged a consciousness of the performance of American life. Critics assessed the film's "technical wizardry" and "mechanical trickery" as a measure of its appeal to all ages.[12] Frank Nugent of the *New York Times* declared that "the wizards of Hollywood . . . had the youngsters' eyes shining and brought a quietly amused gleam to the wise ones of the oldsters." At the same time, he pointed out some failures, limitations, and exposures: "even great wizards . . . are often tripped in their flights of fancy . . . with the best of will and ingenuity, they cannot make a Munchkin or a Flying Monkey that will not still suggest . . . a Singer's midget in a Jack Dawn masquerade. Nor can they, without a few betraying jolts and split-screen overlappings, bring down from the sky the great soap bubble in which the Good Witch rides and roll it smoothly into place." But embracing the imperfect illusion, much as Dorothy's friends accepted the Wizard's gifts, he declared: "It is all so well-intentioned, so genial, and so gay that any reviewer who would look down his nose at all the fun-making should be spanked and sent off, supperless, to bed."[13]

The famous camp style of *The Wizard of Oz* addresses as well a tension between assimilationist and subversive utopian impulses. By making the American fairy tale camp, the film assumes a complex posture toward "America." The movie's relative cohesion and middle-American sentimentality are continually disrupted by queer camp, ethnic schtick, and brash theatricality. These performance practices are evidence of marginal groups navigating a conservative film industry and culture that perhaps permitted them less (or at least different) visibility than the New York stage during the time of the extravaganza.[14] In the intervening time, anti-immigrant, anti-Semitic, and anticommunist sentiments had surged, leading to such measures as the Johnson-Reed Act of 1924, which restricted immigration. Because the Production Code sought to protect children by restricting the portrayal of sexuality, gender nonconformity, and sexual deviance, the classical Hollywood musical and family entertainment flourished in concert with each other as well as with the suppression of difference.[15] Here, as in the extravaganza and earlier musicals, immigrants, ethnic minorities, and other marginal Americans were negotiating whether and how to assimilate in a not always welcoming "America" while encoding their inclusion in its theatrical and cinematic utopias.[16]

Through queer camp and ethnic minority theatrical traditions, the collaborators on *The Wizard of Oz* and other Hollywood musicals both invented Hollywood's version of "America" and subverted it by simultaneously revering and ridiculing normative culture.[17] The camp style in musicals was especially cultivated at MGM. The production team assembled by Arthur Freed later came to be known as the Freed Unit, or more derogatorily, "Freed's fairies," because of its large queer personnel.[18] Set designer Cedric Gibbons and costume designer Adrian presided over design teams that created the camp visual aesthetic of Oz, with its curved lines, plastic flora, whimsical costumes, and iconic ruby slippers. The screenwriters—chiefly Noel Langley, Florence Ryerson, and Edgar Allan Woolf—wrote campy lines that made the film a queer classic.[19] Roger Edens, a gay man, was the music supervisor. He was also Garland's early champion and vocal coach within the studio and is credited with helping to cultivate her style and star image.[20] The deliberately light-hearted songs by Jewish songwriters Harold Arlen and Yip Harburg project assimilated cheerfulness. If the MGM film is an American utopia, it is, to a great extent, a queer-Jewish one passing as a mainstream one. This is something of an inversion of the situation with the extravaganza, in which mostly White actors portrayed overtly ethnic stereotypes.

In the succeeding decades, savvy audiences could decode the film's ethnic and queer performances.[21] Perhaps most famously, Oz and "Over the Rainbow" have become icons of queer identity and utopianism in the United States largely on the basis of the film and its association with Judy Garland, who became a gay icon. By the middle of the century, "friends of Dorothy" was code for gay men to identify themselves to each other, possibly referring to Garland fandom especially (but not exclusively) among White, middle-class gay men, and the journey to the Emerald City served as a metaphor for escaping small town life to live in the queer metropolis.[22] The 1969 Stonewall riots were probably not sparked by Garland's funeral, as the mythology claims, but the coincidence of these events symbolically marked a turning point from the culture of the closet, which included Judy Garland fandom, to liberationist politics.

More deeply suppressed is the cultural influence of Black Americans who could not work on the film or be represented in it. There is no direct acknowledgment of African Americans in either Kansas or the American utopia offered by the Land of Oz, not even among a hundred Munchkins, and Harold Arlen's music is mostly devoid of his usual overt jazz and blues influences.[23] The unmarked category of Whiteness, treated as a standard or universal, is important for what it betrays—the absence of people of color in MGM's Oz. It would take *The Wiz*, decades later, to reinvent Oz in Black terms through the perseverance of a Black producer, Black creatives, Black actors, and an enthusiastic Black audience base.

Out of its multivocal collaborations, MGM's Oz emerged as a film musical with subtly conflicting ideas about home, America, and utopia. The more overtly ethnic and queer performances of the extravaganza are muted here but resurface in the film's darker moments and camp aesthetics. Some of the film's Others appear as a green-skinned witch with angular features and a hook nose, deep-voiced Winkie guards of a similar profile, quaint Munchkins, and a tacitly queer Jewish Lion whose mincing comedic turns pass as eccentricity. Adding to these examples the undeniable exclusions in MGM's White Oz, the dream of a better America for all implied by "Over the Rainbow" remained the unfinished business of the film.

"Over the Rainbow": A Place Where There Isn't Any Trouble

Kansas seems far from utopia, but, for this reason, it is the place where Dorothy expresses her utopian desire in "Over the Rainbow," the quintessential "I want" song. A young person's imagining of a "place where there isn't any trouble," it gives Dorothy her emotional motivation and has become an anthem of longing and belonging within and beyond the film. Sung in a quotidian middle-American farm setting, its dream of a something or somewhere better is implicitly an American one.

The film opens in a Kansas that is nostalgic and familiar like the American fairy tale, but still, as in the book, lacking in color. In the opening credits and first scenes, nostalgic and metatheatrical gestures imply the lyrical retelling of a fairy tale now familiar to American audiences. Over drifting clouds and the music of "Over the Rainbow," a dedication appears to the "young at heart" who have been devoted to the story for "nearly forty years." The cinematic realism of the Kansas scenes that follow provides a suitably everyday setting from which Dorothy can imagine a utopian alternative. Instead of Baum's gray wasteland, the landscape is awash in sepia, the color of both nostalgia and documentary authenticity, evoking old photographs. MGM's bustling farm is different from Baum's bleak landscape or the extravaganza's wordless pantomime. This Kansas evokes the goodness of the common people who were beset by economic and environmental disasters in the 1930s. Its nostalgic ethos also anticipates the patriotic Americana of the 1940s and wartime. Here, Dorothy's character is established by her conversations and interactions with a variety of friends and relatives in Kansas. The absence of song, dance, or color in Kansas, except for Dorothy's dream of somewhere "Over the Rainbow," emphasizes the difference between this America and its musical utopia.

Somewhat misfit and misunderstood in this quotidian American setting, Dorothy is both ordinary and extraordinarily theatrical. On one hand, Dorothy is spirited and spunky, less sober than in Baum's book, reflecting a popular media image of American youth of the time. She fits broadly into the world of the nice teenagers in the kinds of films Garland appeared in with Mickey Rooney. Critics described Garland as a "pert and fresh-faced" girl, praised for her "natural" acting even while recognized as a prodigious young performer.[24] A typical American girl with problems, she's antagonized by a neighbor, Miss Gulch, who hates Toto and wants him destroyed, while Aunt Em, Uncle Henry, and the farmhands are unable to help or offer satisfactory advice. At the same time, sixteen-year-old Garland. in breast binding, pigtails, and a gingham dress, was playing a younger child in drag (Figure 2.1). In the film, she has a wide-eyed, wondering affect, an exaggerated earnestness, as though she is consciously playing a role she has outgrown. Critic Otis Ferguson derided her "thumping, overgrown gambols."[25] In biographer Christopher Finch's description, she is an "adolescent with a grown-up's singing voice *acting* the part of a child" (emphasis in original).[26] Many girls want to play Dorothy in their school musical, but in the movie, even Dorothy seems to be playing Dorothy. She is theatrical in a world of nontheatrical people. She belongs in a musical (as some of us always knew we did) and she is (and we are) deprived of this musical's pleasures until she gets to Oz.

Garland's theatricality reinforces her position as the special and misunderstood young person who longs for something more, a motivating trope of the American musical and fairy tales. Her theatricality in this setting makes both her age and her gender presentation a bit queer, deepening her resonances with the experiences of Americans who are, like her, "musical," a bit different. Garland embodies the queerness of adolescence, its in-betweenness,

Figure 2.1. Judy Garland singing "Over the Rainbow" as Dorothy Gale in MGM's *The Wizard of Oz*, 1939.

its painful transitions, and its fervent longings. She doesn't quite conform to either the innocence of childhood or mature femininity. The attempt to contain her in the body of Dorothy hints that she has agency and desire waiting to burst out in mature expressions of singing and performance.[27] Dorothy is uniquely musical, theatrical, and dreamy in prosaic Kansas—the only person with a song—and her song is about "somewhere" where she might belong.

   Her performance of "Over the Rainbow" further heightens her liminal position as a girl on the verge of bigger feelings. The song mirrors Dorothy's age ambiguity in the combination of Arlen's sophisticated music and Harburg's whimsical lyrics about bedtime stories, lullabies, and dreams: "Somewhere over the rainbow / way up high / there's a land that I heard of / once in a lullaby." The longing octave on the word "Somewhere" is a gesture of desire recognizable as a reaching for big dreams (Figure 2.2). In contrast, the bridge introduces simple, oscillating minor thirds like the calling of a child's voice on the words "Someday I'll wish upon a star / and wake up where the clouds are far behind me," before returning to the yearning melody of the opening. As Gayle Wald notes, "Dorothy sings of lemon drops because she is a girl;

Figure 2.2. Music of "Over the Rainbow" from MGM's *The Wizard of Oz*, 1939. Words by E. Y. Harburg and music by Harold Arlen.

yet the *way* she sings of lemon drops . . . makes it clear that she wants much more."[28]

In a utopian performance, Dorothy transforms herself, her environment, and the entire cinematic soundscape by singing.[29] As the high speaking voice of Dorothy drops into the sensuous alto singing voice of Judy Garland, the sounds of the farm fade away. The orchestra enters the soundscape as progressive narrative time gives way to the lyrical time of song, aided by the technologies of sound and film recording.[30] In response to her singing, clouds open, sunlight streams down, and birds tweet along with the orchestra. This transformation is possible because of her virtuosic expression of sincere emotion through a crafted performance.[31] In this performance, nostalgic, ordinary Kansas and the utopian vision associated with Oz, music, and theater are held together in a lyrical suspension made necessary by their interdependence.[32]

"Over the Rainbow" is a "hymn to elsewhere," in the words of author Salman Rushdie, but its utopian vision also evokes the true meaning of nostalgia, or longing for an imagined or promised home.[33] Harburg chose the image of the rainbow because he imagined it would be the only colorful thing Dorothy would have seen in gray Kansas, but what passes for a mainstream sentimental song may be understood as a promise of inclusion of difference and minority communities.[34] In Judaism, the rainbow is God's promise to preserve the world from destruction after the flood in the story of Noah, and this idea of preservation from destruction may be especially relevant for a song composed by Jewish songwriters in the late 1930s, when the persecution of Jews in Europe was ongoing and the Holocaust was on the horizon. In addition, despite Arlen's downplaying of his usual affinity for Black music, the song remains legible as a secular spiritual, echoing the heavenly promised land "over Jordan" in "Deep River" or "Michael, Row the Boat Ashore" (is the octave leap in "my home is over Jordan" a precedent for "Over the Rainbow's opening leap of desire?) It bears the trace of a symbiosis among Black spirituality, Judeo-Christian traditions, and the propensity of Jewish

Tin Pan Alley writers to draw inspiration from Black music while translating religious ideas for secular consumption.[35]

The continual and inevitable deferral of utopia compels repetitions of the song. By the time of the 1970 March on Washington, the queer mythology of Oz and queer utopianism of "Over the Rainbow" were secure enough that lesbian singer Holly Near pronounced "Over the Rainbow" the "gay national anthem," and it continues to be popular with LGBTQ choruses.[36] Meanwhile the rainbow itself has become a symbol of the community for reasons apparently quite apart from the Oz connection, but the connection is often made when rainbow flags are waved while the song is sung. "Over the Rainbow" does at last become a soulful anthem in the hands of Patti LaBelle, an iconic diva for Black and queer communities. Since the turn of the millennium, a recording by Israel Kamakawiwoʻole expressing Hawaiian indigeneity, sovereignty, and home in a "gentle rebuke of environmental degradation, cultural erasure, and settler colonialism," (and significantly altering Arlen's music) has grown in popularity.[37]

After singing "Over the Rainbow" in the film, Dorothy encounters obstacles to her search for a better life. These play out in a rehearsal of her trip to Oz as she comes up against the Kansas counterparts of divas and humbugs who will reappear on the other side of the rainbow. It begins with the rude intrusion of Miss Gulch's ominous leitmotif at the conclusion of Dorothy's song and the return of narrative conflict as the diva of the county rides up on her bicycle to take Toto away and "have him destroyed." Dorothy presciently calls her a "wicked old witch." After Toto resourcefully escapes from Miss Gulch, Dorothy runs away with him and meets the helpful humbug Professor Marvel. Crossing over a bridge, analogous to going over the rainbow, she comes upon his wagon, emblazoned with words that openly proclaim his skills of juggling and sleight of hand. Humoring Dorothy, he tells her Aunt Em has fallen ill so that she is compelled to return home. In this first encounter with humbug, Dorothy fails to recognize the performance. It's an effective, benevolent trick, and Dorothy immediately heads home. Her full lesson in American performance will come when this scenario is repeated with a difference in Oz.

But before we go on to Oz, let's pause to appreciate Toto, who is an important actor with a role to play in his own right, challenging our assumptions about humanity, animality, and intention in the musical.[38] In pivotal moments of the film, Dorothy's choices are motivated by her affection for Toto. He leads the Scarecrow, Tin Man, and Lion to Dorothy's location so they can rescue her, literally pulls back the curtain on the Wizard's humbug-gery, and, like a magician, is able to escape from baskets and dodge spears. Audiences love him too. The first time I saw *The Wizard of Oz* in a theater, in a special screening during an Oz convention when I was eleven, I was sur-prised that the audience burst into applause when Toto escaped from Miss Gulch's basket. I had never heard people react to a movie in that way. Terry, a highly trained female Cairn terrier who also worked with Shirley Temple, played Toto across the gender line, endearing herself to fans who organized to have her memorialized in the Hollywood Forever cemetery.[39]

When I was a kid, it felt like the Kansas scenes lasted forever. Other people have told me they felt the same way. We really want to get to Oz. We're ready for color and more singing and dancing, and we find it in the musical world over the rainbow.

The Musical Land of Oz

In counterpoint to Kansas, Oz *is* a musical. Rendered in sumptuous Technicolor and music, it has the quality of film musicals Richard Dyer summarizes as *abundance*.[40] The journey from Kansas to Oz effects a change of register from sepia to Technicolor, realism to theatricality, speech to song, narrative time to lyrical time, and pedestrian movement to dance.[41] The mu-sical world of Oz invites audiences' participation, even as it comes with some implicit messages about who does and doesn't belong in this musical utopia.

The tornado that takes Dorothy to Oz makes allusions to American the-atrical and cinematic conventions, implicitly acknowledging the transition from the world of Kansas to the world of musical theater. Arriving home as the storm approaches, Dorothy searches the house for adults, only to have an imploding window knock her unconscious. As she apparently begins dreaming, the bedroom window, as described by Rushdie, becomes a movie screen in which people, animals, and objects fly by, and she realizes she is inside the cyclone (could the mooing cow be Imogene from the extrava-ganza?).[42] This movie within the movie is reminiscent of silent film (in-cluding its not so silent use of musical accompaniment), as the transition from nonsinging Kansas to Oz recapitulates the transition from the silent film era to sound and film musicals.[43] Miss Gulch rides by on her bicycle, transforming into a witch before our eyes. Now riding a broomstick, she emits the first iteration of her famous chill-inducing cackle. Our witness to her transformation is like a peek backstage before the dream performance begins in Oz. We're reminded of the film apparatus when the farmhouse crash lands into the eye of the camera. This series of metatheatrical transitions prepares us for what comes next.

What comes next is a theatrical, cinematic, and musical revelation. As Dorothy opens the door to step outside the crashed farmhouse, there is a rush of music and color, a theatrical gesture equivalent to raising the curtain on a transformation scene. The first camera shot from inside Oz is back on Dorothy, who herself has transformed. In closeup, and now in vivid Technicolor, she's red-lipped, freckle-faced, and wide-eyed. She walks out into the Munchkin village among colorful, obviously plastic flowers. An invisible chorus vocalizes in a wash of impressionistic music. Dorothy utters the film's possibly most quoted line, a camp remark in its obvious but significant observation: "Toto, I've a feeling we're not in Kansas anymore."[44] The music swells on "Over the Rainbow," and on cue she says, "We must be over the rainbow!" More dramatically than in the book or extravaganza, here we have a spectacular revelation of the American utopia as dreamed, and realized, by the Hollywood musical.

In this musical-theatrical place, Dorothy's journey is a ritual performance of an American dream pursued through the conventions of the Hollywood musical. In many film musicals, musical numbers are breakaway moments of song, color, and fantasy surrounded by relatively realist narrative scenes. But Oz is basically all music and color all the time. Musical fantasy is the dominant mode, rather than the exceptional moment in Oz. Even when singing isn't happening, the Technicolor spectacle maintains the dominant aesthetic in what Raymond Knapp calls the *musically enhanced reality mode* of the musical.[45] From the beginning of the Munchkinland sequence to "If I Were King of the Forest," Oz is a series of utopian musical numbers occasionally interrupted by narrative, often in the person of the nonsinging Wicked Witch, who by choice or not is excluded from the musical utopia. The continuous stream of repeating song fragments, verses, and refrains, along with chanted lines (Lions and Tigers and Bears!) and orchestral scoring, has the lyrical forms and feelings of a fairy tale in perpetual telling and retelling.[46] Musical numbers like "Optimistic Voices" and "Merry Old Land of Oz" are reflexive about the utopianism of musicals as manifest in Oz.

Munchkinland introduces Oz's essential musical and theatrical character, presenting it as rooted in childhood and spectacles of difference. Introduced by Glinda as "the little people who live in this land," The Munchkins are related to both the "little people" of European fairy lore and the little people of the American circus. Like Charles Stratton as Barnum's Tom Thumb, they evoke entertainment, fairy tale, and childhood simultaneously, with a child's and a performer's tendency to break into song. Their high-pitched voices are both childish and exotic (actually a dubbed studio chorus played back at high speed). Glinda coaxes the initially shy Munchkins out of hiding, singing "Come out, come out, wherever you are," echoing the singsong call in a game of hide-and-seek (as well as an invitation to embrace a queer identity).[47] She gazes on them in matronly condescension as they emerge from windows, doors, and hedges, tiptoeing to a gentle waltz. The oversized flowers and plants incorporated into their costumes and the set exaggerate their small-ness so that they resemble children playing dress-up as adults in the roles of villagers, soldiers, and city officials. A little person with a fake moustache climbing out of a manhole smoking a pipe burlesques the performativity of age for an audience inclined to view little people as children.

The Munchkins' childlike affect implies the innocence of the American fairyland and our deserving participation in it. The impression of the Munchkins as a race of children is affirmed by their singing and dancing, which emphasize the ABCs of music and simple folk dancing with broad gestures. Songs take the form of basic dances and marches, typically out-lining stepwise, scalar motion and common chords and melodic intervals (Figure 2.3). "Ding! Dong! The Witch Is Dead," includes simple musical instructions like "Sing it high! Sing it low!" on the elementary notes mi-re-do (as in "Three Blind Mice"). Harburg's lyrics revel in the same pleasures of the sounds of words and the interplay of sense and nonsense that are found in

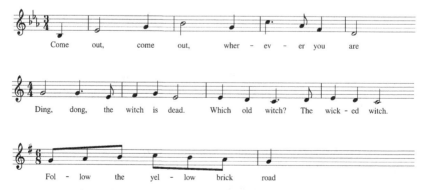

Figure 2.3. Music from Munchkinland in MGM's *The Wizard of Oz*, 1939. Words by E. Y. Harburg and music by Harold Arlen.

nursery rhymes.[48] The popular Lullaby League girls and Lollipop Guild boys are children among children. The sequence climaxes with a series of tra-la-las, as if the performance has reached the point where lyrics are insufficient to express the Munchkins' joy, leaving us only with the metadiscursive sound of singing itself.[49]

Dorothy looks alternately charmed and confused by the uncanny scene. Similarly, as a child, I found Munchkinland to be alternately wonderful and discomforting, although I'm not sure I knew why. The scene is a bit of a Barnumian freak show, with the grotesquery of dwarf performance signifying entertainment itself. As Keri Watson has argued, the use of folk and childlike aesthetics and singing in classical Hollywood depictions of little people, such as the Munchkins and the dwarfs in Disney's *Snow White*, contributes to their simultaneous disabling marginalization as freaks and their potential to subvert normativity.[50] Many of the little people playing Munchkins were recruited and managed by Leo Singer, proprietor of the Singer Midgets. His promotional materials suggest much of vaudeville and the circus (Figure 2.4). The historical mix of disgust and sentimentalization

Figure 2.4. Advertising poster for "Singer's Midgets," ca. 1915. From the Collection of the Public Library of Cincinnati and Hamilton County.

with which little people have been regarded was indulged in rumors about the Munchkin actors' involvement in drunkenness, bar brawls, and orgies during the making of *The Wizard of Oz* (in fact the dominant experience of these little people was of the excitement of working in Hollywood and meeting other little people, in some cases for the first time). Only White, "proportionate" little people were cast, excluding people of color and little people with achondroplasia. In a newspaper article at the time, Jerry Maren, who played the smallest member of the Lollipop Guild, and who would later be a cofounder of Little People of America, attempted to demystify the real lives of little people for readers, but the piece ran under the title, "'Little People' Dislike Name of 'Midgets': Many Odd Facts Are Revealed about Race by One of Them."[51] The description of little people as a "race" points to the complexity of entertainment's Others—White little people were racialized even as Black people were excluded from the opportunity (and exploitation) of playing Munchkins in the musical.

In the musical-theatrical setting thus established in Oz, the Witches are divas whose magic is performance. Glinda, the "good" diva, played by Billie Burke, a former Ziegfeld girl, personifies theater, flying in on a bubble to the accompaniment of her own delicate musical theme. In response to this display of theatrical magic, Dorothy remarks with camp innocence, "Now I know we're not in Kansas." Glinda waves her wand decoratively more than she uses it for magic (this bothered me as a kid), and her twittery voice and artificial manner are attractive but suspicious. She affirms her own beauty, saying only bad witches are old and ugly right after she has asked Dorothy, "Are you a good witch or a bad witch?" This is an important question, not only dividing the world into good and evil but also confirming that Dorothy should take Glinda's perspective on which side is which. Ultimately, she sends Dorothy on a quest to destroy a rival witch and expose the Wizard, possibly in the service of her own political goals. In the extravaganza, the transparent performance of the Good Witch, a member of the Witches Union, is trustworthy because we know she's not fooling us. Doubts about Glinda's motives and seemingly flawless performance in the MGM film prompt *Wicked*'s rethinking of the Oz repertoire. Regardless, her influence is a power that can't be denied. She acts as the *diva ex machina*, the diva in the machine who directs much of what happens on screen.

If Glinda is a possibly duplicitous performer in the role of good witch, the Wicked Witch of the West, played by Margaret Hamilton, is unambiguously wicked. She makes a diva's entrance in a theatrical blaze of fire and billow of smoke, interrupting the climax of the celebratory Munchkinland operetta. Lacking Glinda's conventional glamour, she retains the essential quality of a diva—she is a remarkably, even perversely, powerful woman with a penetrating voice. The Witch does not, possibly cannot, sing and seems to resent when other people do it by the number of times she interrupts them midsong. Nonetheless, she projects awe-inspiring feminine power in her signature evil laugh, operatic in its total engagement of the voice. Children and adults alike are frightened by it. A dark Other in greenface, like her latter-day incarnation, Elphaba, she has her own kind of vocal excess.[52] In the exchange with Glinda and Dorothy that ensues, we have no doubt that the Wicked Witch revels in her reputation.

The Wicked Witch and Glinda, clearly old rivals, engage in a well-rehearsed battle of divas. Because the MGM film is the first adaptation to introduce the Wicked Witch this early in the story, the ruby slippers, which she claims the right to have, become central to the movie's camp drama (internet memes characterize the film as a story about women fighting over shoes). Camp lines fly in their competition over the shoes and Dorothy's role in the scenario. When Glinda uses her magic to transfer the shoes onto Dorothy's feet, they are shown in close-up as Dorothy moves them into elegant poses displaying their fashionable, sparkling magic. The Wicked Witch warns, "Stay out of this, Glinda, or I'll fix you as well," to which Glinda twitters, "Oh, ho-ho, rubbish! You have no power here! Begone before somebody drops a house on you too!" The orchestra strikes a "Mickey-Mouse" chord as the Wicked Witch looks upward warily, but she has her last word on a classic exit line, addressed to Dorothy: "I'll get you my pretty, and your little dog too!" as she twirls around and disappears in a blaze of fire and smoke. Amid such theatrical pyrotechnics (if you watch closely, you can see her fall through a trap door), there is rather more posturing than magic in this exchange.

This scene is the beginning of an increasingly prominent role for the Wicked Witch in the repertoire of the American musical. In Baum's book, she makes no appearance before Dorothy and her friends set out for her castle, and she doesn't appear in the extravaganza at all. But here she's a formidable villainess who wastes no time making extravagant threats and chasing Dorothy across Oz from the moment she arrives. In *The Wiz*, she finally gets a showstopping villain's song, and in *Wicked*, this diva gets to tell her story in full throated, belted vocals as the complex heroine of her own musical. It is the MGM film—and Margaret Hamilton's performance—that turns her into a character eventually deemed worthy of her own musical.

Throughout, Dorothy maintains her innocence, declaring of her killing of the Witch of the East, "it was an accident. I didn't mean to kill anybody." Armed with her blamelessness and the protective ruby slippers, she goes on to gain access to the Wizard and eventually depose both him and the Wicked Witch of the West. Along the way, she dances down the yellow brick road, making friends and enemies, causing accidents, and liberating the native inhabitants without being asked. We might see her as an immigrant or a colonizer, or just a simple girl from Kansas, but many are the ways in which her journey models the performance of an American quest in all its good intentions and wicked outcomes.

Taking the Show on the Yellow Brick Road

The journey through Oz is a performance ritual, and along the way, Dorothy and her friends learn confidence in their performances, using the gestures of the musical in the (at first naïve) pursuit of an American dream. While Dorothy performs American goodness—innocent but capable and occasionally morally outraged—her queer friends struggle to achieve performances that will allow them to fully assimilate in the American fairy tale. The Wizard's humbug is a lesson in self-aware execution of these performances, while diva witches assure everyone that the choices made are righteous. The gestures of musical theater—song and dance—linger on in the embodied rituals that allow audiences to recapture these performances when they need to be remembered, repeated, renewed, revived, and revised.

Glinda initiates the performative journey, and the theatrical nature of the endeavor is evident in the way she, the diva in the machine, sets things in motion. Withholding the information that the ruby slippers can send Dorothy home right away (something she clearly knows at the end of the film), she seems to manipulate Dorothy into killing the Wicked Witch and exposing the Wizard.[53] Advising Dorothy to keep the ruby slippers on, because they "must be very powerful," she puts her in danger of the Wicked Witch as she sets out to get help from the Wizard.[54] Glinda's behavior is a rupture of adaptation, because she's a conflation of the Good Witches of the North and South from the book, only one of whom knows the shoes' power. But if we think about Oz as a theatrical place, we might note that Glinda, a consummate diva, is simply committed to the principle that the show must go on. To reveal the power of the shoes right away would end the movie prematurely.

Therefore, her motives may be dramaturgical as well as pedagogical. Indeed, in Oz these are the same thing. It's not enough for Dorothy to have the desire to return home. She must first demonstrate her ability to perform.

The gestures of musical theater are not incidental to this American journey. Song and dance are *how* one travels in Oz. In Munchkinland, Dorothy is a mostly a bewildered observer, but as the Munchkins see her off, they teach her the first steps to participation in the musical community (companion website 0.1). Musical tones sound on Dorothy's tentative first steps as she muses, "Follow the yellow brick road?" and a Munchkin responds, "Follow the yellow brick road!" There is call and response on this utterance as Munchkins come forward encouragingly reiterating Glinda's instruction, "Follow the yellow brick road!" The phrase repeats like a magical incantation as Dorothy's steps become more assured. She walks to the beat, until the Munchkins' chanting finally bursts into song on a musical phrase that merrily "walks" up and down the first four notes of a major scale to the words, "follow the yellow brick road" (Figure 2.3). The musical elements congeal in a bouncy jig as Dorothy's walking becomes skipping, and finally a progressive *pas de basque* (as described in the Introduction), a step ambiguously between skipping and dancing, simultaneously pedestrian and wonderful.[55]

As usual, objects that are both everyday (shoes and roads) and magical (ruby and yellow brick) are the enchanting scripts of American choreographies of performance. While the yellow brick road maps out the route, the ruby slippers script movement and mobility. Both magical and commonplace—modern shoes covered in what are clearly sequins—the ruby slippers have captured the imaginations of generations of American children. In the movie, their prompting of song and dance makes them appear singularly and perfectly magical. But because of the rigors of these very acts of performance, there had to be several pairs—some that could be worn out in dancing, some reserved only for close-ups—to maintain the illusion of their magic. Desire to possess the ruby slippers and their theatrical magic has led people in our world to pay hundreds of thousands of dollars for any of the several pairs that exist, while those who can't afford the genuine item make exquisite replicas.

As Dorothy and her friends join together on the road, they grow in self-inventive virtuosity through song and dance, demonstrating brains, heart, courage, and, in Dorothy's case, the goodness of American childhood. These capacities are explicitly produced through the body in performance. For each of Dorothy's friends, early steps to bodily mastery in performance are set to

the same tune, "If I Only Had . . ." (a brain, a heart, the nerve). This song, recurring with differences, constitutes an "I want" song for each of Dorothy's
friends within Oz. The Scarecrow first appears immobile on his pole,
recalling Fred Stone's virtuosic stillness, but after some falls and experiments
he begins to be able to use his flimsy body. "If I Only Had a Brain," like the
subsequent iterations with heart and courage, suggests something of a crisis
of masculinity manifest as a disability in its slightly awkward rhythms and
phrases culminating in a type of cadence formerly known as a "feminine
ending," with unstressed final syllables on "flowers" and "hatching," and the
word "brain" providing the solution on a stressed ending:

> I could while away the hours, conferrin' with the flowers
> Consulting with the rain
> And my head I'd be scratching, while my thoughts were busy hatching
> If I only had a brain.

The necessity of a brain for the Scarecrow's full embodiment is suggested
when he sings, "I could dance and be merry / life would be a dingaderry /
If I only had a brain." Importantly, however, the realization in the end that
Dorothy's friends already have what they need suggests that any perceived
physical or character deficiencies are not in need of curing.

The rusted Tin Man can't even speak at first, but with encouragement and
lubrication from his new friends, he too sings and dances with virtuosity. He
croons about emotional feeling as a role to be performed, imagining himself in the part of Romeo, singing "Picture me, a balcony, above a voice sings
low." In a metatheatrical gesture not out of place in Oz, an offstage voice that
happens to be that of Disney's Snow White, Adriana Caselotti, interjects,
"Wherefore art thou, Romeo?" The Tin Man continues, "Just to register emotion, jealousy, devotion, and really feel the part," affirming his essentially theatrical orientation to the workings of the heart. When Dorothy says at the
end of his song and dance, "That was wonderful!" He replies, "I'm afraid I'm
a bit rusty yet," suggesting the importance of practice and rehearsal in the
demonstration of a loving heart.

The Cowardly Lion's version of the song is the shortest (he gets a big solo
later), but, if anything, it's more endearing in its queer vulnerability. The
character of the comic dandy was an established part of Bert Lahr's performance repertoire, and Arlen and Harburg, who had worked with him before,
knew how to write to his strengths in "If I Only Had the Nerve": "Yeah, it's

sad believe me missy / when you're born to be a sissy / without the vim and verve. . . . I'm afraid there's no denyin' / I'm just a dandylion / a fate I don't deserve . . ." Lahr's lispy enunciation of *sissy* and flop of the wrist on the accented first syllable of *dandy*, and somehow even his eye rolling on the last iteration of "da nehve" convey connotations of sexuality, class, and ethnic minority status in simple, singular gestures. Dorothy, the Scarecrow, and the Tin Man welcome him on the journey. At the end of his song, they all restate their desires in turn, recalling similar repetitive passages in Baum's book: "Then I'm sure to get a brain / a heart / a home / the nerve." Then off they go, dancing down the road in solidarity and the pursuit of their dreams.

The foregrounding of the musical act of dancing down the road in the film gives the journey a new measure of American optimism. While the journey on the road in the book is central, much of the trip is arduous, long, and exhausting. The road becomes broken and treacherous, and dangers and barriers are encountered. The extravaganza only briefly presents Dorothy, the Scarecrow, and the Tin Woodman, marching to "When You Love, Love, Love." In the MGM film, the journey is joyful, hopeful, and optimistic because of the impetus provided by song and dance and the general optimism of the Hollywood musical. "We're Off to See the Wizard," which is reprised at each leg of the journey after Dorothy sequentially encounters the Scarecrow, Tin Man, and Cowardly Lion, affirms simple faith in the Wizard's power and benevolence in repetitive assertion: "If ever, oh, ever a wiz there was / the Wizard of Oz / is one becoz / becoz, becoz, becoz, becoz, becoz / becoz of the wonderful things he does!" Dotted rhythms provide uplift and optimism in synchronized movement, inviting audiences to join in or extemporize their own playful performances after the movie is over. Toto participates too, trotting merrily along beside the human(oid) members of the group.

These performances remain embedded, overtly and subtly, in the immigrant, queer, and minority traditions of the American musical, implying the participation of different groups in different degrees of visibility. Ethnic vaudeville and minstrel cross-chat inform the dialogue, as when the Tin Man pleads through his rusted jaw, "Oilcan!" and the Scarecrow responds "Oil can what?"[56] An Irish Bostonian who received formative training in Jewish theater and the Irish and African American milieus of his hometown, Bolger performed loose-limbed choreography as the Scarecrow that also owes much to the legacy, mentorship, and minstrel practices of Fred Stone, whom he admired and with whom he reportedly consulted in developing his performance.[57] Lahr, for his part, shows no restraint in his vaudevillian delivery of comic lines from the moment he bounds on screen, growling, "Put 'em up, put 'em up!" and making pointed personal remarks like "Get up and fight ya lopsided bale of hay," and "How long c'n you stay fresh in that can?" to the Scarecrow and Tin Man.

Dorothy's friends carry on the tradition of homoerotic comedy teams. The queer manners of the original "friends of Dorothy," are often remarked upon, and as she travels with them Dorothy seems like a diva backed up by a trio of queer chorus boys who link arms with each other for the dance. Their non-normative bodies are a focal point of their interactions as the Scarecrow constantly has to be restuffed, the Tin Man has to be oiled up by his friends, and they cling to each other in moments of difficulty (as the Tin Woodman holds onto the Lion's tail while they climb to the Witch's castle, the Lion says, "I hope my strength holds out," and the Tin Man replies, "I hope your tail holds out!"). These antics are accompanied by queer double-entendres: the Scarecrow advises Dorothy at the crossroads, "People do go both ways." In the Emerald City's Wash and Brush Up scene, while the Scarecrow and Tin Man are stuffed and buffed by muscular men in tight-fitting shirts, the Lion is surrounded by women in short skirts who give him a manicure. These attentive chorus girls provide some cover for his fey mannerisms when he sings of "that certain air of *savoir faire* in the merry old land of Oz," ending his refrain with a big flop of the wrist on "Ha!" When they are turned away from the Wizard, he protests, "But I got a permanent just for the occasion!" These queer gestures are permissible because of their comedy, their Otherness, and the deniability afforded by the innocence of a children's fairy tale film.

The Cowardly Lion is especially virtuosic when it comes to the coding of multiple identities in performance, a skill he displays musically in "If I Were King of the Forest." A burlesque of opera with its gender and class pretensions, this song was written to the specifications of Lahr's persona by Arlen and Harburg. In this respect, it resembles the specialty numbers that performers in the extravaganza incorporated from their own acts.[58] The Lion's queerness elides with Lahr's coded Jewishness in the old tropes of the effeminate homosexual and the neurotic Jewish male. In addition, Lahr employs a repertoire of gendered, classed, and ethnic gestures merging with childishness and animality.[59] The first phrase, "If I were king of the forest," is executed with masculine pomp, an upraised fist, and a comically wide vibrato (maybe more of a tremolo) on the high note of "forest." This rising phrase is followed by a delicate falling one ("not queen, not duke, not prince"), on which Lahr holds his palms out daintily with a smiling expression. This is followed by another bravura phrase ("My regal robes of the forest") and then flouncing on the next ("would be satin, not cotton, not chintz"). Contrasting grand gestures and clasped hands continue through the song. At the end of the number, Lahr's performance is fractured, productively and comically, by the failure of his last sung gesture, an operatic melisma on "mo-ha-ha-ha-ha-ha-ha-ha-narch. Of all I survey!" which causes him to run out of breath. But the Lion's limitation in one skill, singing, is his virtuosity in another, comedy. Critics overwhelmingly praised Lahr's performance, but some felt it broke the fairy tale spell with its modern (and perhaps ethnic) flavor.[60] It's just these elements, though, that invite diverse participation in the American fairy tale.

The characters' evident theatricality inheres not only in their costumes, makeup, and musical performances, but also in their haunting by actors who played them before, or who might have.[61] We may know this casting history because it makes up a significant part of Oz and Hollywood lore. Some viewers in 1939 would remember Anna Laughlin or other actors from the extravaganza. It's not clear how seriously Shirley Temple was considered for the role of Dorothy, but she was a dominant image of girlhood at the time, to which teenage, brunette, belting Judy Garland may be seen as either an insufficient substitute or a preferable alternative.[62] Ray Bolger was almost the Tin Man, and his Scarecrow shows the influence of Fred Stone, as mentioned. Buddy Ebsen, another eccentric dancer, was originally cast as the Scarecrow and then briefly played the Tin Man until his aluminum dust makeup damaged his lungs, sending him to the hospital and off the film. Ebsen still haunts this role, ultimately played by Jack Haley, as his voice remains, disembodied, in group singing in the prerecorded vocals on the soundtrack. In addition to surrogating the Wizards of the book and the extravaganza, as well as humbugs back to Barnum himself, Frank Morgan's mildly bumbling portrayal of the Wizard hints at the performances that might have been given by others considered for the role, especially Ed Wynn, or W. C. Fields, for whom the dialogue was likely initially written. All of this role-switching might encourage us to think of the parts in the Wizard of Oz as ones we can play interchangeably in our own performances.

Accidents and failures make the performances relatable, and accounts of *The Wizard of Oz* love to indulge in retelling the hazards encountered in making the film.[63] The Lion's virtuoso failures, such as those in "If I Were King of the Forest," endear him to audiences, who may identify with his combination of vulnerability and perseverance. The rigors of performance are obscured by the ease with which Dorothy and her friends dance down the road, but audiences like breaking this spell by repeating the backstage stories of the suffering everyone went through in making *The Wizard of Oz*.[64] We know how Jack Haley got eye infections from his aluminum make-up and napped on a board because he couldn't lie down in his costume. Bert Lahr's costume was heavy, and he had to sip soup through a straw because of his jowly makeup. Terry the Terrier was trampled by a Winkie Guard and spent some days recuperating. Margaret Hamilton was seriously burned and hospitalized when a trapdoor dropped too late for her to clear the blaze of fire meant to obscure her descent as she disappeared from Munchkinland. All of this might prompt us to think over the Witch's warning to Dorothy, "I can cause accidents too!" Ruptures of the cinematic illusion presage the "accident" that exposes the Wizard's performance when Toto pulls back his curtain at the end of the film.

When our friends arrive in the Emerald City amid their trials and errors in performance, they find a utopian theatrical scene, virtually a one-man show plus chorus, with Frank Morgan in all the major roles as the Guardian of the Gate, the Cabby, and the Palace Guard as well as the Wizard (Figure 2.5). His transformations and affected accents recall the changing outfits and ethnic specialties of the Wizard in the extravaganza. As the Wizard, he appears using the technology of cinema—projections on a (smoke) screen.

Figure 2.5. Frank Morgan in various guises in MGM's *The Wizard of Oz*, 1939. Clockwise from center: The Wizard of Oz, the Cabbie, Professor Marvel, the Palace Guard, and the Guardian of the Gate.

"The Merry Old Land of Oz," is an explicitly utopian musical number inside of Oz, whose lyrics hint at Harburg's prolabor and socialist politics: "We get up and twelve and start to work at one / Take an hour for lunch and then at two we're done."[65] As with the Lion's Queer-Jewishness, such political commentary could go unnoticed in the film because of the patina of innocence in a children's fairy tale.[66] As was the case in the Munchkinland sequence, at the end of the song, the utopian feeling exceeds the limits of semantic language and can only be expressed as sung laughter ("Ha ha ha, ho ho ho"). This purely affective musical climax is once again interrupted by the Wicked Witch, who appears overhead skywriting "Surrender Dorothy."

Thus, the musical utopia envisioned in the "The Merry Old Land of Oz" is explicitly threatened by the nonsinging Wicked Witch, an Other who must be destroyed to restore harmony. Following the Wizard's order to kill her and bring back her broomstick as proof, Dorothy and her friends venture into the Wicked Witch's domain. This carries us into the film's final scenes, which lack singing except for the eerie syllabic chanting of The Witch's Winkie Guards in oscillating fifths over primal percussion. Slaves of the Witch, they are grateful to be freed when Dorothy melts her, by accident of course. Whether dangerous and in need of destruction or helpless and in need of liberating and taming, the Other in the film recalls the contradictory genocidal and paternalistic policies of the United States toward the Indigenous people it sought to either forcefully assimilate or relegate farther and farther to the wild, wicked, and untamed West. The restoration of harmony to the musical utopia was originally shown in a reprise of "Ding! Dong! The Witch Is Dead," begun by the Winkies and transitioning to the Emerald City, but it was cut for time in the final edit, leaving the film feeling a bit incomplete as a musical.

The return to the Emerald City takes us backstage, as Toto pulls back the curtain on the Wizard's humbug performance, and the Wizard awards each of Dorothy's friends their symbols of brains, heart, and courage—a diploma, a heart-shaped ticking clock, and a medal for bravery. Each of these props is presented with a theatrical little speech that rhetorically imbues the thing with its power to inspire confident performances. This scene, originally conceived as a song, was ultimately written in dialogue by Harburg. Perhaps, at the end of Dorothy's journey, there's no longer a need to keep up the song and dance. The scene exhibits Harburg's ironic sense of humor in its simultaneous satirizing of people's investment in symbols over substance and validation of the necessity of the performance. Director Victor Fleming constantly admonished Frank Morgan to tone down the vaudevillian impulses in his

performance of the Wizard, making him a more sympathetic and less duplicitous character than in the extravaganza or in *Wicked*. The Wizard's performance satisfies Dorothy's friends, but his inability to return Dorothy home
betrays the limits of his act.

After the Wizard leaves in his balloon, Glinda returns to reveal the power
of the ruby slippers. When the Scarecrow asks her why she didn't tell Dorothy
before, Glinda responds, "Because she wouldn't have believed me. She had
to learn it for herself." Here, she reveals that she has been the goddess in the
machine, who has not only appeared at the end to save the show in its final
moments, but has been directing events and scripting the performances
all along.

In a difference from the book, the MGM film gives us an emphatic moral
about home, articulated by Dorothy in response to the Tin Man's direct
prompt, "What have you learned Dorothy?" She replies, "I've learned that
it wasn't enough just to want to see Auntie Em and Uncle Henry again, and
if I ever go looking for my heart's desire again, I won't look any further than
my own backyard, because if it isn't there, I never really lost it to begin with."
This speech, described by Rushdie as a "conservative little homily," is performative, educing the meaning of home in its recitation.[67] Further emphasizing ritual performance as an act of believing, Dorothy clicks her heals and
repeats, "There's no place like home" as the ruby slippers carry her back to
Kansas.

Back in Kansas, Dorothy wakes up surrounded by family and the old
Kansas versions of her friends. As though removing their masks and
appearing for their curtain call at the end of the show, they appear one at a
time at Dorothy's bedside. Dorothy declares, "Now I'm home. And this is my
room. And I love you all. And I'm not going to leave here ever, ever again! . . .
Oh, Auntie Em, there's no place like home!" The homely sentiment is reinforced by the omniscient orchestra's final sweeping gesture, which accompanies the words "The End."

A Real Truly Live Place

Whether and how musicals and their gestures bring Dorothy (and us) home
matters. Whereas, in Baum's book, getting home is a rather practical matter,
and in the extravaganza it is an afterthought to indulgent performance (it's either not shown or abandoned), in MGM's Oz, home is of utmost sentimental

significance. But the film's collaborators had different attitudes about the return home. There were those like Arthur Freed and producer Mervyn LeRoy, both Jewish but essentially conservative, who were invested in the sentimental ending. LeRoy reportedly insisted on the "home is best" moral with Dorothy waking up repeating, "There's no place like home." Harburg, an unapologetic leftist steeped in Jewish traditions of social justice, hated it, saying, "The picture didn't need that 'Home, Sweet Home,' 'God Bless Our Home' tripe."[68]

Ambivalence about home lingers in the film's ending and its reception. After all the fun of Oz, Dorothy seems to choose to assimilate in Kansas.[69] Yet, at first, she insists that Oz is "a real, truly live place," only relenting when the adults clearly don't believe her.[70] Is she humoring them when she says she'll never leave home again?

The melody of "Over the Rainbow" lingers in the score during this scene. The lack of any songs in the final scenes of the movie may make us long for the musical utopia of Oz, prompting our own repetitions of the songs we remember. After Oz, we and Dorothy have the gestures of the musical and know how to use them. The film's moralizing about home, while not insincere, feels more obligatory than conclusive. Its spoken platitudes don't have the force of song that "Over the Rainbow" does and are more easily forgotten or ignored than the promise of something on the horizon offered by the immanently repeatable song of "I Want."[71]

The MGM film doesn't simply promote American nostalgia directed toward the restoration of an ideal past. It makes camp of it even while holding it as aspirational, exposing it as a performance, but one worth joining. At popular sing-along screenings, the film is embraced both by those who find its message affirming and those who view it as camp, as well as many who do both at once. Alongside "innocent" viewings are those that look for hanging Munchkins in the background and use the film for drug-induced psychedelic experiences while syncing the film with Pink Floyd's *Dark Side of the Moon.*[72] By questioning nostalgia for "America," while also celebrating it, the film is simultaneously a conventional and radical text. In this respect, it carries on the legacy of humbug and the carnivalesque extravaganza after all, leaving cracks that can be exploited in more expansive visions of the American fairy tale to be offered by *The Wiz* and *Wicked.*

The return home isn't the end of the story. The failure of utopia keeps audiences coming back to the film and its musical gestures. My father was the first to point out to me that there's nothing to stop Miss Gulch from coming back to get Toto, raising the possibility of needing to escape to Oz again (as Dorothy does in the books). We don't have to believe that Oz was "only" a dream. Nine-year-old critic Mary Diane Seibel, reviewing the film in 1939, mused, "Everybody but Dorothy and Toto thought it was a dream. I don't know what to think."[73] I always imagined that the magic of the ruby slippers was to make it appear that Dorothy never left, because there are certain things adults just can't know. As long as we can find reasons to repeat the performance and the journey, there is the possibility not only of return but of revision.

Home and Oz are interdependent, in the imagination and in the embodied gestures of the musical. Dorothy wants to get to Oz when she's in Kansas and wants to go home when she's in Oz. In Kansas she sings about the "somewhere" of Oz on a rising octave. In Oz, Glinda, who assumes that Kansas is a star from which Dorothy has fallen, sings the name of the state on a falling octave: "Kansas she says is the name of the star." Musically, home and Oz are linked by this elementary yet extraordinary interval that contains the magical and the mundane in a single motion. In Oz, it's Kansas that is the dream Dorothy can hardly remember. In a moment of vague recognition, Dorothy says to the Scarecrow and Tin Woodman. "I feel as if I've known you all along." This has its equivalent moment back in Kansas, when she says "you were there!" as the melodies of "Home Sweet Home" and "Over the Rainbow" mingle in the score, suggesting they are aspects of each other.[74]

Repetitions of song and story make it possible to return to Oz, or to go back and forth between Oz and home in the constant reinvention of the American utopia. The annual television broadcasts assured this possibility, seeding a familiarity that enabled constant quotation and reenactment. These repetitions are lyrical moments out of time, utopian performatives oscillating between the magic of Oz and the accessibility of home. In practice, audiences find home and Oz without having to choose one in exclusion of the other. These repetitions make space for America's Others to keep finding their way into the story. Utopia is always becoming.

The influence of the MGM film can scarcely be overstated. It secured the form of the American musical as the form in which the American fairy tale comes. The annual television broadcasts made the movie a classic and allowed Americans to feel ownership of it through ritual viewing. The stage adaptation of the film has entered the canon of school and community theater musicals, where it represents the American musical itself as one of the most frequently programmed. The film is influential abroad, where it represents Hollywood and American film to international audiences, who participate in its performances of an idea of America. Subsequent musicals are always managing audience expectations on the basis of MGM's version of Oz, America, and musical theater. Among these adaptive performances are those that, like *The Wiz* and *Wicked*, re-envision Oz for new purposes.

3

Easing Down the Road

The Soul of *The Wiz*

During a recent summer, I attended an outdoor performance of *The Wiz* in Philadelphia's Malcolm X Park. Here, in a Black neighborhood, *The Wiz*, a staple of Black culture, was framed as a cookout and family reunion, with food served off the grill. A yellow brick road was drawn in chalk on the sidewalks that crisscrossed the park so that Dorothy and her friends moved through the audience, seated in lawn chairs, welcoming them into a performance of the American fairy tale as fashioned by and for the Black community. Racially conscious and gender-fluid performances of the Oz characters included a bearded Good Witch of the North played by one of the few White actors in the production and a more than usually gender-queer Wiz (this musical's version of the Wizard). This was a local performance of a musical whose circulations in wider networks of Black community have expanded the possibilities of the American fairy tale.

I first encountered the film version of *The Wiz* (Lumet, 1978) on TV at my cousin's house. "It's the Black *Wizard of Oz*" she said. At the time I got little more than a fleeting glimpse of Michael Jackson as the Scarecrow, and we didn't have cable at home, so I had to wait for another chance to see the whole thing. During my Thanksgiving break from school in seventh grade, my parents took me on a road trip to tour the South Carolina textile mill where the cotton grown on our Louisiana farm was spun and woven into cotton-polyester fabric. Somewhere along the way, traveling in reverse one of the routes through the Black Belt that both Black people and my White ancestors likely followed across the South, we stopped at a small motel on a night when *The Wiz* was on TV. This was no coincidence. *The Wiz* has been a Thanksgiving tradition on Black television. It was an imperfect experience watching it on the motel's very small television set, but I could finally say I'd seen it. Later, when the movie was released on home video, I rented and made a VHS copy. The video quality was poor, but the songs were the best

Oz and the Musical. Ryan Bunch, Oxford University Press. © Oxford University Press 2023.
DOI: 10.1093/oso/9780190843137.003.0004

part anyway. I recorded them on a cassette tape by holding a recorder up to the TV, as one did in those days. In my early teens, "Home" and "Believe in Yourself," became part of an interior soundtrack that boosted my private self-esteem when I felt different and isolated. Like many White Americans before me, and with all the attendant complications, I was drawing inspiration from songs that were deeply rooted in Black life and the Black, queer, Jewish, and other American experiences of the people who made *The Wiz.*

On Broadway (1975) and on film (1978), *The Wiz* makes an African American claim on the American fairy tale, reimagining Oz and the musical through Black performance legacies. Combining Black soul with the utopianism of the musical, it performatively revises Oz and home through forms of Black knowledge emerging from roots and routes of migration, oppression, and freedom. Its politics are those of optimism in the joy of being Black. It revels in Black difference. By acknowledging the contributions of Black people to the American musical, it makes Oz more fully American, as Dorothy, a Black girl, claims the role of diva.

As a Black musical, *The Wiz* belongs to a long tradition, from shows that were contemporaneous with the Oz extravaganza, such as *Clorindy, or the Origin of the Cake Walk* (1898), *A Trip to Coontown* (1898), and *In Dahomey* (1903) to a series of Black musicals in the 1970s that dealt openly with Black politics and culture, such as in *Purlie* (1970), *Raisin* (1973), *Ain't Misbehavin'* (1978), and *Dreamgirls* (1981).[1] While *The Wiz* was less overtly political than some of these shows, its celebration of Black culture made a lasting impression. Like many Black musicals, *The Wiz* involves negotiations of authoritative Black performances out of the minstrel tropes that come already embedded in the American musical.

The Wiz exemplifies the collaborative, multivocal, and contested nature of the American musical. Black people from different backgrounds came together to make it a reality. Radio administrator Ken Harper pitched the idea of *The Wiz* for years, first for television and then as a Broadway musical despite having few contacts and no experience in the theater profession.[2] With grit and humbug confidence, he wrote audacious letters to potential investors. Initially, Geoffrey Holder was to direct and star as the title character, but his role was soon limited to costume designer while Gilbert Moses took over as director. During rocky out-of-town tryouts, Holder again took over as director, although some disputed amount of Moses's work seems to have remained.[3] *The Wiz* faced challenges of long gestation, changing personnel, and rough preview performances. Yet, in the end, the stage version of *The Wiz* conveys its racially conscious vision of America with a cohesive sense of purpose.

The Wiz was promoted as a "soul musical," which put it broadly in the category of the then-emergent rock or pop musical, which drew on American popular music genres such as rock and soul that had been previously ignored or denigrated on Broadway. This was another aspect in which *The Wiz* positioned itself as a work of Black musical theater for contemporary audiences. Harper promoted *The Wiz* as a soul counterpart to *Hair* (1968), *Pippin* (1972), and other recent pop-oriented shows, and the cover of the original Broadway cast recording bore the tagline, "Super Soul Musical."[4] More than any other element except for the actors' vibrant performances, the songs expressed *The Wiz*'s soulful philosophy. Soul music was the key to authoritative Black performance in *The Wiz*'s transformation of the of the American fairy tale.

The feeling of soul is also key to *The Wiz*'s concept of home. The "souls of Black folk" have been a matter of some historical urgency in America, where, as W. E. B. Du Bois famously formulated, it has been necessary for Black people to perform a double-conscious strategy of being Black and American.[5] Questions about the status of Black souls informed debates about slavery and the place of African Americans within Christianity, eventually resulting in the formation of distinct Black churches, spiritual practices, and musical traditions. By the 1960s and 1970s, arising from the civil rights, Black Power, and Black Pride movements, soul became a powerful signifier with special cultural currency. Soul food, soul music, and soulful ways of dressing, talking, and performing served as automatic markers of Black cultural identity.[6] In *The Wiz*, brains, heart, and courage can be summed up under this concept of soul, a Black sense of self that at the time was both specific to Black culture and influential in popular music and society.

The Wiz's Black style drew on Black diasporic traditions within and beyond the geopolitical borders of the United States. Collectively, the collaborators were influenced by the Black Arts and Black Theater movements.[7] Harper described the musical conception as integral to a pan-African vision:

> we're going to do a new version of *The Wizard of Oz* with a contemporary score and an all-black cast. It will be fun, and it will be spectacular, with the music expressing every phase of the various rhythms associated with black culture, including West Indian, Afro-Cuban, blues, jazz, rock and even gospel.[8]

Geoffrey Holder created costumes in colorful designs influenced by African mask art and the Carnival traditions of his native Trinidad. In the musical, these designs also aligned with a camp taste for the exotic.[9] Gilbert Moses was associated with the Black Theater Movement and had directed the Broadway musical *Ain't Supposed to Die a Natural Death* (1971). George Faison, whose choreography critics compared to that of Alvin Ailey, devised a spectacular tornado ballet performed by a dancer with an immense strand of black fabric emerging from her head, swirling and filling the stage. Set designer Tom H. John invented a group of men in yellow tuxedoes and luxurious afros, representing the Yellow Brick Road, who guided Dorothy and her companions along their journey (Figure 3.1).

The score also emerged from diverse sources. Initially, Harper had conceived of a compilation score by numerous popular songwriters. In the end, composer Charlie Smalls received credit for most of the music and lyrics. However, the celebratory number, "Everybody Rejoice/Brand New Day," was written by a young Luther Vandross, while Larry Kerchner, a young Jewish songwriter at the beginning of his career, sold three songs to Harper that Smalls was given credit for: "No Bad News," "So You Wanted to Meet the

Figure 3.1. Deborah Malone with Yellow Brick Road dancers in the touring production of *The Wiz*, 1978. Photo by Martha Swope. © Billy Rose Theatre Division, The New York Public Library for the Performing Arts.

Wizard," and the show's theme song, "Home."[10] That these songwriters were at the beginnings of their careers may help to account for the score's youthful idealism about the search for identity. Authorship notwithstanding, or perhaps as a result of consonances, however historically fraught, between Black and Jewish experiences of homesickness, "Home" became a Black anthem. Stephanie Mills, who played Dorothy, made it her signature song and a Black music standard, much as "Over the Rainbow," became a signature for Judy Garland.

The Wiz's musical syntheses express varied Black experiences of oppression and freedom. In both the stage and screen versions, The Wiz's celebration of divas, dancing, and disco highlights the roles of women and young, queer, and multiracial subjects who participated in urban social scenes. Black gay men at all levels of production included Ken Harper, André De Shields, and Luther Vandross, whose "Brand New Day" pulses with the celebratory sound of disco combined with gospel. Considerations of The Wiz in scholarly literature tease out some of the strands of Black life that run through the musical. La Donna Forsgren, for example, expanding on Stacy Wolf's reading of Dorothy as mother to an assembled black family, reads The Wiz as a queer Black adolescent fantasy in which Dorothy constructs an interior queer world as an alternative to heteronormative futures.[11] Songs like "Believe in Yourself," "Be a Lion," and "Home," express feelings of difference and self-acceptance familiar to queer people, girls, and women, but in The Wiz they speak specifically to the Black experience of those differences.

Performers were important collaborators in investing The Wiz with authority as a work of Black musical theater and American myth-making. Many of the cast members of The Wiz, including Stephanie Mills, Mabel King, Ted Ross, André De Shields, and Clarice Taylor, were established or rising figures in Black theater, film, and television.[12] The role of The Wiz, initially conceived for Holder, was at some point to have been a bumbling Midwesterner like Baum's and MGM's Wizards, but André De Shields's eye-popping audition in platform shoes and hot pants prompted scriptwriter William F. Brown to rewrite the character for De Shields's mercurial queer Black persona.[13] Brown was the only White member of the credited creative team, and his authority to write the dialogue, complete with Black vernacular, was questioned by the cast, so Holder had Brown seek their input during preview rehearsals.[14] The Scarecrow, originally meant to be played by comedian Stu Williams, became a dance role in the Stone-Bolger tradition when Williams became ill and dancer Hinton Battle stepped out of the chorus and into the role.[15]

The Wiz makes its claim on the American fairy tale in the Black vernacular tradition of signifying. Classic examples of this practice involve playfully improvising on an existing formula to outwit an opponent, as in "signifying the dozens," in which combatants trade "your Mama" insults, or the toasting tradition of the Signifying Monkey tales, in which the Monkey tricks the Lion into insulting the Elephant who summarily trounces the Lion. One aspect of signifying, as described by Henry Louis Gates Jr., involves making a Black commentary or an authentically Black revision on a White text or trope, " 'authentically,' with a black difference, a compelling sense of difference based on the black vernacular."[16] *The Wiz* revises and comments on the American fairy tale and the American musical, using Black expressive practices to perform Blackness itself. The jivey shortening of the title of the American fairy tale from *The (Wonderful) Wizard of Oz* to the very hip *The Wiz* signals a certain attitude even before the curtain goes up. The signifying style carries through in "Ease on Down the Road," a funk-inflected travel song that, as we'll see, reframes "Follow the Yellow Brick Road" and "We're Off to See the Wizard" in terms of Black performance.

Taking a cue from *The Wiz*'s signifying and soulful style, the reviews manifested contemporary attitudes about race in American culture, particularly in their descriptions of the musical performances. Those who praised the show heaped enthusiasm on its "blazing high spirits" and "its piping hot servings of soul."[17] However, some influential White critics displayed an inability to fully grasp or embrace the show's signifying acts. Clive Barnes of the *New York Times* was ambivalent, saying, "There are many things to enjoy in *The Wiz*, but, with apologies, this critic noticed them without actually enjoying them."[18] He hastened to add that he was "respectfully unmoved, not insultingly unmoved." Rex Reed's frankly racist review for the *New York Daily News* called it an "all-black sacrilege" capable of starting a race war.[19] Unfavorable comparisons to the MGM film and Judy Garland implied a loss of "innocence" in the musical's up-to-date Black style and references to street life, sex, drugs, and androgyny. Varied reactions to *The Wiz* evidence contested visions of America, the American fairy tale, and Broadway musicals. The broadening of participation was resented or dismissed by some and celebrated by others.

It took the advocacy and determination of Black people to save *The Wiz* from an early closing date.[20] In a concerted effort that Stacy Wolf describes as mirroring the performance of community within the show, fans and supporters of *The Wiz* asserted their influence in making it a success.[21]

Enthusiastic notices appeared in the Black press—notably the *Amsterdam News*, which also ran opinion pieces asserting that mainstream critics had been unable to understand *The Wiz*'s Black style of theater.[22] The newspaper urged Black theatergoers to actively support the show, and church groups and Black theater parties boosted attendance. In addition, Twentieth Century Fox, which had invested in the show, redoubled its promotional efforts with a television advertising campaign. In the end, *The Wiz* won seven Tony awards and ran for four years.[23]

Many of *The Wiz*'s advocates located the show's potency in an allegory of Black life. Jessica Harris's assessment in the *Amsterdam News* emphasized its *feelings* of Blackness arising from the experiences that shaped Black Americans' contributions to American musical theater.

> The American musical theatre originated with Black people; with the Broadway production *The Wiz*, it has been reclaimed by Black people. *The Wiz* . . . is soul food. . . . Just as Black people took cast offs from white kitchens and turned them into something uniquely theirs, so William F. Brown and Charles Smalls have taken a mediocre story (The Wizard of Oz by L. Frank Baum) which has been canonized by the memory of Judy Garland, and created something uniquely Black. . . . From the moment that Aunt Em (Tasha Thomas) opens her mouth it is clear that the people who wrote and the people who perform this musical know all about grandmothers and aunts and Aretha and LOVE. . . . The Wiz is a microcosm of Black survival in America, it must be seen in all of its splendor and richness to be truly believed—and "Over the Rainbow" hasn't got a chance.[24]

Reflecting on the success of *The Wiz* several months later, Black columnist Bryant Rollins wrote in the *New York Times*, "The main themes running through the show are slavery and emancipation, the black church and religion, the great black migration from rural south to urban north."[25] Black music and performance practices gave expression to these themes.

The Wiz's status as a Black classic was secured by the film adaptation, despite perceptions of its box-office failure.[26] Transferring Dorothy's home from Kansas to Harlem, the film portrays the heroine as a young schoolteacher who goes to an Oz much like New York City. Jewish director Sidney Lumet added commentary on Black social realities, transforming on-location sites in New York City into the landscape of Oz so that the World Trade Center became the Emerald City, stylized repetitions of the Chrysler Building formed

Figure 3.2. The yellow brick road leading to the Emerald City in Universal's *The Wiz* (dir. Sidney Lumet), 1978.

part of the skyline, and Munchkinland was set amid the remains of the 1964 World's Fair Pavilion. The yellow brick road meandered through this city like a roller coaster track (Figure 3.2).[27] The urban locales look empty, like Harris's cast-offs, as if by consequence of White flight or some other form of abandonment or neglect. These visual evocations of the city reinforced the cultural work of the soul music, which was rearranged under the supervision of Quincy Jones with a more lustrous sheen and thumping, four-to-the-floor disco pulse than Harold Wheeler's Broadway orchestrations. The songs remained the heart of the movie, and iconic performers like Diana Ross, Michael Jackson, and Lena Horne ensured the film's popularity with Black audiences. Joel Schumacher, a White Jewish gay man who shared Diana Ross's interest in Werner Erhard's est system, wrote a screenplay expressing a self-help philosophy that explicitly defined home as a metaphor for self-knowledge.[28]

Kansas/Harlem: The Feeling

The stage and screen versions of *The Wiz* begin respectively in Kansas and Harlem. These two locales already represent geographic poles in Black life—the farms Black people worked as enslaved people, sharecroppers, and independent farmers, and the thriving Black neighborhoods of cities that were nurtured by the Great Migration. In the search for home, Dorothy's journey into Black Oz recapitulates in spirit the historical migrations of Black people. At the end of this performative ritual, she takes her place as a Black diva. As a consequence of the cultural specificity of this journey, the "I want" of *The Wiz* is different from the straightforward longing for escape expressed in MGM's "Over the Rainbow." The first song in *The Wiz* is sung not by Dorothy, but by Aunt Em, the matriarch, who expresses a desire for "The Feeling That We Have," the feeling of Black family and community that is the true meaning of home, transcending the circumstances of place. The idea of home or utopia as "no-place" is especially salient to a Black experience that is both deeply rooted in the places people have lived and uprooted from the place they've had to leave.

The Wiz affirms that, through the gestures of the musical, Black girls have the same claim to American girlhood and its promises as Baum's Dorothy or Judy Garland. Stephanie Mills's performance was as earnest as Garland's, projecting an image of a post–civil rights Black girl entitled to childhood and its innocence. The stage libretto describes her as a farmgirl of thirteen or fourteen, "bright and alive as can be. Somehow, it would seem she's built a life of her own on this dreary farm, and would probably rather remain a child as long as possible instead of accepting the responsibilities of adulthood."[29] But, unlike MGM's Dorothy, whom Aunt Em implores to stay out of the way on the farm, *The Wiz*'s Dorothy is expected to help with the farm work. To Aunt Em's frustration, however, Dorothy is too busy playing with Toto and daydreaming to do her chores. On the family farm, Dorothy is caught between her desire to remain a child and the pressure to grow quickly into the responsibilities of Black womanhood.

In the tradition of Laughlin and Garland, Mills was a prodigious young woman playing dress-up as a younger Dorothy so that her talent seemed all the more precocious. Although she was almost eighteen when the show opened on Broadway, she was consistently portrayed as fifteen going on sixteen in the press.[30] Her costume was a frilly white Sunday dress with a short skirt, which made the already diminutive Mills look even younger so that kids in the audience believed she was their age (Figure 3.3).[31] The dress, impractical for farm work, positions Dorothy as a dreamer and an eternal child playing dress-up as a fairy tale princess, its pure white color making a claim on childhood innocence for a Black girl.[32] At the same time, the Sunday dress represents church, spirituality, and soul. If Laughlin's minstrel performances

Figure 3.3. Stephanie Mills in the Broadway production of *The Wiz*, 1974. Photo by Martha Swope. ©Billy Rose Theatre Division, The New York Public Library for the Performing Arts.

excluded Black girls while holding them up to ridicule, and Garland is the innocence of unmarked White girlhood, Mills's Dorothy performs the innocence and perseverance of Black girls with their own empowering vocality derived from gospel and soul music. Mills herself was aware that she was providing a role model and message for Black kids, saying that she was giving them "something to look up to. It gives them a fantasy. And our version has more to say than the original."[33]

In *The Wiz*, home is a feeling, and the feeling for home motivates the show from beginning to end. Unlike Dorothy in the MGM film, Dorothy in *The Wiz* does not sing about going elsewhere. There is no counterpart to "Over the Rainbow" in *The Wiz*. Dorothy never expresses a desire to leave home, but rather to better comprehend the feeling of family and community. Dorothy's navigation of Black girlhood is guided by divas who teach her to become one of them.[34] With little preceding dialogue Aunt Em sings "The Feeling We Once Had" to reassure Dorothy that she loves her, even though she is often frustrated with her. Recognizing that Dorothy is experiencing complicated feelings associated with growing up, Aunt Em implores that they retain the "feeling" of love.

And I'd like to know that it's there
The feeling we once had
Knowing that you can come to me
Whenever you're feeling bad

Song is how this feeling is expressed, in reiterative emotional argument, exemplified by the backup singers who chant imploringly, if not prayerfully, "Don't lose the feeling that we have / Don't lose the feeling that we have." Feeling will sustain the interdependent relationship of children and adults in the racial family of Black people. In the movie, Aunt Em sings the song while presiding over the dinner table during a warm scene evoking love through food and song at a large family holiday gathering. Swaying and singing soulfully while everyone clasps hands around the table, she represents the women who are pillars of Black family and community—the Auntie as inspiring diva. "The Feeling That We Have" expresses a different desire than "Over the Rainbow," not to escape home, but to feel it more deeply.

Dorothy's failure to fully return this feeling is the problem her soulful journey to Oz's Black musical-theatrical world will address. She lacks what philosopher Tommy J. Curry, in writing about *The Wiz*, calls "that old tyme feeling of race," knowledge of oneself through knowledge of Black history and community, which in *The Wiz* is also the meaning of home.[35] This problem is especially pronounced in the movie. A 24-year-old Harlem schoolteacher played by 33-year-old Diana Ross, Dorothy steals away to the kitchen during Aunt Em's solo, singing "I don't even know the first thing about what they're feeling." In the movie, this feeling comes with a strong implication of the need to "grow up." Aunt Em wants Dorothy to leave a job she likes teaching kindergarten so she can make more money teaching high school students who are "almost adults" and in "such an important time in their development." What Aunt Em is really thinking about is Dorothy's development into heteronormative adulthood.[36] She declares, gently, that it's time for Dorothy and Toto to move out. Dorothy is about to have the Black experience of displacement, on a fantastical scale, and it will lead her to learn something about soul. On stage, she's caught up in a tornado represented by expanses of black fabric in a disco ballet. In the movie, as in the MGM film, Glinda, the diva, and Toto, the girl's animal familiar, instigate the journey, as Toto runs into the street, causing Dorothy to chase after him and get caught in a cyclonic snowstorm sent by Glinda (on stage, Toto doesn't go to Oz). And so the familiar journey begins again, repeating with a Black difference.

Oz: Black Style and the American Musical

In Oz, we again find a fully musical landscape, but now it's thoroughly embedded in the performance practices and feelings of Black music, theater, and acting. The adventure begins in Munchkinland, where, as usual, the musical-theatrical character of Oz is established. In the first of many encounters with the inhabitants of Oz, who perform in Black vernacular, the Munchkins greet Dorothy in spirited jive talk and an exuberant musical number, "He's the Wiz." In the movie, The Munchkins are Black youth of the "inner city" in colorful streetwear who have been turned into living graffiti as punishment for tagging the park. Dorothy doesn't speak as much in the "jivernacular" of the other characters, and as played by Ross in the film, she seems as out of place here as she did at home. But we'll soon see that her latent soulfulness is abundant.

The witches of this Oz are Black divas whose magic, like that of witches in other Oz musicals, is performance. They appear out of the machinery of the theater (in the movie, Miss One descends from the sky in a shiny elevator), openly acknowledging their magic as conscious Black performance. Addaperle, the stage version's Good Witch of the North, advertises herself as a magic act, acknowledging that she does "tricks," theatrical and otherwise. Of Glinda, the Good Witch of the South, Addaperle remarks, "You oughtta see her act, honey." The humbug of her magic is transparent in its limits and failures. She is unable to divine Dorothy's name and can't send her back to Kansas because "that comes under the heading of transporting a minor across state lines." When she's unable to magic herself home, she shrugs and takes the bus. Miss One, in the movie, admits, "my powers don't amount to much," but "Glinda's a real star." The idea of Black women as almost magical figures might be at work here, but the work and performance that go into the magic is acknowledged and displayed in the American tradition of humbug. This is a different kind of theatricality than that shown by Billie Burke's Glinda, more honest, arguably, because it's manifestly a performance, one that wins an audience's affection and trust largely through its disarming failures.

When the Wiz is invoked, his magical powers are extolled in song as the Good Witch and the Munchkins sing "He's the Wiz," which Miss One inaugurates with the theatrical pronouncement, "That's this number, honey." When Addaperle or Miss One starts to sing, she shows her true magic. Her divinity as a Black woman who sings is affirmed by the vocal and choreographic backing of the Munchkin chorus. Whereas, in the MGM film, Glinda leads the Munchkins in a song celebrating the death of the Wicked Witch of the East, in *The Wiz*, it's a song praising the Wizard. Her vocal authority lends credence to the legend of his power, which we know will be shown to be humbug. In contrast to Billie Burke's warbling to the Munchkins in the MGM film, *The Wiz*'s Good Witches sing with a power deriving its authority from Black soul.

Black style is the essence of performative magic in *The Wiz*, and the silver shoes, given to Dorothy by the Black witch-diva, are its necessary accessories. The ineffable essence of Black style is suggested by Addaperle, who says the shoes have a secret, but she doesn't know what it is—"that's why it's a secret." They are, as Addaperle admits, "second-hand shoes." But as Jessica Harris tells us in her review of *The Wiz*, Black people can make magic with hand-me-downs. The shoes' Black difference from the ruby slippers is in the way they script embodied performance in the co-presence of music and dance. In distinction from the ruby slippers' skipping motion to the jig of "Follow the Yellow Brick Road," in *The Wiz*, the silver shoes script a cool shuffling movement. Black style has been a key to mobility for Black artists, musicians, and entertainers, enabling the survival of Black culture. In the movie's running joke about cabs not stopping for Black people, taxis putter away when Dorothy approaches them. But if Dorothy has to walk, she does it in style in her silver shoes, moved by the soulful pulse of "Ease on Down the Road." The shoes enable social mobility too, gaining her access to see the Wiz and ultimately taking her home. The danger that her Black style can be stolen or appropriated comes in the form of Evillene, the Wicked Witch of the West, a slave driver who covets the magic shoes.

Oz: Soon as I Get Home

Left alone after the departure of the Good Witch and the Munchkins, Dorothy shows the first hint of her soulful potential, singing her "I want" song "Soon as I Get Home." The inclusion of this number is a change from the MGM film, where a medley of "Follow the Yellow Brick Road" and "You're Off to See the Wizard" are sung as Dorothy first starts off on the road from Munchkinland. "Soon As I Get Home" evokes the confusion of being displaced (not unlike Black people finding themselves in the "New World") as Dorothy walks among the Yellow Brick Road dancers, indicating the importance of the "I want" song and the journey home. As an "I want" song, "Soon as I Get Home," functions similarly to "Over the Rainbow," but with the destinations reversed and the mode of desire transformed from the gentle, Tin Pan Alley escapism of the MGM film to the feeling of soul. It also shares with "Over the Rainbow" a juxtaposition of childlike and sophisticated elements. The verse begins with a carousel waltz evoking Dorothy's disorientation: "There's a feeling here inside / That I cannot hide / And I know I've tried / But it's turning me around . . ." She gains confidence as the music transitions into a more soulful 4/4 time and modulates to a new key in the transition from the verse to the refrain: "I'm gonna be alright / Soon as I get home / Soon as I get home." This transition is complete on the word "home" where the harmony finally lands squarely on the tonic chord of a new key (what would also be thought of as the "home" chord). The juxtaposition of a European-derived waltz and Black soul suggests the performance of double-consciousness Dorothy must be able to execute in order to navigate life as a Black girl. The carousel waltz also evokes childhood ("I'm acting just like a baby"), transforming to the soulful maturity Dorothy is expected to achieve at the end of her journey. In the movie, Diana Ross's transformation is more incremental. She begins "Soon as I Get Home" without instrumental accompaniment, her voice breathy and breaking. Ross's performance grows in confidence, vocally and physically as she walks toward the camera at the start of the more determined chorus.

The unmistakably Black gestures of musical theater in *The Wiz* affirm the place of Black girlhood in the American fairy tale. In *The Wiz*, Dorothy's ability to belt like a Black girl, a new sound in the repertoire of Oz musicals, introduces a powerful mode of singing and transformative possibilities. Dancer and sociologist Aimee Meredith Cox describes Black girls as shapeshifters, inhabiting bodies that mark them as outsiders to White, middle-class normativity, who transform social spaces as they move through them.[37] As she moves through Oz, belting along the way, *The Wiz*'s Dorothy transforms not only herself and those with whom she comes into contact, but also the predominantly White spaces of the Broadway stage and Oz. These transformations conjure what activist CaShawn Thompson has called Black Girl Magic, the ability of Black women and girls to get things done. However, the pressure to live up to the mystique of the strong Black woman can be overwhelming without recognition of the work involved.[38] The gestures of musical theater have the potential to foreground the physical and emotional rigors in the performance of Black Girl Magic, making visible the virtuoso performances behind the "natural" strength, power, and beauty of the Black girls and women who are the providers and visionaries of their communities.

For one listening especially to Mills belt this song—and it's all the more striking because it's the first time we hear her sing—there's no question that Dorothy has soul. Like her friends who already have brains, heart, and courage, she only needs confidence and the opportunity to perform. It is not enough to perform alone, however. To fully realize her soulfulness, Dorothy will need to perform with others.

Come on and Ease on Down: Participatory Black Performance on the Yellow Brick Road

Dorothy and her friends practice soul on the yellow brick road as they revise the theatrical ritual familiar from the MGM film. They demonstrate their soulfulness by singing gospel, soul, funk, vaudeville, blues, jazz, and soul idioms reflecting the routes of the middle passage, the underground railroad, the great migrations, the blues highway, and Broadway. *The Wiz* invites audiences to participate in this journey by drawing on inherently participatory Black performance traditions.[39] Contemporary reviews and bootleg recordings of the Broadway production reveal that audiences cheered and applauded in middle of the stirring musical performances.[40] This was not something that typically happened on White Broadway. Audiences seemed to be responding to a direct invitation extended to them to participate in the performance as suggested by the refrain, "Come on and Ease on Down, Ease on Down the Road."

In *The Wiz*, participatory Black performance traditions invite each character into the center of the circle to have solos as well as participate in group numbers. In contrast to the MGM film in which they share the same tune ("If I Only had a Brain/a Heart/the Nerve"), each of Dorothy's companions gets his own unique song. However, instead of singing about the abstract qualities of brains, heart, and courage, as in the MGM film, each of these characters sings about their material experiences and particular desires arising from the experience of being Black.

After leaving Munchkinland, Dorothy first meets the Scarecrow, whose songs in the stage and screen versions relate the challenges of Black mobility and the importance of collective memory in performance—particularly in the repurposing of second-hand resources and the reclaiming or rejection of theatrical minstrel tropes. On stage, Dorothy finds the Scarecrow stuck on his pole, where, he notes, he's literally not getting anywhere. Referencing the importance of capital, he asks Dorothy for some spare change so he can save up to buy some brains. In "I Was Born on the Day before Yesterday," he sings about how he was put together from discarded materials, such as rubber bands, old gloves (evoking minstrelsy), and a "suit that had been thrown away." Using theatrical metaphors of makeup and costuming, he adds that "to top off the drag" they penciled in his eyes and nose, before putting him up on a pole and directing him, "strike me a pose." Despite just having been "born," the Scarecrow sings of hard experiences, as though he has inherited the cultural memory of Black struggles through the second-hand materials he's made of: "I had holes in my shoes / and I was cryin' the blues." The racial question of who qualifies as a person in American performance takes on vivid significance in the Scarecrow's composition out of cast-off junk come to life. The Scarecrow's position is even more pointed in the movie's "You Can't Win," in which crows, reminiscent of minstrel characters, tell him he is too stupid to get down from his pole. In gambling metaphors, they describe a hapless Black person up against a system designed to keep him immobile. They deceive Scarecrow by blaming the individual ("you've only got yourself to blame") for systemic racial inequality.

As performed by Hinton Battle and other Black actors on stage or Michael Jackson on screen, the Scarecrow reconfigures the appropriated Black eccentric dancing of Stone and Bolger as authoritative Black performance. In "I Was Born on the Day before Yesterday," the Scarecrow sings about discarding his old shoes and standing on his own feet. Similarly, as musicologist Jacqueline Warwick has argued, in the film, Jackson's Scarecrow rejects the blackface minstrelsy personified by the crows.[41] Dorothy helps him banish these figures by shooing them away. Inviting him to join her on the yellow brick road, she sets him on the path to confidence and self-discovery through the physical expression and mobility of song and dance. After some initial fumbling, Jackson's Scarecrow dances with stunning virtuosity to the propulsive beat of the first iteration of "Ease on Down the Road."

"Ease on Down the Road," is a fulsome example of how *The Wiz* signifies by reworking the tropes of *The Wizard of Oz*, revising the square melodies and Anglo-American folk rhythms of MGM's "Follow the Yellow Brick Road" and "We're Off to See the Wizard" using the tropes of Black music (Figure 3.4). It opens with an instrumental motive that seems to reconfigure the ascending and descending walking figure from "Follow the Yellow Brick

Figure 3.4. Music of "Follow the Yellow Brick Road" from MGM's *The Wizard of Oz* (1939, words by E. Y. Harburg and music by Harold Arlen) and "Ease on Down the Road" from *The Wiz* (1975, words and music by Charlie Smalls).

Road," using the notes of a blues scale with strong syncopation and expressive changes of direction. This assertive motive serves as a call to hit the road with a soulful attitude, while somewhat thumbing its nose at the "original." The melody proper is composed predominantly on the pentatonic scale (a basis of Black music from the traditional folk spirituals to the riffs improvised by contemporary R&B singers) with the addition of blue notes. In providing an alternative to the skipping *pas de basque* of the MGM film, *The Wiz* invites us to "ease on down the road" to a motion whose manifest coolness is emphasized by setting the word "ease" on a syncopated blue note.[42] The soulful backup vocals, syncopated bass line, layered rhythms, and percussive instrumental effects are typical of soul and funk-influenced Black popular music of the 1970s. But what's important about this music is not just that it has Black style, but that it has it with a certain kind of self-aware audacity.

"Ease on Down the Road," expresses optimism in collective mobility on the road of Black American life. Echoing the spiritual, "Down by the Riverside," the song urges the listener to lighten their burden and travel with a feeling of ease made possible by journeying together: "Don't you carry nothin' that might be a load / Come on, ease on down, ease on down the road." The first iteration, sung by Dorothy and the Scarecrow, emphasizes the individual's perseverance ("pick your left foot up while your right one's down"), while the final verse, sung when the whole party is assembled with the addition of the Lion, emphasizes group support: "You stick with us / And we'll show you how to smile." Whereas "Follow the Yellow Brick Road" and "We're off to see the Wizard" in the MGM film anticipate the meeting of the Wizard who will solve our friends' problems, "Ease on Down the Road" focuses more exclusively on the persevering performances of its singers and their solidarity on the journey. The same song is repeated with a different verse for each new character added to the group, making it also the nearest thing to "If I Only Had a . . ." in function, replacing those expressions of individual desire with collective effort. There are references to losing your mind (but stated in the Tin Man's verse) and courage (more predictably, in the Lion's), but these are meant to encourage the whole group, perhaps recognizing that these qualities are connected.

The Tin Man's performance is strongly linked to his ability to feel (the soulful theme of the show)—something that he claims to be unable to do because of a lack of a heart, even as he sings one of the show's most heartfelt songs, "What Would I Do If I Could Feel." Still, in his introductory solo, he focuses on his physical and material conditions, much as the Scarecrow did. In the movie, he's a washed-up carnival performer, an "old flimflammer" who attracts Dorothy and the Scarecrow by calling, "Hurry! Hurry! Hurry! Step right up and save a life!" In an allegory of the abandoning of the inner city, he was left behind when the amusement park closed. "Nobody home in soulville," the Tin Man says when Dorothy calls into his echoing, empty chest. As with the Scarecrow, song and dance enable him to regain mastery of his body in confident performance in the vaudevillian "Slide Some Oil to Me." As he goes into a tap dance, he exclaims, "Now watch me dance!" in a direct command to the audience to watch his performance. His soulful delivery of "What Would I Do If I Could Feel," sung during this scene in the movie but to the Wizard in the stage show, leaves no doubt that he already has deep feelings. Whereas in the MGM film the Lion gets a bonus comedic number ("If I Were King of the Forest"), in *The Wiz* the extra number is this ballad for the Tin Man, reflecting *The Wiz*'s prioritization of feeling and the capacity of song to express it.

The Lion's first appearance is musicalized in a complex performance of queer Black masculinity. Singing "Mean Ol' Lion," the failed king of beasts, played by Ted Ross on both stage and screen, performs virtuosic ferocity and feyness, recalling Lahr's queer gestures in "If I Only Had the Nerve" and "If I Were King of the Forest," but in strutting Black vernacular. He fluffs and tosses his mane ("I just had it touched up this morning") while checking himself in a mirror, then, roaring, violently tosses the mirror away. "If I happen to let you slide," he sings, "you just done caught my better side," doubly referring to his temper and his vanity. Reduced to tears by a bite on the paw by Toto, he confesses that he has been exiled from the jungle because of a "terrible secret." At this confession, Dorothy and the others lean in expectantly as if expecting him to come out of the closet, as he reveals, "That I'm a lion without any courage!" In the stage version, he makes references to his Owl therapist and an overbearing mother, and the Scarecrow calls him a "pretty mixed up cat," which can be heard as a term of mental illness, homosexuality, or both. Nonetheless, the others bring him into the group and encourage his participation in "Ease on Down the Road." Dorothy and her friends thrive in spite of their inability or refusal to perform norms of femininity, masculinity, or able-bodiedness. Ultimately, their queer performances are sufficient, and Dorothy herself doesn't need a heterosexual love plot to perform friendship, or even a mothering role, to the others.[43]

Before reaching the Emerald City, Dorothy and her companions endure trials of their group cohesion, the Lion's courage, and Dorothy's capacity to care for her queer friends. In the stage show, the Lion fails to show courage in a fight with ferocious beasts called Kalidahs. In the film, he bravely rescues the others from an attack by a subway station come to life, only to lead them into danger again when he falls for the seductive Poison Poppies in a red-light district. To comfort and encourage him, Dorothy sings "Be a Lion," which evokes the iterative performativity of courage in rhetorically repetitive lyrics and music: "If on courage you must call / then just keep on trying, and trying, and trying / you're a lion; in your own way, be a lion." Dorothy's singing makes an emotional argument more persuasively than words alone could, but the intensity of the performance reveals the work involved, as the quiet ballad builds into a belted anthem and then a powerful duet for the two of them.

Humbugs and Divas

When they arrive in the Emerald City, it is, on both stage and screen, a night-club, a spectacle of light and sound where Dorothy and her friends find "the beautiful people" preening and posing.[44] As usual, we can interpret the show put on here as one that is managed by and in service to the Wiz himself. In the MGM film, "The Merry Old Land of Oz" is inclusive and welcoming. In *The Wiz*, Dorothy and her friends are out of place in the stylish night club of the Emerald City. This difference may reflect *The Wiz*'s skepticism about utopian illusions and empty promises. It evokes, as well, the continued discrimination encountered by Black people migrating to the city, who might, in addition, be regarded as bumpkins. Called "trash" and "riff-raff," Dorothy and her friends are initially denied entry.[45] More than in the MGM film, there is a hint from the time Dorothy arrives in the Emerald City that the town and its Wizard are not what they are cracked up to be.

On stage, the character of the Wiz is a dynamically Black and queer performance of the American humbug. Charismatically portrayed by André De Shields in the original production, the Wiz performs various stock characterizations inspired by television preachers and politicians of the time,[46] while his musical language incorporates Black pop sounds and James Brown funk. Once again a master of props and disguises, he hides not behind a screen or curtain this time, but a mask, as he appears in person singing "So You Wanted to Meet the Wizard." The Kabuki-inspired style of his makeup (Figure 3.5) evokes the gender fluidity of the Japanese theatrical tradition as well as the "kabuki theater" of politics.[47] In an interview, De Shields spoke about the mask of double-consciousness in the negotiation of theatrical stereotypes and residual minstrel tropes: "It's literal change in order to survive, what the chameleon does. All Black people in this society have this quality, this ability to wear the mask, to play a variety of roles."[48] The interviewer goes on to call him "a master mask changer, a character wizard par excellence," but says it's "hard to find the core of the man." Perhaps this core, particularly a core queerness, is something De Shields could reveal and conceal depending on the audience. In an interview with activist and film historian Vito Russo, he revealed,

> At auditions, they kept reminding me that nobody in the play was gay. I guess they were telling me to put on my butch act. . . . It *says* up there—André De Shields is the Wiz . . . and *this* is who I am. . . . They never know what they mean when they say something is too gay.[49]

The tension between De Shields's performance and producers' expectations exemplifies the multivocal negotiations of identity and expression at the core

Figure 3.5. Carl Hall in makeup as the Wiz in a publicity shot for the replacement cast of the Broadway musical *The Wiz*, 1977. Photo by Martha Swope. © Billy Rose Theatre Division, The New York Public Library for the Performing Arts.

of America and its collaborative art form, the musical. Without queerness being explicitly named in the show or the songs, De Shields was able to invite queer participation in the fairy tale and the musical through his barely coded queer performance of an iconic American character.

The Wiz in the movie, by contrast, is unable to perform the gestures of the musical. He is nonsinging, at first disembodied, and ultimately a lost soul. He appears to Dorothy and her friends as a mechanical head, and "So You Wanted to Meet the Wizard" is reduced to one line spoken in the voice of Richard Pryor. His inability to perform in his own body makes the film's Wiz a far more tragic character than the stage version's. Frank Morgan's nonsinging turn as the Wizard in the MGM film makes him lovably bumbling and trustworthy. But lacking either the MGM Wizard's charm or the stage Wiz's virtuosity, the Wiz of the film is simply a fraud.

Notwithstanding the nonsinging Wiz in the film, in both versions of *The Wiz* the spirit of participation in the Black musical prevails. Even Evillene, the Wicked Witch of the West gets a showstopping solo. The tyrannical slavedriver and formidable church lady sings the gospel of her own perpetual moodiness in "No Bad News." She makes clear her intolerance of nonsense when she reprimands a Winged Monkey by warning, "Don't come signifying to me, little ape." Her rousing gospel style is a reminder that soul, historically, derives from profane lyrics set to Black church music. Like MGM's Wicked Witch, she derives her power from vocal prowess, but in the soul musical, that power is necessarily displayed in song. She's a dangerous feminine Other, however,[50] and, also like MGM's Wicked Witch, must be destroyed. As usual, Dorothy eliminates her by accident, melting her with a bucket of water in the stage show and by desperately setting off a fire sprinkler in the movie when Evillene threatens to roast Toto into a "hot dog." As in other versions, it is Dorothy's righteous indignation at injustice and the threat of harm to her friends that justifies the act.

The extinguishing of the Witch is immediately followed by "Everybody Rejoice/Brand New Day," a celebration of freedom from oppression. An exhilarating dance number, it brings to mind the importance of disco in Black, women's, queer, Latinx, and other communities in the optimistic 1970s following civil rights advances and the Stonewall rebellion. In the movie, the freed slaves unzip their cumbersome costumes to reveal their Black bodies and dance to the extended "Liberation Ballet." Having defeated the musical's most vocally powerful Witch, Dorothy takes her place as diva and leads the celebration. If Judy Garland's "Over the Rainbow" was a more covert gay expression in the 1950s and 1960, Diana Ross's "Brand New Day" represents a more confident attitude of queer liberation in the post-Stonewall 1970s.

Bringing It "Home"

Believing in oneself is a matter of performance in *The Wiz*, as it is in MGM's Oz, but here, the Black difference matters. Back in the Emerald City, the lesson about the performance of selfhood is offered by both the humbug Wizard and the good diva. After being revealed as a humbug in the stage show, The Wiz gives the Scarecrow cereal for brains, the Tin Man a plush heart, and the Lion a liquor of courage. He sings "Believe in Yourself," declaring that "the miracle is what you allow your eyes to see" before delivering a sung a sermon ("Y'all Got It?") and leaving in his balloon without Dorothy. On cue, Glinda makes her *diva ex machina*. In this role, it is Glinda, not the Wizard, who can "restore Dorothy's confidence."[51] The secret to working the magic of the silver shoes, and everything, according to Glinda, in a reprise, is to "Believe in Yourself." She sings, "believe what you feel," which rings true both for soul and for musicals.

Together, the Wiz's and Glinda's renditions of this song show the vital relationship between theatricality and belief in the performance of selfhood and community. Glinda reveals that the silver shoes could have taken Dorothy home the whole time, while Addaperle justifies not having told Dorothy the secret of the shoes by saying, "look at all the people I'd have put out of work." Dorothy herself demonstrates her newly acquired knowledge of the cycle of Black suffering and redemption through faith and acting when she declares, quoting a well-known spiritual, "Nobody knows the trouble I've seen!"[52] At the same time, the soulful expression of belief in song is the ultimate proof of knowing oneself and finding home, in contrast to the MGM film, which communicates these messages with speeches by the Wizard and the lesson Dorothy rehearses for Glinda.

The importance of believing in yourself is even more pointed in the film, where home is explicitly portrayed as self-knowledge. Without the showman's confidence, the Wiz of the movie is unable to help Dorothy and her friends, and without soul, he is unable even to sing.[53] Here it's Dorothy, having learned her own lessons, and importantly not the humbug Wiz, who sings "Believe in Yourself," revealing to her friends that they have had brains, heart, and courage all along. When the Wiz asks if she can help him, she replies,

> I don't know what's in you. You'll have to find that out for yourself. But I do know one thing. You'll never find it in the safety of this room. I tried that all

my life. It doesn't work. There's a whole world out there. And you'll have to begin by letting people see who you really are.

This is another revision of MGM's idea of the backyard, emphasizing the importance, and for Black people, necessity, of moving through the world with a strong sense of self. Glinda, played by legendary Black diva Lena Horne, who *can* sing (Forsgren calls her the *mother of all divas*, italics included),[54] advises Dorothy that she too already has what she is looking for: "Home is a place we all must find, child. It's not just a place where you eat or sleep. Home is knowing. Knowing your mind, knowing your heart, knowing your courage. If we know ourselves, we're always home anywhere." She then sings "Believe in Yourself" back to Dorothy. The pairing of the song between Dorothy and Glinda instead of the Wiz and Glinda de-emphasizes humbug, implying a more authentic, interior belief in personal integrity. Whereas the Wizard leaves more or less triumphantly in the book, the MGM film, and the stage version of the *Wiz*, in the film, he simply recedes silently into darkness on screen.

Dorothy's ultimate mastery of soul and self-knowledge are revealed in the final song, which assures us that this is the meaning of the "home" we've been searching for. Facing out to the audience (the camera in the movie), she sings a new rendition of "Soon As I Get Home," refashioned simply and assuredly as "Home," a song of being, becoming, and life lessons learned in contrast to the "I Want" of "Over the Rainbow" or "Soon as I Get Home," whose waltz is abandoned here for pure soul. Dorothy sings that she has learned to love others and believe in herself.

> When I think of home, I think of a place
> Where there's love overflowing . . .
> Suddenly, my world's gone and changed its face
> But I still know where I'm going . . .
> . . . And I learned that we must look
> Inside our hearts to find
> A world full of love
> Like yours, like mine
> Like home.[55]

The Wiz's message repeats the theme from the MGM film with a difference, and the difference is soul, which, unlike MGM's homily about the backyard, must be sung. "Home" is a song type and mode of performance unavailable to Judy Garland or any other previous Dorothy. A second-act song of self-affirmation, it's a feature of contemporary musicals, amplified by Dorothy's belting, virtuoso melodic riffs, and the authenticating roots of soul performance in gospel music. The obvious skill involved in such emotional singing reveals the relationship between materiality and make-believe as Dorothy sings, "Living here in this brand new world / Might be a fantasy / But it's taught me to love / So it's real to me." As an alternative to Garland's spoken moral at the end of the MGM film, Dorothy, fully embodying the role of diva, makes "home" for herself in the act of soulfully singing about it. Singing the song works the magic of the shoes, replacing the MGM incantation, "There's no place like home." In the MGM film, the backyard might be a metaphor for selfhood, but it can still be interpreted as contentment with a given place: "If I ever go looking for my heart's desire again, I won't look any farther than my own backyard; because if it isn't there, I never really lost it to begin with!"[56] In *The Wiz*, the place is less important than the feeling. After Dorothy clicks her heels, the return to Kansas or Harlem is brief. We don't know what Dorothy does after she walks back into the house at the end of the film or embraces Toto at the end of the stage show.[57] Whether she stays home with Aunt Em and Uncle Henry or goes out to make her own version of home, she knows herself, and that is the real point. Maybe we can recite the "backyard" speech from the MGM film, or maybe we can't, but many people, especially in the Black community, can sing "Home" by heart.

Keep on Keepin' on the Road That You Choose

The Wiz belongs to Black people, who affirm its importance in the community. For many Black families, the film is a ritual television viewing experience alongside or in place of the MGM film and likewise resembling a holiday.[58] As with the MGM film, people often can't remember the first time they saw *The Wiz*, but they have memories of seeing it, usually on Black television networks at certain times of the year, such as Thanksgiving. A Black woman I interviewed told me, "It is a cultural, iconic movie. People gather the family together and pop popcorn and take a Saturday night and introduce children to *The Wiz*. And everyone at the end is singing the songs. It's such a community staple." When asked to identify any musicals they know,

Black students in my classes mention *The Wiz* as readily as White students come up with *The Sound of Music*, *The Phantom of the Opera*, and *Wicked*. One student told me how her mother had introduced her to the movie and called her Evillene when she was in a bad mood. She now watches it with her six-year-old son. Across generations, *The Wiz* is the primary version of the American fairy tale for many Black families.

As in the case of the MGM film, the songs ensure the staying power of *The Wiz*, in this case reinforced by their association with the Black community and revered Black performers. The film version is valued for the importance of seeing iconic Black bodies in the Oz roles. According to the director of a community theater production of *The Wiz*, songs like "You Can't Win," "Believe in Yourself," and "Home" speak to Black people, not only because of Michael Jackson, Lena Horne, Diana Ross, and Stephanie Mills, but also because they resonate with people's experiences. One college student with whom I spoke remarked, "I saw [*The Wiz*] and it was like, this is people like me. And I think it's better than the original." Another described the music as something she could "bop my head to," compared to the MGM film, suggesting that the kinetic experience of the musical is integral to the appeal of *The Wiz*.

The Wiz is important for Black performers, posing an opportunity to play Black roles while also playing the iconic characters of the American fairy tale. A Black theater director spoke to me about how important it is for Black actors to play these roles:

> It's important to have the opportunity to just sing one of those songs and just get it in their body and play one of these characters that doesn't really have to deal with the quote-unquote oppressions of the Black community directly . . . it's fun to be able to explore a Lion written for the Black body. And a Scarecrow written for the Black body. And this evil Wicked Witch written culturally for it. It's connecting with and getting that character in your body in a particular way, in your spirit that's most comfortable. . . . As performers, we get in our head about whether we're being too ghetto, too inarticulate, not authentic enough to ourselves. [Do you] have too much soul, not enough soul, and stuff like that. . . . [In *The Wiz*] there's no such thing as too much soul, there's no such thing as being too big in making those choices and throwing some flava on it. They can just continue to explore what is most authentic in their personal selves.

Because of the importance of these roles for Black participation in musical theater, there can be tremendous pressure on performers and others involved in a production of *The* Wiz to get it right. Many Black fans of *The* Wiz are deeply protective about the film or stage show and how any new production should be handled. Audiences and cast members alike already have deep personal connections with *The Wiz*.

The continued popularity of *The Wiz* necessitates negotiations of Blackness, race, and performance. Multiethnic and even all-White productions raise questions about who can or should perform in *The Wiz*. A quick search for school productions of *The Wiz* on YouTube reveals how often *The Wiz* and its songs are performed divorced from their Black context. White reception of *The Wiz* ranges from well-meaning but often appropriative enthusiasm to dismissive criticism. Unsurprisingly, *The Wiz* is popular with White gay men, as borne out by personal experience, anecdote, scholarly literature, and fandom for it in the Oz Club, a nearly all-White organization.[59] Conversely, some I've spoken to dismiss *The Wiz* as "unnecessary," regarding the MGM film as a classic that should be sufficient for all.

The continued relevance of *The Wiz* in Black communities and in discourses of race was evident in the social media engagements surrounding the broadcast of NBC's *The Wiz Live!* In 2015.[60] During the televised event, Black, queer, and theater people posted humorous commentaries to Twitter and other platforms about *The Wiz*, Black culture, and musical theater. Many expressed racial and familial pride in the performance of newcomer Shanice Williams in the role of Dorothy and exulted in the Black excellence of established singers and actors like Mary J. Blige, Ne-Yo, Queen Latifah, and Stephanie Mills, who returned to play Aunt Em. Cast members spoke about the importance of *The Wiz* to them personally and in the community.[61] The Black Twitter response indicated that the broadcast was a balm in the midst of the violent attacks on Black people that prompted the Black Lives Matter movement, from the shooting death of Trayvon Martin to the deaths of Michael Brown, Eric Garner, Freddie Gray, and Sandra Bland. Even internet trolls, who, ignorant of what the show even was, complained about the "racism" of an all-Black *Wiz*, couldn't rain on the parade. Ridiculed, they were simply informed of the existence of the all-White MGM film and the token White person in *The Wiz Live!*'s chorus.[62]

The performance of *The Wiz* I attended in the park foregrounded the role of family and community, transforming the communal space into a utopian one where home and Oz were coextensive. The actors, wearing family reunion t-shirts, which were also available to purchase for fundraising, hugged and greeted each other and members of the audience warmly, making the audience part of the family. Cast members who spoke before the show called each other "cousin" and led us in singing "Lift Ev'ry Voice and Sing," so that the musical was framed by two Black anthems, the official one at the beginning and "Home" at the end. Dorothy, not fitting in at first, did not wear the reunion t-shirt in the opening scene in which Aunt Em sang about "the feeling." But after her experience in Oz, she put the t-shirt on as she finished singing "Home," clicked her heels and rejoined the reunion scene ready to be part of the family. A bucket was passed for offerings after the show. Describing the effort as mission work, a member of the production team expressed the hope that Black children in the audience would find positive representations of themselves in the show to counter the media's coverage of violence and crime in the community.[63]

Any perception that *The Wiz* lacks overt political commentary overlooks its potent affective politics as a musical celebration of Black life and culture, in which the right to feel is, in the moment of song, at least, a form of resistance to racial oppression through hope and joy. The director of this production explained her reason for choosing *The Wiz* by saying,

> I think our community needs something that feels good. . . . I'm in a state of needing to reclaim our joy, as a community, and I think it's important for our people to not just ingest oppression that we face everyday, theatrically, but rather, also balance it out with some of the joy of being within the Black community and celebrating our culture.

The Wiz is both a respite from heavier theater about Black issues and a corrective to negative representations.

Originating in a moment of Black optimism in the 1970s, *The Wiz* makes a bold assertion of African American access to the American fairy tale—not by assimilating to the existing text, but by transforming the text to accommodate Black difference. *The Wiz* helped expand what Oz could be, loosening the exclusive hold of MGM and Garland on Oz. By recasting Oz as a celebration of a specific community, affirming their participation in America, the American musical, and the American fairy tale, it possibly helped pave the way for *Wicked*, which takes a broader, and vaguer, position on difference in America while turning the mythology of Oz on its head.

4

Wicked

The Witch's Turn

Margaret Hamilton was something of an outsider during the making of the MGM film. She had no scenes with her only friend in the cast, Frank Morgan, and she was excluded from Bolger, Haley, and Lahr's boys' club. She was self-deprecating about being chosen to play the Wicked (i.e., "old and ugly") Witch, and loved to tell stories about how differently she and Billie Burke, the Good Witch, were treated. Burke's pink and blue dressing room was stocked with powder puffs. Hamilton's was a black canvas tent where she ate her lunch alone—a peanut butter sandwich wrapped in wax paper to prevent swallowing the copper-based green makeup that got on everything she touched. After the Munchkinland accident in which she was seriously burned by a ball of fire meant to cover her disappearance through a trapdoor, a friend had to drive her to the hospital, and the studio expected her to return to work the next day. When Burke sprained her ankle on another production, the press reported that she was carried out on a stretcher and transported to the hospital in an ambulance. In good-natured accounts of her abuse, told years after the movie became a classic, the Wicked Witch became the sympathetic figure in her own story.[1]

The Wicked Witch has always had her fans, so it's fitting that an iconic musical of the new century gives the Witch her turn. While many people were frightened by the Witch as children, many also claim her as a favorite character. Filmmaker John Waters recalls dressing as the Wicked Witch for a birthday party when he was a child, composer Fred Barton created a one-person musical entitled *Miss Gulch Returns!* (1985), and a friend of mine has a four-year-old son who dresses up in a witch costume with red shoes to pretend that the Wicked Witch has won and gotten the ruby slippers from Dorothy.[2] It's little surprise, then, that composer-lyricist Stephen Schwartz and book writer Winnie Holzman were each drawn separately to Gregory Maguire's 1995 novel *Wicked: The Life and Times of the Wicked Witch of the*

Oz and the Musical. Ryan Bunch, Oxford University Press. © Oxford University Press 2023.
DOI: 10.1093/oso/9780190843137.003.0005

West, a sympathetic portrait of the Witch, as a property for musicalization, even before reading it.[3]

Encountering Maguire's novel in my college years, I found it to be a sophisticated retelling of the fairy tale with compelling acknowledgment of philosophy, politics, and sexuality. The portrait of the Wicked Witch of the West as a misunderstood outsider, specifically a socially conscious young person, appealed to my youthful idealism as well as my emergent understanding of Oz fandom as a queer phenomenon. The novel's themes are dark, dystopian, and "adult."

Wicked (2003) the musical, billed as "The Untold Story of the Witches of Oz," imagines difference as redemptive in a new century with new anxieties. Exploring themes of integrity, justice, and friendship, it tells the story of Elphaba, a misfit green girl who becomes the Wicked Witch of the West after experiencing rivalry and friendship with Glinda. The musical's setting is dystopian, but its feelings, typical of the form, are utopian. Musical theater scholar Jake Johnson has identified a recent turn in the American musical in which audiences seek exploration of dystopian worlds reflecting the current state of American crises rather than of a now tarnished utopia.[4] *Wicked*, which remains popular, holds utopia and dystopia in tension and interdependence. Like *The Wiz*, *Wicked* challenges the MGM film's canonical authority, addressing its gaps by inverting and complicating the trope of the monstrous, nonsinging witch, repositioning the Other as a heroine capable of full expression and participation in the musical. Focusing on the relationship between the Good and Wicked Witches, it elevates them from secondary characters and gives them the good songs.

The question of who can be a full participant in the American dis/utopia is related to the ability to perform the gestures of contemporary musical theater, including highly emotional contemporary pop-influenced Broadway singing. *Wicked*'s ideal of tolerance is complicated by its corporate "diversity" mentality, its lack of explicit representations of racial difference in conception and casting, and its regrettable ableist subplots. With its adult themes and complex relationships, it's tremendously popular with tween, teen, and young adult audiences. *Wicked* has been playing on Broadway, internationally, and in North American tours since 2003 and is currently the fifth-longest running musical in Broadway history. Its influence is set to continue with a two-part film adaptation, which will presumably be released while stage productions are ongoing.[5]

Wicked brings the inherent optimism of the American musical to its source material, reworking Maguire's darker and more fully dystopian novel according to the musical's conventions and utopian feelings. When I first heard there was going to be a musical adaptation of *Wicked*, I had difficulty imagining what such a musical would look and sound like. Even after hearing the cast album, I was somewhat underwhelmed until I saw the fully staged show on Broadway a few weeks later. Repeated listening has revealed the score and lyrics to be thoughtful and sophisticated in equal measure to their pop-rock accessibility. The musical's focus on the two women, which is in keeping with the musical's emphasis on feminine performativity, is a key aspect of its artistic success and popular appeal.

Wicked mixes styles and genres of musical theater to speak to contemporary audiences and invite their participation. In this mix of influences, *Wicked*'s performances combine intense feeling with critical irony. As noted by musicologist Jessica Sternfeld, *Wicked* includes elements of both megamusical and musical comedy.[6] Like a megamusical, it has an epic story, technological spectacle, international replica productions, global marketability, a broadly appealing pop score, and universalizing themes in its treatment of social tolerance.[7] Concurrently, its musical comedy elements acknowledge audience involvement and foreground performativity, as actors at times play to the audience for a response, occasionally with winking references to the MGM film. This element of musical comedy alleviates the megamusical's tendency, described by Stacy Wolf, to overwhelm its actors, especially women, in immersive music and spectacle.[8] The revelation of the theatrical technology behind the performance is aptly represented by the exposed clockwork machinery of *Wicked*'s stage design. The alternation of songs and dialogue, in distinction from the typical sung-through megamusical, allows *Wicked*'s divas to perform with reflexive theatricality and acknowledgment of the audience's presence while yet retaining megamusical-sized emotions in powerful singing.[9]

Wicked can also be seen as an influential entry in an emergent genre of "young adult musicals" marketed to teens, tweens, and young adults.[10] Combining the conventions of girls' stories with those of the American musical, *Wicked* addresses political and social matters of concern to young people, specifically girls and young women, in contemporary US society. In this respect, *Wicked* resembles teen and youth fantasies like *Buffy the Vampire Slayer* (1997–2003), *Sabrina the Teenage Witch* (1996–2003), and *The Craft* (1996) that use magic, witchcraft, and girl power to explore young people's relations to adults, peers, and social institutions.[11] In turn, *Wicked*'s success may have led to the trend of adapting such girls' films as *Clueless* (1995 film, 2018 musical), *Legally Blonde* (2001 novel and film, 2007 musical), *Heathers* (1988 film, 2013 musical), and *Mean Girls* (2004 film, 2018 musical) as musicals. *Wicked*'s recognizable girl story conventions serve as both emotional hooks and winks to the audience.

In *Wicked*, American ideas of goodness and wickedness are matters of performance inextricable from the performatives of gender, externalizing girls' interior experiences through sung soliloquy and embodied performances of femininity.[12] While Dorothy represents the innocence of America, *Wicked*'s divas, Elphaba and Glinda, are aware of the ethical implications of their performances and the challenging navigations they require. In *Wicked*, the American girl or young woman acquires the right to be wrong, to be conflicted, and to make imperfect choices in impossible circumstances. The range of songs and the contradictory emotions they convey enable performances of American girlhood and womanhood from conventional to queer, with ambiguous implications for racial difference and disability. What an "I want" song means in this musical is different, and more ambitious, and more complicated, than the apparently straightforward desire expressed in "Over the Rainbow." *Wicked*'s broadly appealing, empowering music and performances, and its accessibly human divas, invite participation by audiences who can identify with and emulate the performances.

Wicked's ambivalence about home and utopia/dystopia arises from the kinds of questions that motivated Maguire's novel at the time of writing, questions about good and evil in the propaganda surrounding the Persian Gulf War of 1991.[13] By the time the musical opened in 2003, similar questions surrounded the response to 9-11 and the US invasion of Iraq. Critic Ben Brantley noted that the show's portrayal of the "illusion of doing good over a genuinely noble act," was reminiscent of political photo-ops, possibly in reference to the Bush administration's misleading banner prematurely proclaiming "Mission Accomplished" in the Iraq invasion.[14] The scapegoating of talking Animals (with a capital *A* as opposed to non-speaking lowercase-*a* animals), has been identified by the show's creators, commentators, and scholars as a metaphor for the Holocaust, the Gulf War, and the post-9-11 environment. It also aligns with American experiences of queer marginalization and race-based experimentation.[15] During its illustrious Broadway run, *Wicked*'s performances of humbug and redemption have taken place against the backdrops of the "postracial" discourses of the

Obama era, the racial violence leading to the Black Lives Matter movement, and the strains of xenophobia, authoritarianism, paranoia, official deception, self-delusion, and fraudulence that run from "mission accomplished" to Trumpism, climate change denial, and COVID skepticism.

Wicked's girl-centered politics and theatrical style were baffling to many critics (often middle-aged, White, and male), who positioned themselves as the curators of the American musical and gatekeepers of its quality.[16] John Lahr (son of Bert, the Cowardly Lion of the MGM film) dismissed *Wicked*'s prioritizing of young women's relationships with sarcasm: "The Wicked Witch, Elphaba . . . turns out to be good, while Glinda the Good Witch . . . is exposed as a smug, ambitious, manipulative bitch. . . . So you see, the emotional stakes are very high indeed." Using the stereotype of feminine hysteria to foreclose any further discussion of the show's feminine politics, he continued, "For reasons both of critical responsibility and of sanity, I think this is far as I should go with the plot."[17] Finally, Lahr assessed the show and its audience as vapid: "It is only fair to report that on the night I saw *Wicked* the spectators gave this fourteen-million-dollar piece of folderol a standing ovation, a phenomenon that the musical inadvertently explains in a number called 'Dancing through Life': 'Life is painless /For the brainless.'" Ben Brantley similarly derided the story formula "in which the adversarial women learn from each other and which recalls sobfests about female friendships like the movie *Beaches*. (You keep expecting Glinda to start singing, 'Did you ever know you where my hero, Elphaba?')."[18] These reviews misrecognize the coexistence of the personal and political in women's experiences while dismissing the show as crassly commercial in its feminine and presumably infantile qualities.[19] Taking a defensive position meant to protect a high art concept of the musical from "bad" shows like *Wicked*, such critiques recall those of other Oz musicals—White critics failing to appreciate the racial commentary of *The Wiz*, classist complaints about the extravaganza, and adult critiques of the MGM film's unabashedly playful phantasmagoria.

But as with other Oz musicals, audiences, especially girls and young women, ignored the critics and embraced the show's camp performances of femininity as both celebratory and reflexive about their own real-life performances. Audiences have welcomed *Wicked* for its ambivalent mix of pleasurable spectacle and serious politics. The actors, seen as theatrical divas but also ordinary young women, are coauthors of the roles, inspiring audience participation in *Wicked*'s performances of feminine politics.

Wicked explores anew the questions of difference in America that were caricatured in the extravaganza, sanitized in the MGM film, and restored from a particular perspective in *The Wiz*, but just what kind of difference Elphaba represents is less than clear. Her green complexion and magical powers function metaphorically, as Stacy Wolf notes, making her an individual whose "'difference' stands in for all difference" rather than a specific racial or social representation.[20] *Wicked* carries on the tradition of queerness as an open secret in Oz and musicals, positioning Elphaba and Glinda as, first, the homosocial competitive comedy duo, and then a queer (not necessarily lesbian) couple in the musical's marriage trope.[21] Elphaba is a social misfit but magical/musical prodigy, whose difference turns out to be both a superpower and a limitation as she grows into the role of Wicked Witch.[22]

Perhaps more than anything else, Elphaba's difference is that of the unusually theatrical or musical person. Describing the character, Schwartz used the metaphor of the misunderstood artist, akin to the misfit theater kid, as a metaphor for every kind of difference:

> Anyone who is an artist in our society is going to identify with Elphaba. Anyone who is of an ethnic minority, who is black or Jewish or gay, or a woman feeling she grew up in a man's world, or anyone who grew up feeling a dissonance between who they are inside and the world around them, will identify with Elphaba. Since that's so many of us, I think there will be a lot of people who will.[23]

Affirming the "musical" nature of this difference, a White high school fan of *Wicked* told me she identified with Elphaba because, as an aspiring musician, she felt different from her peers. In style, the music that represents this difference in the show doesn't have the cultural specificity of anything like the soul music in *The Wiz*. Its pop style is easily assimilable, making broad claims about tolerance without specifying exactly who is being included, allowing the show to be palatable to audiences, including conservative ones, who might see in Elphaba the kind of individual they prefer.

Wicked represents ideas about "America" at home and abroad, closing a circle in which Oz and musicals, cobbled together from disparate international and immigrant influences are exported back out across borders that have never been secure. The musical's dystopian setting and utopian aspirations serve, as palpably as ever, as a theatrical allegory of American actors and their role in the world.

Glitter and Belt: When Witches Sing in Oz

Wicked begins and ends in Oz, and because we start in Oz, we jump right into the question of what kind of musical world this Oz/America is. *Wicked's* Oz belongs to diva-witches whose powerful singing and theatricality are models for American performances of gender and unique individualism in a topsy-turvy mythology and global context. By singing the important song types, the Witches become the heroines of the American fairy tale. While the MGM film's Glinda twitters and its Wicked Witch shrieks, in *Wicked* both women draw on varied vocal gestures as evidence of their psychological complexity. Access to the songs of the American musical—"I want" songs among others—and the expressive possibilities of contemporary musical theater conventions, including pop singing and belting—allow the Witches to be powerful, complex subjects. Only the soulful Dorothy of *The Wiz* rivals them for sheer technical and expressive power. As both a villainess and a new incarnation of the girl protagonist of the American musical, Elphaba destabilizes the distinction between hero and villain, good and evil, in American theatrical, political and social life.

These divas live in the machinery of the theater, which is their source of power and the reflexive proof of their authority to be the central figures of Oz and musicals. References to previous theatrical and filmic renditions of the American fairy tale authenticate the divas' story and invite audiences to remember their participation in the mythologies of Oz and musicals. *Wicked* displays its theatrical machinery and sense of Ozian history from the beginning. A map of Oz reproduced from Maguire's *Wicked* but also resembling those included in the endpapers of Baum's *Tik-Tok of Oz* (1914), serves as the curtain before the show begins. To the dissonant opening chords of the musical, the Time Dragon, within whose clock the story is framed, operated by visible strings, swings its head above the stage, drawing the audience's attention to the proscenium that frames the action, while a winged monkey turns a crank, activating visible gears to move the scenery. The opening number that follows is a repeated performance of the moment in the MGM film when Dorothy has just melted the Wicked Witch of the West and the people of Oz are rejoicing. Filling a gap where a reprise of "Ding Dong the Witch Is Dead" was cut from the film, Ozian chorus members appear on stage singing, "Good News! She's Dead! The Wicked Witch Is Dead!" However, this variation on the classic song sets the stage for a much more ambivalent perspective on the Wicked Witch's life and death and what it means for participation in the American fairy tale. This more ambivalent outlook is provided by Glinda, who arrives at the celebration not just to affirm the Ozites' rejoicing, as Billie Burke does in Munchkinland, but ultimately to tell a more complicated story.

In her revised performance of the role as played by Billie Burke in the MGM film, *Wicked*'s Glinda performs anew the role of musical theater diva and the *diva ex machina* in Oz. Literally riding the machinery of the theater, she makes the quintessential diva's entrance, descending in an industrialized version of the bubble from MGM. The significance of her entrance is reflected in its use in promotional videos and press materials.[24] Positioning herself as a star and authoritative narrator she simultaneously addresses the crowd assembled on stage and the audience in the theater, declaring with a twinkle, "It's good to see me, isn't it? No need to respond, that was *rhetorical*." In this utterance, Glinda speaks her role into being, not only as Glinda but as the diva in a musical, acknowledging to an appreciative audience that the diva (Glinda herself as well as the Broadway star who plays her) is in fact who we've come to see. Her entrance is momentous simply because of her importance in the art form and in Oz.

Glinda's gestures draw attention to her metatheatrical self-presentation, inviting us to take a critical stance toward her performance even as we accept it as proof of her divine status in the theater. Like any good public figure, she is a master of her modes of communication. She sings in the *bel canto* style she uses when performing for the masses (drawing on the same encoding of class pretensions burlesqued by Lahr in his use of operatic conventions in "If I Were King of the Forest").[25] She rhymes cleverly while making truth claims ("Isn't it good to know / that good will conquer evil / The truth we'll all believe'll by and by / outlive a lie . . ."). By playing to the audience, she reminds us of the artifice of theater, foregrounding her role as the privileged narrator. Glinda is on her way out when someone shouts, "Is it true you were her friend?" forcing a deviation from her official script. She motions to someone above to lower her bubble.

As she begins to tell Elphaba's story, Glinda asks us to consider whether wickedness is an essence or a performance mapped onto one in repeated performatives, a question highlighted by her own gendered performance in the role of the diva. "Are people born wicked," she muses, "or do they have wickedness thrust upon them?" This is a significant revision of Billie Burke's simple question, "Are you a good witch or a bad witch?" Beginning with Elphaba's childhood, she relates how Elphaba was born green and ultimately killed by Dorothy, an innocent "female child." Right away, it's implied that innocence and wickedness, essential character traits in previous iterations of Oz, may be called into question here. The choices Glinda and Elphaba make (or can't) in the unfolding of the musical result in their performances of goodness and wickedness.

As the story proceeds, questions of goodness and wickedness are inextricable from the performance and performativity of gender. Meeting in college, Elphaba and Galinda (as she is called in the beginning) represent competing styles in these performances, as demonstrated in their vocal gestures—Glinda glitters and Elphaba belts. Glinda is the social aspirant and Elphaba is the misfit young person with hidden special powers. Glinda heralds her own arrival on the first day of school with a little vocal cadenza as she rolls in on top of her luggage (this must have required a virtuosic change of costume after descending from her bubble!). When she has no words, Glinda randomly lets out high notes to express exuberance (as so many sopranos I know do!).

As divas in the spotlight, Elphaba and Glinda embody postfeminist tensions between power and objectification and between individual choice and collective good. *Wicked* was called a "girl power" musical by some critics, not necessarily complimentarily.[26] Taken seriously as one, though, it challenges and complicates notions of how to be a girl, woman, or feminist capable of both pleasure and power in the American musical and contemporary society. Glinda's glittery artifice—her sparkling costumes, wand, and tiara—are a conscious indulgence in feminine performance, the kind of girl-oriented feminist camp that film scholar Mary Celeste Kearney calls "sparkle culture."[27] As Stacy Wolf notes, Glinda's performance of conventional femininity "sustains a critique of those behaviors even as she plays them out."[28] Glinda's adorned sparkle has its counterpart in her singing, described by critics as bright and agile in its *bel canto* upper register. Like her sparkling outfits, it projects both femininity and power, in a more obviously self-aware way than MGM's Glinda. The acknowledged theatricality of their performances make Elphaba and Glinda seem like accessible and relatable divas as they take on the roles of women singing the songs and emotions of the American musical in their respective styles.

"Making Good": The Witch's Want

Elphaba is a contrast in style and character to Glinda, her own musical personality and gestures positioning her as the misunderstood and underestimated heroine of the musical. Oz for her is no more utopian than

Kansas is for Dorothy. She enters in a cap, braided hair, and glasses, a picture of a studious young college woman. She's also green. Glinda makes jokes about Elphaba's complexion to the amusement of the other students, and headmistress Madame Morrible is simply patronizing toward her. Elphaba is hardly more at "home" in her family, having only been sent to university to care for her sister Nessarose, who uses a wheelchair and is her father's favorite. Clearly ashamed of Elphaba, he gives Nessarose a pair of magic shoes that sparkle in ambiguous colors under the theatrical lighting. Are they silver or ruby? MGM's lawyers will never be able to tell, but the audience knows their power. To Elphaba, they represent the love and acceptance she doesn't get from her father. We understand why she feels entitled to them after Nessa, who will become the Wicked Witch of the East, is crushed by Dorothy's falling house.

Elphaba, however, demonstrates her virtues and her powers immediately. Protective of her sister, she expects to share a room with Nessarose, but Madame Morrible has arranged to see after Nessarose in her own quarters. In an involuntary emotional response, Elphaba telekinetically rolls Nessarose's wheelchair from Madame Morrible's grasp to her own. Recognizing her natural talent, the previously dismissive Madame Morrible declares that she will introduce Elphaba to the Wizard. In the meantime, she will take no other students in sorcery, dashing Glinda's hopes of studying with her.

On hearing this news, Elphaba displays a power greater than telekinesis. She breaks into song. Elphaba's difference is ultimately revealed as a source of power manifest equally in magic, emotion, and singing. "The Wizard and I" (companion website 4.1) expresses not only her desire and her power but also the power of desire itself. An "I want" song in the lineage of "Over the Rainbow," but a world away from it, it communicates the feelings of a special young person and her vision of future triumph with an intensity only possible in high-powered belting. The conventions of the "I want" song script the performance and constitute the form of the desire. Elphaba starts the song alone on stage facing the audience, in a signal that an "I want" song is beginning. In a reflective verse she anticipates the transformation of her difference into something good: "This weird quirk I've tried to suppress or hide / is a talent that could help me meet the Wizard / If I make good / So I'll make good." The word "good" lands decisively on the tonic harmony, the "home" chord of the song's key, and the driving rhythm of the refrain begins, projecting confidence in the vision—she make-believes being with the Wizard, singing "when you're with the Wizard, no one thinks you're strange." Belting, in its technical and emotional virtuosity, makes the dream seem limitless. When Elphaba sings about "feeling things I've never felt," with the Wizard, she might as well be singing about the large feelings and vocal empowerment of musical theater. Big feelings like this belong to contemporary musicals like *The Wiz* and *Wicked* and are an important part of how audiences participate.[29] A young woman I interviewed remembered how the show made her feel overwhelmed with emotion to the point of holding back tears. My voice students requested songs from *Wicked* so they could reproduce these feelings by singing like Elphaba.

With her ability to magically transform by belting, Elphaba answers the question, "What happens when the Wicked Witch is allowed to sing?" Although Evillene, the Wicked Witch in *The Wiz*, gets a showstopping number in "No Bad News," it's a villain's song. As the hero of her story, Elphaba gets to sing the kinds of songs a heroine gets, with the depth of character and motivation they allow—"I want" songs, "I am" songs, becoming songs, eleven o'clock numbers, dynamic songs of friendship, love songs, sentimental ballads, and duets. If at the same time she represents a different image of the American girl, her contemporary vocal performance makes of that character a complex and empowered, if ultimately limited, subject.[30] As a musical-theatrical type, an alto-belter with an 'I want' song (not to mention the protagonist of an Oz musical), Elphaba is aligned with Judy Garland's Dorothy as well as Hamilton's Witch. It makes sense that Idina Menzel played Dorothy in her school production of *The Wizard of Oz* before growing up to be Elphaba.[31] This connection is encoded in "The Wizard and I," which contains the first sung iteration of a recurring musical motif set to the words, "Unlimited, my future is unlimited" (Figure 4.1).[32] This musical phrase subtly borrows its first several pitches from "Over the Rainbow," disguised in a new rhythm. Stacy Wolf suggests that this borrowing positions Elphaba as a "Dorothy-like heroine."[33] It might also imply a transformation of the classic

Figure 4.1. Music of "Unlimited" motive in "The Wizard and I" from *Wicked* (2003, words and music by Stephen Schwartz) using the first seven notes of "Over the Rainbow" from *The Wizard of Oz* (1939, words by E. Y. Harburg, music by Harold Arlen).

"I want" song, with Dorothy's yearning becoming Elphaba's ambition and the famous octave of Dorothy's "Somewhere" now giving flight to Elphaba's "Unlimited." As with *The Wiz*'s Dorothy, it's clear from her first song that Elphaba is a natural-born diva who will take her place in the musical theater pantheon by the end of the show.

"The Wizard and I" is an ambitious dream about difference and validation. It demonstrates an American belief in the strength of the individual amplified by the power of personal expression. At its best, this expression takes the form of a moral defense of what's right, whether in Elphaba's devotion to her sister, Dorothy's defense of the Scarecrow with a bucket of water, or a citizen's sense of fairness. It's the sense of righteousness that gives a Dorothy or an Elphaba the entitlement to sing, dance, and act in the world. Elphaba's power in unabashed singing is vindicating for those who are always being told to stop singing and being different, inviting participation from anyone who has longed to belong. Elphaba's dream that her father and sister will no longer be ashamed of her resonates with queer and immigrant adolescence as well as the experience of the misfit theater kid.[34]

The question remains however, from what position this power of expression comes, and who it benefits. As an "I want" song "The Wizard and I" is analogous to "Over the Rainbow," but its vision is one in which the intense feeling of difference will be vindicated by a presumed American meritocracy, supplemented by the endorsement of a well-placed public figure. If "Over the Rainbow" is a dream, or even a temporary escape from the problems of the world, and *The Wiz*'s "(Soon as I Get) Home," is about finding the dream in yourself, "The Wizard and I" is a song about the fulfillment of an American dream through personal ambition. This ambition and its fulfillment are evidenced by even more intense feeling at the high point of the song: "And I'll stand there with the Wizard / feeling things I've never felt." Thus far, Elphaba's difference is situated in the context of family and peer dynamics, divorced of any explicit politics, making her a sympathetic character to audience members who can imagine that they are the good guys, regardless of their politics.

The utopian performative of the "I want" song is impossible without the inevitable failures that will require its repetition, and there are hints of Elphaba's limitations in the song. Elphaba's asserted personal limitlessness will prove insufficient by itself to change the world. She is ultimately rejected by her community, and she is literally never able to fill Dorothy's shoes. These events are foreshadowed ironically when she imagines "a celebration throughout Oz that's all to do with me," not realizing it will be a celebration of her demise (but we know!), when she declares, "I'd be so happy I could melt!" Elphaba's faith in the Wizard is misdirected, as it was for Dorothy. She daydreams that the Wizard will "degreenify" her, reflecting ambivalent feelings about the pleasures of performative femininity. But her real "I want" is to be accepted, and she will soon learn that meeting the Wizard is not the answer to her problems. In the meantime, she rehearses with her peers the types of personal and social performance that will enable her future transformation into the Wicked Witch.

What Is This Feeling? The Road to Divadom

During their time at Shiz, Elphaba and Glinda teach each other their respective styles of girlhood using the gestures of musical theater and conventions of girls' stories, eventually becoming friends and inviting audiences into the performance along the way. Elphaba finds a measure of acceptance among her peers prior to meeting the Wizard, mainly by performing girl-centered bonding with Glinda in the course of act one. The school setting offers a rehearsal space where young people can practice the codes of American performance before going out into the larger world. The gestures of musical theater express the intensities of emotion and relationships among young people as they navigate their social environments and try to establish their place in the community. This period in Elphaba's story is loosely analogous to Dorothy's journey on the Yellow Brick Road, in which she learns the virtues of performance while making new friends. Here, however, it is prelude to Elphaba's larger journey, one in which her arrival in the Emerald City and confident performance of "Defying Gravity" at the end of act one will be complicated by the events of a second act. Brains, heart, and courage remain at the center of these performances, as Glinda and Elphaba in their different ways teach each other compassion and intelligence and Elphaba ultimately acts on the courage of her convictions.

Elphaba and Glinda begin in a state of "total detestation" for each other, in a recognizable encounter between the popular girl and the outsider. Complete opposites, they have predictably been forced to room together. In "What Is This Feeling?" they compose, in their separate ways, letters home, facing the audience as they sing about each other. Glinda struggles to describe Elphaba in her letter to her parents; Elphaba quite simply sums Glinda up as "blonde."

Indirect cross-talk continues as Glinda declares her loathing of Elphaba's face and clothing while Elphaba loathes Glinda's voice (in a musical, it's especially harsh to insult someone's voice, don't you think?). Elphaba gets a final jab in at the end, shouting "boo!" at Glinda and laughing when she squeals and jumps in shock. As counterpart to the rivalry between Glinda and the Wicked Witch of the West portrayed in the MGM film, this exchange is not only set as a song, making it singable and imitable, but also transferred to a situation that is relatable to modern audiences.

At the same time, in scenes such as this, they are girl counterparts to the comedy teams of Montgomery and Stone; Bolger, Haley, and Lahr; and Dorothy's friends in *The Wiz*, complete with the erotic charge that comes with the business of same-sex comedy duos. As Stacy Wolf notes, "What Is This Feeling?" begins as a parody of love songs describing the physical symptoms of love.

> What is this feeling / so sudden and new? / I felt the moment / I laid eyes on you / my pulse is rushing / my head is reeling / my face is flushing / what is this feeling? / fervid as a flame / does it have a name? / Yes!

The twist is that this feeling turns out to be "loathing," but we know from musical conventions that this kind of conflict signals that Elphaba and Glinda will eventually end up as friends, or as Wolf argues, a queer couple.[35] Fiyero, their mutual love interest, ostensibly triangulates and diffuses the possibility of their same-sex attraction, but the focus of the musical remains dominantly on their relationship as they experience intense love/hate emotions and intimate situations together. Moreover, Fiyero himself is potentially queer, as noted by Steven Greenwood, occupying something of the role of feminine-performing chorus boy, queerly rejecting normative time in his "it's just life" attitude, and playing the queer best friend to the two leading ladies.[36]

Elphaba and Glinda's generically inevitable friendship develops through the gestures of musical comedy and conventions of youth narratives. Glinda, as a mean joke, gives Elphaba an ugly, pointed black hat. In addition, for selfish reasons, Glinda has set Nessarose up on a date with the Munchkin Boq, who is, in reality, in love with Glinda. Seeing how happy Nessarose is, Elphaba convinces Madam Morrible to take Glinda on as a student. Wearing the ugly hat, Elphaba arrives at the Ozdust Ballroom, where all the students have gathered. She realizes she has been humiliated when her entrance causes the music to stop and everyone to laugh at her. Mustering her dignity, Elphaba descends the staircase in silence (an iconic diva entrance but without the music) and begins to do a strange solo dance, pretending not to care. Remorseful, Glinda joins Elphaba in her eccentric dance. This dance, reminiscent of Tony and Maria meeting in the dance at the gym in *West Side Story*, another musical about American youth and difference, shows a form of sincere connection that that could not be expressed in dialogue or even song. This gesture recalls similar moments in the MGM film and *The Wiz* when Dorothy and her friends help each other find their footing in the journey's dance.

Now that they're friends, Elphaba teaches Glinda something of a conscience, while Glinda teaches Elphaba social and gender performances that will help her choreograph a pathway through *Wicked*'s dystopia. In a scene inspired by the movie *Clueless*, Glinda determines to make Elphaba popular by giving her a makeover.[37] Although the transformation is only partially successful, it serves as a lesson in performance that helps Elphaba prepare for her future role as the Wicked Witch. Employing some of her clever lyricizing ("when someone needs a makeover / I simply have to take over"), Glinda emphasizes the details of performance.

> Popular, you're gonna be popular / I'll teach you the proper poise when you talk to boys / Little ways to flirt and flounce / I'll show you what shoes to wear, how to fix your hair / Everything that really counts to be / Popular

She proceeds from these personal gestures to social ones: "You'll hang with the right cohorts / you'll be good at sports / know the slang you've got to know." The performance is acknowledged by the comedy of Glinda failing to execute Elphaba's kind of magic. She tries to use her wand to turn Elphaba's frock into a ballgown, but it doesn't work for her. Following her instincts as a performer, she taps it like a microphone and asks, "Is this thing on?" She succeeds in her own kind of magic all the same. She takes Elphaba's glasses off and lets her hair down, and handing Elphaba a mirror, she declares her beautiful, "just not quite as popular as me!"

"Popular" is not just a superficial performance of girlishness, although it somewhat presents itself as one. It's an important ritual of feminine bonding. Inspired by bubblegum pop, with its youthful and feminine associations, "Popular" prominently features Glinda's bubbly vocal style and use of extralinguistic vocalizations. Not mere silliness, these vocal sounds constitute what Jacqueline Warwick has described as *ecriture feminine* in embodied feminine performance that is both consciously constructed as girlish and assertive of girls' expressions beyond patriarchal control.[38] In displays of her performative prowess, Glinda alternately belts and flips into her head voice on the word "popular." She indulges in pure physicality and vocality, dancing and flouncing around, singing "La, la, la, la, I'm gonna make you popular."

The comedic acting in this number acknowledges the audience and invites its participation in the blossoming friendship while sending up the performance of femininity and the conventions of girls' stories (companion website 4.2). Glinda practically mugs for laughs, and Elphaba laughs along with the audience at her antics. In this scenario, audiences might recognize the challenge of always having to execute gendered performances. One woman told me "Popular" was her favorite song from the show when she was in high school, not only because it was "annoyingly catchy," but also because of its obvious superficiality and its "making fun of being popular." Unlike Glinda in the MGM film, Chenoweth's Glinda shows us her flaws and the honesty of her performance by breaking the illusion and the fourth wall. Whereas the perfection of Billie Burke's Glinda may seem out of reach, *Wicked*'s Glinda invites us to imagine that we, too, could pull off the role of the Good Witch. Such a performance invites us, in our own moments, to become Glinda, to sing her songs, and to occupy her position as the American diva. The first time I saw *Wicked*, Chenoweth was in a neck brace after an injury. In showing Elphaba how to flip her hair, she couldn't toss her head with the neck brace on. After an uncertain pause, she managed the task by moving her whole body from the waist in a crowd-pleasing improvisation. I learned later that it was not the first time she had performed in a neck brace, and while the injury wasn't faked, the performance was surely rehearsed. An accident becomes an opportunity to demonstrate virtuosity and bond with the audience. Girls and women might especially appreciate Chenoweth's ability to carry on with this demanding performance of femininity in the face of inevitable complications. Thus presented, the performance of a gender role is both pleasurable and a demonstration of a honed skill.

Themes of friendship, rivalry, and empathy are politically relevant as Elphaba, Glinda, and their peers navigate their performances. They demonstrate contemporary ideas of brains, heart, and courage in ways that may resonate with the political concerns of young people in a twenty-first-century America resembling *Wicked*'s dystopian Oz. Elphaba's commitment to justice for Animals dignifies a form of political empathy, animal rights, that is often trivialized and ridiculed, all the more because of its association with girls. To a sympathetic Elphaba, Dr. Dillamond, a goat and the only talking Animal professor remaining in the college, reports that Animals have been losing their power of speech. He unexpectedly bleats while trying to sing the word "bad" ("Something bad is happening in Oz"). It's a worrying development when people lose their voice, both politically and in the musical, where the elevated speech of singing is evidence of performative power, so Elphaba plans to ask the Wizard for help.

As the day of Elphaba's departure for the Emerald City approaches, friendship, romance, and politics twine with musical theater and romantic comedy conventions. Fiyero appears first as Glinda's natural match because he is so much like her, "Dancing through Life" without thinking too deeply. (Fiyero, we eventually learn, is the future Scarecrow, so this is his "If I Only Had a Brain.") Musical theater and romantic comedy conventions tell us that this is a match that will not hold, however, because it's opposites that attract. Glinda and Fiyero both occupy this role for Elphaba, who changes them. In the case of Fiyero this is accomplished quickly, almost as a theatrical obligation, when he helps her release a captive lion cub (the Cowardly Lion). Still, Elphaba can't yet believe that he could love her. Until now, one could hardly imagine the Wicked Witch of the West singing about unrequited love, but in "I'm Not That Girl," Elphaba sings a type of ballad distinctly belonging to the young heroine of a musical. Meanwhile, Boq, the lovelorn Tin-Man-to-be, partners with Nessarose only to please Glinda, his true love. Fiyero brings Elphaba flowers at the train station, where she is leaving to meet the Wizard. Recognizing that Fiyero is attracted to Elphaba's political conscience, Galinda tries to impress him by changing her name to Glinda in solidarity with Dr. Dillamond, who had been unable to pronounce the "Ga."

All of this culminates in Elphaba's arrival in the Emerald City to meet the Wizard. Glinda accompanies her there for "One Short Day," and in the glow of the metropolis, their bond of best friendship is cemented in tropes of feminine bonding activities, such as shopping and going to see a musical. Bright costumes, acrobatic choreography, and flashy Broadway show music greet them. In fulfillment of the queer myth of going to the Emerald City, Elphaba finally feels at home where everything is green. As a parallel to "The Merry Old Land of Oz" or the Emerald City ballet in *The Wiz*, this number is Elphaba's dream come true. She seems to have arrived in the place where she belongs after some successful performances with new friends.

Encountering the Humbug and Defying Gravity

In her encounter with the humbug, Elphaba embarks on a spectacular diva's journey and performance for which everything up to now has served as rehearsal. Deciding after her meeting with the Wizard that she must look to herself and her own powers, she takes flight through the power of singing and theater magic. Elphaba's acceptance of the role of "wicked" emerges from personal choices and compulsory performances, and the gestures of musical theater are the terms on which she makes these negotiations.

Unlike Dorothy, Elphaba is immediately taken backstage of the Wizard's throne room, where she discovers that he is a fraudulent despot who is responsible for the silencing of Animals. The Wizard acknowledges his deceptions but maintains his good intentions as a "Sentimental Man," who only wants to be a father to the people of Oz. He and Madame Morrible trick Elphaba into reading an incantation from the *Grimmerie*, the book of transformations, so that the monkeys the Wizard holds in captivity grow wings to serve as his spies. Already, the curtain is pulled back on the Wizard's true intentions. Rather than the helpful humbug of the extravaganza or MGM film, this is a humbug for contemporary audiences who are well aware of the Oz mythology and of being given the song and dance by politicians and the media. Elphaba is as indignant as Dorothy and her friends who angrily accuse the Wizard of his humbug on their second visit. She refuses to join the Wizard's circus, and Madame Morrible declares her an enemy of Oz, a "Wicked Witch."

Resolutely, Elphaba transforms in "Defying Gravity," a song that has secured a reputation as one of the most powerful performances of selfhood in the musical theater canon (companion website 4.3).[39] Using musical gestures and the technology of the theater, Elphaba takes control of her own performance, at least for the moment of song. After singing to Glinda that she no longer wants to be with the Wizard, Elphaba performatively pronounces her transformation: "Something has changed within me / Something is not the same / I'm through with playing by / The rules of someone else's game." The music supports her declaration as high notes spin in the accompaniment, anticipating her ability to take flight by breaking into song as she sings, "It's time to try defying gravity / I think I'll try defying gravity." In Menzel's performance, audible gasps for breath between phrases evince the intensity of her feeling. As the energy of the song builds, she declares that she's "through accepting limits," and acknowledges that she's making something of a humbug choice to believe the better of two options when she sings that she'd "sooner buy defying gravity" in the attempt to change things than rely on love that "comes at much too high a cost." Having accumulated sufficient power through singing up to this point, she pauses to read some magic words from the *Grimmerie* as the Wizard's guards attempt to enter the room to capture her. Following the incantation, she yells, "Stop!" The stage apparatus and omniscient orchestra comply, yielding to her authority as a diva taking command of the theatrical machinery. The theater falls silent and still. A broom, enchanted by her words, emerges from a trap door. Elphaba invites Glinda to join her, and for a moment they sing about being "unlimited" and "defying gravity" together, but Glinda is incapable of Elphaba's type of transformation, so they part ways. As suits her talents, however, Glinda gives Elphaba a cape that, together with the hat, completes the familiar witch habit. The costume change, as it does for divas in musical theater, affirms Elphaba's ability to finish her musical number with authority.

The transformation is complete as Elphaba takes flight through the powers of song and theater magic in the remainder of the song, which brings act one to a forceful close. She fully assumes the role of diva, taught to her by Glinda, but on her own terms and in her own style.[40] As guards rush in and grab Glinda, Elphaba cries, "I'm the one you want. It's meeeee!" On this elongated self-proclamation, in a transitional vocalization between shouting and singing, Elphaba rises above the stage surrounded by streaks of light and fog, taking flight with her broom for the first time. The stagecraft of her flight is obvious. She is simply hoisted vertically, taking a stationary position above the stage, but the gesture is effective. It draws the audience into her expression of selfhood, yet reminds us, through its spectacle, of its being a performance. She belts out the climax of the song, asserting her abilities of self-determination and a go-it-alone strategy.

> And if I'm flying solo / at least I'm flying free / to those who'd ground me / take a message back from me / Tell them how I'm defying gravity / I'm flying high defying gravity / and soon I'll match them in renown / And nobody in all of Oz / no Wizard that there ever was / is ever gonna bring me down!

Menzel has sung the first two solo iterations of the hook (containing the words "defying gravity") in her head voice or in semibelted head tones. Now, in a fully chest-dominant belt she reaches an F5, setting a new standard for how high women are expected to belt in a musical. She ends in a wordless vocal display, a defiant riff that, like Margaret Hamilton's Witch cackle in the MGM film, is pure affect, at the top of her range and teetering on the edge of control.[41]

This is the height of achievement for the Witch's expanding range of musical expression in the repertoire of Oz musicals. After being erased from the extravaganza, prevented from singing in the MGM film, and finally getting to be a strong voice of villainy in *The Wiz*, now she gets a defining song of selfhood and becoming in the American musical. In a display of subjective power deriving its authority from its performance of personal authenticity, Elphaba defies and physically exceeds the frame of a narrative intent on containing her.

During the song, the "unlimited" motive has returned, but the second act shows how this performance of individual defiance is ultimately constrained by Elphaba's relationships and larger social forces. Elphaba tries out several different tactics to use her powers for good—reconciliation with family, compromise with the Wizard's regime, heterosexual trysting with Fiyero—but each leads her to ever more limited options. In what has become somewhat infamous as an ableist episode in the musical, she enchants Nessarose's shoes so that she can walk, but Nessarose is ungrateful when Boq, as a result, sees an opportunity to leave her to her newfound self-sufficiency.[42] When Nessarose botches an attempt to cast a spell to make him love her, inadvertently depriving him of a heart, Boq himself is ungrateful to Elphaba for saving his life by turning him into the Tin Man.

Despairing, Elphaba momentarily reconsiders the Wizard's offer of a partnership. Charming her with the old song and dance, the Wizard characterizes his role as accidental, declaring that he accepted the job of Wizard because "the folks in Oz needed someone to believe in." Singing about how they proclaimed him "Wonderful," he claps his hands, much as Baum's Wizard rubbed his hands together on being called a humbug, a gesture that encapsulates his own glee and implies the applause of an adoring public. He insists that the lies he told the people were lies they wanted to hear, adding "Where I'm from [America], we believe in all sorts of things that aren't true. We call it history." He goes on to sing about how notions of good and evil are performative and historically determined: "A man's called a traitor or liberator / A rich man's a thief or a philanthropist / Is one a crusader or ruthless invader? / It's all in which label / Is able to persist." The allusions to crusaders and invaders recalls George W. Bush's ill-advised description of the War on Terror as a crusade, implying a war on Muslims, and the performative transmogrification through repeated assertion of this campaign into the invasion of Iraq.

In a show in which pop music and belting signify truth and authenticity, the Wizard's vaudevillian style is crafty and duplicitous. He offers to make people see Elphaba as wonderful too, seductively setting his next words to her music from "The Wizard and I":

> At long, long last receive your due / Long overdue / Elphaba, the most celebrated / Are the rehabilitated / There'll be such a whoop-de-doo / A celebration throughout Oz / That's all to do with you.

Reciprocating, Elphaba sings his tune, ("It does sound wonderful, I must admit") and briefly dances with him. When people dance together in a musical, as Elphaba and Glinda did earlier, it's usually an indication of some kind of coming together. Momentarily drawn into the Wizard's song and dance, Elphaba says she will join him on the condition that he set the monkeys free. However, as he does so, it is revealed that he has been keeping Dr. Dillamond, now completely speechless, in captivity. With the curtain pulled back once again, Elphaba vows to fight the Wizard to her death.

Elphaba becomes more recognizable in the role of the Wicked Witch we know as she masters her performance. In the process, she becomes more glamorous and sexually expressive, finally getting to be "that girl" in committing the "wicked" deed with Fiyero.[43] Even in "As Long As You're Mine," however, their love has queer potential as it takes place in an ephemeral moment which ultimately holds little promise for a normative outcome under the circumstances.[44] When, as expected, Dorothy's house crashes in Oz, killing Nessarose, Elphaba's confrontation with Glinda repeats the Munchkinland scene from the MGM film, with knowing comedic references to the film. When Fiyero allows himself to be captured by the Wizard's guards and is hung on a pole to die, Elphaba, in "No Good Deed," saves him by transforming him into the Scarecrow, while declaring, "I'm the witch," and "no good deed will I do again." Speculating that she may have been punished for insincere good deeds, and that sincere actions may be impossible, she grapples with the relationship between "truth" and performance: "Was I really seeking good / or just seeking attention? / Is that all good deeds are / when looked at with an ice-cold eye?"

The resolution of Elphaba's journey in the musical, as for Dorothy, is in her final encounter with Glinda. In previous Oz musicals, Glinda has been the authoritative diva who emerges from the theatrical machinery to teach or affirm Dorothy's lesson, but here there is mutual learning and understanding between the two divas. Whereas in the MGM film Dorothy recites a homily in Glinda's presence and in *The Wiz* she sings "Home" as a solo after being encouraged by Glinda's version of "Believe in Yourself," in *Wicked*, Elphaba's final lesson comes in a duet with Glinda, a conversation or dialogue, about how to be and how to act. "For Good," as Wolf has shown, has the form and vocal relationships of a couple's duet, reconciling two contrasting personalities according to the musical's marriage trope.[45] Elphaba and Glinda sing about how bodies—people and objects— affect each other and the lessons about performing selfhood and doing good they have learned from each other: "Like a comet pulled from orbit / as it passes a sun / like a stream that meets a boulder / halfway through the wood / who can say if I've been changed for the better? / But because I knew you / I have been changed for good." Elphaba sings the "unlimited" motive again, now set to the words "I'm limited," a familiar theme heard differently. Even diva-witches have limited powers in their gestures toward an unfinished utopia.

In her final act, Elphaba does provide something of her own *diva ex machina*, literally using the machinery of the theater to remove herself from a scene in which she is threatened by a gathering mob. Her final performance plays out like a peek backstage during the events of the MGM film, as she stages her death by melting, using a curtain, lighting effects, and theatrical trickery worthy of the humbug Wizard. In silhouette, we see the familiar shape of the Winkie Guards' spears as Dorothy throws water on a witch who appears to melt. The freaks take command of the performance, as Chistery the monkey pulls back the curtain, revealing that only Elphaba's hat remains. In the MGM film, the Wicked Witch warns Dorothy, "I can cause accidents too!" Here she delivers on that promise, intentionally staging Dorothy's ultimate accident for her own purposes.

Home for Elphaba is as impossible as utopia, but we are left with hope. Much as MGM's Witch had to be destroyed because of her vocal nonconformity, Elphaba has to be expelled from the community to restore peace as a consequence of her powers manifest as a vocal excess more appreciated by fans of the musical than by the citizens of Oz. But for Elphaba there is an escape route. Another trapdoor in the stage floor, reminiscent of the one that failed Margaret Hamilton in her injury in the MGM film, is the way out for Elphaba and Fiyero, who emerge from their hiding place to escape into exile and what Steven Greenwood describes as their own queer partnership between a legally deceased witch and a nonhuman scarecrow.[46] In the end, Elphaba is, as Wolf says, "triumphant to the audience if not in the musical's world."[47] Elphaba's powers, we learn, were the result of her being the child of two worlds, the issue of an affair between the Wizard, an immigrant from America, and Elphaba's Ozian mother. The liminality of home and elsewhere, Oz and America, that inspires audiences was the source of her magic. The musical ends with Elphaba and Glinda, unseen by each other, singing a reprise of "For Good" and the chorus declaiming "Wicked!" over a dissonant tritone in the orchestra.[48] Remaining after the applause and the curtain call are the bonds of friendship and the entangled performances of good and wicked. The tense coexistence between Oz and America, goodness and wickedness, home and exile, hangs over the ending of the musical as if to suggest that the audience leaves the theater with all the complexities and ambiguities that *Wicked* represents within and beyond "America."

What a World: *Wicked* at Home and Abroad

Wicked stages American self-inventive performance for domestic and international audiences. Its border crossings are facilitated by the emotional impact of its popular score, its dynamic performances, and its corporate, international marketing. Fans identify with Elphaba, Glinda, and the actors who play them, adopting their performances.

Wicked's emotions enable the formation of intimate publics and collective identities among fans of the musical.[49] As Stacy Wolf has shown, *Wicked's* initial success was fueled in part by young fans who invested emotional identification in the two divas, Elphaba and Glinda, while sharing their perspectives and experiences online.[50] *Wicked* also became the iconic musical for a generation of musical theater fans. As an object of fandom, it simply was the thing around which a community was formed. As one young woman said, "*Wicked* was to a certain group of people what *Rent* was to me and my friends." *Hamilton* (2015) is undoubtedly the next musical in this sequence. The musical itself binds fans together. Finally getting to see *Wicked* is a rite of passage for many. For others it remains a dream, but one through which fans can still feel connected to each other through the show. Many people encounter such inspiring songs as "Defying Gravity" through the cast recording before seeing the musical. *Wicked*'s appealing score affords kinesthetic and vocal participation in a similar way to the MGM film, but with an especially intense identification with the characters and the actors.

As an act of pilgrimage, attending a live performance of *Wicked*, with New York or Broadway as the Emerald City, is the ultimate goal in a quest for the musical theater experience. *Wicked* stands in for Broadway itself, with the spectacle and general "Broadwayness" of the show being a major part of the appeal, just as the extravaganza is about theater and performance, the MGM film is about the Hollywood musical, and *The Wiz* is self-consciously about Black performance traditions. The longing of a theater kid or misfit person for the city is an important component of the whole experience, just as Dorothy longed for a place over the rainbow, which turned out to be a version of the Hollywood musical. In New York, according to a young woman I interviewed, you could feel like you were part of a place where people were more "interesting and creative" than in your hometown. In an episode of the television series *Glee*, Kurt and Rachel, the representative gay boy and Jewish girl (and as such, representative of core audiences of musicals), have their Broadway dreams come true on a trip to New York when they sneak into the Gershwin Theater, where *Wicked* plays, to sing "For Good" in front of the iconic set.[51] In a further measure of the significance of *Wicked* and its divas, Menzel and Chenoweth both had recurring roles on the show. *Wicked* is a touchstone for musical theater kids, but the intensity of identification is sufficiently strong that the show itself indexes Broadway beyond these fan groups.

Menzel's image as something of a misfit might be an especial point of identification for the underestimated.[52] Her underdog status is reflected in *Wicked*'s reviews, many of which offered more praise for Chenoweth as the Good Witch.[53] Menzel has a reputation for always pushing herself to the limit—often to the point of flubbing notes in live broadcasts, as she did in her performance of "Defying Gravity" during the Tony Awards. Her appeal is that we do know she's "limited," but unafraid to test what the limit is, even at the risk of failure in front of an audience. Elphaba/Idina's ability to perform her way to authenticity might inspire girls who are also subject to judgments about their bodies and voices. When asked about her favorite character in *Wicked*, a former girl fan responded, "I think my favorite character was, like, Idina Menzel." Menzel's vulnerability is something she shares, in a different way, with Judy Garland, both in her early career as a teen star and in her middle-age concerted career, which was so closely associated with her struggles and triumphs, deepening her endearment to queer subcultures.

Chenoweth's star power casts its own spell as she plays the role of the home-grown American diva in her public appearances and interactions with fans. In concert performances, Chenoweth routinely invites an aspiring singer or musical theater actor on stage to sing "For Good" with her. Reenacting Glinda's tutelage of Elphaba in "Popular," Chenoweth plays the more experienced diva with the young singer. An ordinary girl (a Dorothy, if you will) gets to connect with the star to whose divadom she aspires, while the lyrics of the song position the girl as learning from Chenoweth. Chenoweth points out the moment when the performance "clicks," and the ordinary girl transforms, becoming the diva in her performance. These performances illustrate the ability of women to change, empower, and support each other with their voices, specifically in the pursuit of singing and musical theater. Viewing several of these videos in succession reveals that they are more scripted than they might at first appear, but this doesn't diminish their power.

Who gets to play Elphaba or Glinda, and have access to her expressive and empowering musical gestures, matters in the composition of *Wicked*'s implied America. Elphaba's color invites analogies to race, but her greenface makeup might tend to reinforce the Whiteness of the actor beneath it, despite influences of Black musical practice in the belting and improvised riffs of the contemporary musical theater idiom.[54] Whiteness is routinely assumed when race isn't specified. When she's played by a Black actor such as Alexia Khadime or Saycon Sengbloh, or a Latina such as Eden Espinosa, there might be a change in our understanding of the social constraints and marginalization she encounters. As Donatella Galella argues, context, performance choices, and audience reception matter in racially conscious casting.[55] When Brittney Johnson became the first Black Glinda standby in 2018, fans speculated that having a Black actor in the role would make Glinda a fellow outsider to Elphaba, implicitly changing the dynamic of their friendship in performance. Others felt that it might compromise the perception of Glinda as socially privileged.[56] Johnson herself remarked,

> I think Elphaba being green gave us a chance, as an audience, to empathize with her character and apply it to our lives while still allowing us to

be somewhat removed because, I mean short of Comicon, you don't encounter many green people! When Glinda is a person of color, it forces us to look at the similarities in their struggle and to really notice Glinda's growth in a way that maybe we didn't quite see before.[57]

That casting decisions may change the understanding of a character in this way complicates the assumption of "universality" in Elphaba's experience of difference or Glinda's "goodness." Recent news that the film adaptation of *Wicked*, directed by Asian American director Jon M. Chu, will be released in two parts with Cynthia Erivo, who is Black, queer, and British, as Elphaba and Ariana Grande, who is Italian-American, as Glinda, suggests a broadening of *Wicked*'s portrayal of American and international divadom in the still unfinished American musical.[58]

Globally, Broadway musicals represent "America," and *Wicked* invites international audiences to participate in its performance of Americanism.[59] *Wicked*, like many contemporary corporate musicals, is a transnational brand, bringing the American musical, and an internationalized ideal of acting American, to the global stage.[60] Part of what makes *Wicked* so "American," according to Willemijn Verkaik, who played Elphaba in the Dutch production, is the "passionate expression of how you feel."[61] This emotional quality makes the show, and its performed American values, whatever they are, marketable across borders. While many US critics found *Wicked*'s standard Broadway pop style unnoteworthy, it's undoubtedly responsible for much of the musical's international appeal. Whatever the score lacks in a "timelessness" that might be associated with Oz, it makes up for in its marketable utopian placelessness. The tendency of international productions to be replicas of the original assists in translation. When I had the opportunity to see *Wicked* in the Hague, with prior knowledge of the Broadway show and cast recording, my inability to understand Dutch was no impediment to enjoying the show.

When Elphaba and Glinda arrive in the Emerald City, they attend a Broadway-style show called *Wizomania*, a piece of the Wizard's propaganda. A show within a show, it metatheatrically reminds us of the man behind the curtain, as does the popular backstage tour of *Wicked*'s Broadway production, "Behind the Emerald Curtain."[62] As ever, seeing the curtain pulled back does not diminish belief in the performance known to be one. It is bought happily, along with souvenir booklets and CDs. *Wicked* warns us to be careful what we buy even while functioning as part of a global commercial enter-tainment apparatus supported by many of the same power structures as the American economic, political, and military hegemony it tacitly and explicitly critiques. The ability to navigate such contradictions by seeing both sides of the curtain, embracing the show while aware of its humbug, is as American as Oz itself.

5

"And Then There Was Oz Again"

Making Believe between Oz and Home

For the fiftieth anniversary of MGM's *The Wizard of Oz* in 1989, Downy produced an ad featuring middle-class American kids dressing up to put on a home performance of *The Wizard of Oz* (companion website 5.1).[1] To the music of "We're Off to See the Wizard," a girl retrieves a red sneaker from under the bed and a large funnel from the kitchen drawer. She informs two boys, one White and one Black, that they are playing the Scarecrow and Tin Man, placing the funnel on the Tin Man's head for a hat. She auditions her little brother for the role of the Lion and naturally plays Dorothy herself, wearing the red sneakers. The family dog is Toto. The music transitions into "Over the Rainbow" as they all get into costume (this is where the laundry comes in), and the commercial ends with a tribute to "everyone who believes dreams can come true" as a curtain is pulled back from an arched doorway to the living room and the four kids skip forward in iconic formation, singing "We're Off to See the Wizard," as choreographed for them by the familiar film text. This is a cross-generational performance too, as Dad teaches the boy how to move like the Scarecrow and Mom plays the piano.

This ritual is recognizable to many Americans who grew up in the latter half of the twentieth century, when television broadcasts of the MGM film were an anticipated annual event and playing Oz afterward was common. During this time, *The Wizard of Oz* was a touchstone of American childhood and an automatic marker of belonging to the community of American children. Film scholar Alexander Doty's recollection of Oz play touches on the significance of performance with material objects, casting negotiations, role-playing, and gender dynamics.

> Almost every year the telecast of *The Wizard of Oz* inspired my siblings and me to stage an impromptu version of the film using the sidewalk around the block as the Yellow Brick Road. . . there were only two essential props: one sister's sparkling red plastic high heels and a suitably messy old broom.

Oz and the Musical. Ryan Bunch, Oxford University Press. © Oxford University Press 2023.
DOI: 10.1093/oso/9780190843137.003.0006

My sisters and I would then argue about who would play the two star parts [Dorothy and the Wicked Witch]—leaving the loser and our two turned-out-to-be-straight brothers to play Glinda and whatever male roles they fancied.[2]

Wicked author Gregory Maguire similarly recalled leading groups of local kids and his six siblings in what Dee Michel calls "backyard play," playing the Scarecrow because Dorothy didn't seem to be an option.[3] Much as the girl in the Downy ad enlists her brothers and friends in her production, as a kid, I recruited my niece and nephew in my Oz play and home movies.

After every musical, we have considered how Oz and home are integrated in the "real" world after the return. The relationship between home and Oz is enacted explicitly in everyday performances such as home Oz play, school musicals, themed environments, and community events. These performances of the American fairy tale express identity and community, drawing on the performance gestures and characterizations available in the repertoires of Oz and musical theater. Musical theater conventions make these performances possible by providing the sounds, scripts, and choreography that shape bodily movements and transform the environments through which the participants move. Informal and playful performances transform the backyard, the living room, the school auditorium, and main streets into hopeful visions of utopia. In these utopian performatives, home and Oz are simultaneously transportive and rooted in their places. As these performances take place in different American communities, they reflect local values and histories of inclusion and access.

Playing Oz at Home

Playing Oz at home is an American tradition. I often have to explain it to people from abroad, and sometimes to Americans born after the era of broadcast television, but Americans who experienced childhood in the second half of the twentieth century know the practice well. In Oz play, home *becomes* Oz, as the songs and dances, even if imperfectly remembered the day after the broadcast or months later, provide a kinesthetic script for twice-performance and participation. Playing Oz is performative participation in American childhood, binding a common identity through its very acts while making the American fairy tale and its wonders available for daily use.

Beginning in the 1950s, television presentations of the MGM film became so embedded as an American ritual that many people can't remember the first time they saw the movie.[4] According Paul, one of my informants, "It feels like it's just always been part of my life."[5] There was only one chance to see it each year, and you didn't miss it. If you didn't have TV at home, you went to a neighbor or relative's house.[6] The highly anticipated broadcasts formed something of a collective childhood experience and common culture for many American kids. Gregory Maguire has described how kids would "thrill in simultaneous shock and delight" and "experienced the story at the same time, in a hundred thousand households."[7] It had "an almost sacramental aspect."[8] These annual broadcasts were almost like a national holiday. Paul says, "Oz was a tradition for us. I feel bad that it's no longer a national cultural event. We didn't have a lot of customs that we followed as a family, really. It was a family thing, and we were all excited to watch it." In many homes, the normal rules were relaxed for Oz night. Paul was allowed to stay up later than usual, and popcorn was popped. It would be inaccurate to say that this experience has been universal, but it was common. At this level of participation, surely the MGM film alone made a significant contribution to the concept of the family musical as well as to the experience of the American fairy tale.

Consequently, home Oz play is scripted by the conventions of the musical. Before home video, MGM's Oz was an ephemeral experience that had to be recreated through singing, dancing, and play between annual broadcasts. Amelia, who first saw the movie in theaters in the 1950s, recalls, "Every chance I got to see it, I would wander around and sing as many bad versions of the songs for as long as it would stay in my head. . . . I couldn't remember the words exactly. I think that my enthusiasm made up for my lack of accuracy." Choreography of performance with others might require negotiations of family and peer relations. Linking arms to perform "We're Off to See the Wizard" or chant, "Lions, and Tigers, and Bears, Oh My!" forms a symbolic social unit among the people engaged in the performance. One person told me how she linked arms with parents and siblings while skipping around to "We're Off to See the Wizard" on family hiking trips in the woods. After her middle school did *The Wizard of Oz*, she and her friends sang "Were Off to See the Wizard" and recreated bits from the show around the neighborhood. In performing the same routine with his peers, one person told me he always had to be on the end of the group, so that he was only holding hands with his girlfriend and not her friend.

Even the theatrical or make-believe act of putting on a costume or finding a prop can imply getting ready to sing or perform in a musical. We see this in musicals when Elphaba completes her witch outfit for the first time to sing "Defying Gravity," when Dorothy and her friends get makeovers while singing "Merry Old Land of Oz," or in Montgomery and Stone's constant changes of costume in the extravaganza. Once a costume element is in place, it may prompt breaking into song as an essential trait of the character. Karin, an eleven-year-old Black girl who was Dorothy for Halloween one year, carried a basket and skipped on the sidewalk as she went trick-or-treating. Much as Doty's play involved a sister's shoes and an old broom—all the more magical because of its antiquated state—David is certain he must have put a funnel on his head like the Tin Man in play. How in this act could one not be compelled to launch into "If I Only Had a Heart," or "We're Off to See the Wizard?" In such scenarios, everyday objects script the musical performance of the American fairy tale through their associations with the musical and its gestures. Acquiring magical properties in performance, any pair of red shoes can be the ruby slippers, prompting skipping and dancing by knowledge of how they behave in the musical.

Home media and material culture transmit the scripts of the American musical for Oz play. As children's music scholar Ingeborg Vestad has noted, recordings afford the opportunity to act out a familiar story to the scripting of sound and movement.[9] Coinciding with the broadcast era, the soundtrack of the MGM film was released in 1956, so kids could play and sing along to the record, just as people likely performed to newspaper lyrics and sheet music from the extravaganza. Similar activities are available with recordings of *The Wiz* and *Wicked*, and singalong edition DVDs and Blu-rays of the MGM film have been released, offering further affordances for singing and playing along.[10] The centering of these media on the home made the American fairy tale accessible, collapsing home and Oz into a singular performative space. As a child in the 1980s, Paul recorded songs from movie musicals, including *The Wizard of Oz*, on audio cassette by placing the recorder near the TV speaker. He recalls playing the recorded Oz songs in the backyard while singing and playing along, pretending to be the characters with other kids from the neighborhood. Here, the backyard or suburban neighborhood, a typical place for American children in the twentieth century to meet up and play, serves as the setting and point of access for the performative ritual of going to Oz. Maybe Dorothy was right about finding some measure of your heart's desire in the backyard.

Playing Oz is making utopian theater at home. When Jonathan and his sister made home Oz movies starring their dolls, they used double doors separating one room from another as their curtain, opening and closing it to reveal different scenes. Like magical objects in the fairy tale, or props in the theater, material things, in conjunction music, suggest movement through the spaces of home reimagined as Oz.[11] As their Dorothy doll traveled through Oz, they sang "We're Off to See the Wizard," which, according to Jonathan, was important because it scripted mobility from one place to another. That their movies were otherwise not musical suggests the integral importance of the song in the transmission and repetition of the story. The found-object and do-it-yourself performances of home have their more elaborate counterparts in community theater, which accomplishes its own transformations of everyday spaces into the fairy-tale realms of Oz and musical theater.

Playing Oz on Stage

School and community theater performances are counterparts to home play, in which going to the theater is like going to Oz. Oz musicals have a prominent place in the musical repertoire as part of what Stacy Wolf describes as an ecosystem of community, regional, and professional theater that defines the American musical beyond Broadway.[12] The theatrical version of the MGM film consistently ranks among the top ten or twenty musicals produced by grade schools in the United States.[13] As a result, it significantly contributes to the definition of what school or community theater is. As the characters in musicals do, actors in community performances use the gestures of musical theater to act out their identities and social relations with others. Stage versions of the MGM film and *The Wiz* bring community members into the performances, with different implications depending on the demographic makeup of the community and the extent to which Oz and musicals are understood to stand in for a sense of America and how to be part of it.

Because of the prominence of Oz in the school and community theatrical repertoire, playing its roles, for many young people, amounts to "doing" theater as well as implicitly acting American. In these performances, kids are virtuoso performers of the repertoires and gestures of musicals, Oz, and American childhood. These performances not only expand young people's opportunities to participate in the performance of the American fairy tale, but also transform the American fairy tale itself, envisioning and realizing more inclusive and less conventional embodiments and performances of the roles, the songs, and the musical gestures.

Like playing Oz at home, doing an Oz musical in your school or community is participating in an American tradition. That Idina Menzel played Dorothy in school before becoming Elphaba in *Wicked* is more expected than surprising, and even Margaret Hamilton was in a Junior League production of an Oz play as a youth.[14] When actor Kristen Bell tweeted an old picture of herself as Dorothy in her school production, users replied sharing pictures from their own school shows, which included many of them in Oz costumes.[15] The shared experiences of Oz and musicals engender feelings of inclusion and recognition, serving as social and cultural currency and binding relations among participants. School Oz musicals are nostalgic for adults, while kids use them for their own expressive purposes.

In order to observe some of these performances, I attended several middle school and high school productions of *The Wizard of Oz* and *The Wiz* in urban and suburban settings in the northeast corridor of the United States. In these spaces, it was sometimes necessary to navigate my presence in a community to which I was an outsider. Usually, I blended in with the crowd, but in an accident of poor timing, I arrived an hour and a half early for one show. A parent volunteer asked me which child I had I had come to see. I said, "I just love *The Wizard of Oz*." We had a conversation about how many times I'd seen the movie (a few) and whether I'd ever been in the show (yes, but I didn't mention I was in the Lullaby League as an adult). My demonstrated experience with Oz and musicals gave me entrée as easily as if I were wearing the ruby slippers. She directed me to a nearby pizza restaurant where I could have dinner and return at showtime.

School and community theaters work with the available official and unofficial scripts, the often limited production resources, and audience expectations, making their local performances of the national fairy tale distinct. The scripts licensed for community performance may measure up to performer and audience expectations in varying degrees. An irreverent, vaudevillian 1942 script used by the St. Louis Municipal Theatre with the MGM songs interpolated was the only official script available for decades.[16] The text now commonly used is the 1987 Royal Shakespeare Company (RSC) version, adapted directly from the MGM screenplay, which fulfills expectations for a musical even better than the film by including verses, reprises, and songs by Arlen and Harburg not included in the film. Working with these scripts, some school productions add in details from the film adaptations, with which audiences may be more familiar. *The Wiz* is available in the Broadway version, but "You Can't Win," more familiar to many from the film, may be substituted for Broadway's "I Was Born on the Day before Yesterday." Set designs and choreography are often based on the familiar film versions while dialogue and songs follow the official stage librettos.

Out of necessity, school productions employ do-it-yourself theatrical humbug resembling home play. Some schools may have well-equipped theaters while others must adapt to the available spaces of auditoriums and gymnasiums with folding chairs. Scenery may be elaborate or minimal. Music may be provided by a single piano, a recording, a small pit band of volunteer adults and students, or in well-resourced schools, a full orchestra. But playful engagements with the American fairy tale through the practices of the musical transform the school as they do the home. Low-tech special effects resemble both the Wizard's humbuggery and the improvisations of kids' play, as Munchkins crowd around to hide Dorothy's feet while somebody "magically" puts the ruby slippers on her or the Witch melts by crouching down to the floor while slipping out of her dress and hat behind a set piece or a little fog. In one show I attended, the Wizard, when exposed, emerged from behind the proscenium curtain, which happened to be emerald green, making the analogy of Oz as theater explicit. When he departed in his balloon, he simply scooted it off the stage while still inside, to the amusement of the audience. The often simple props, costumes, and choreography in school productions resemble the everyday objects used in Oz play. Red or silver sneakers frequently suffice for ruby slippers or silver shoes. Some productions faithfully reproduce Dorothy's *pas de basque* step, while others use everyday skipping.

Audience participation is enabled by the gestures of the musical and the rituals of theater. The impulse to sing and move is evident as people mouth or quietly sing along to the songs. The audience may clap along to favorite up-tempo numbers, on the downbeat of "We're Off to See the Wizard" or the backbeat of "Ease on Down the Road," while bouncing children on their knees. It was a relief to me during these shows to be able to indulge in this impulse to participate once the local audience affirmed that it was allowed. Audience members show affection for the familiar songs and the young actors performing them. Applause and shouts of appreciation are offered for a soulful rendition of "Home" by an accomplished high school vocalist or, equally, for a performance of "Over the Rainbow" by an aspiring Judy

Garland who is still finding her voice. Other opportunities for participation are plentiful, as parents, siblings, classmates, and community members help with rehearsals, costumes, and sets. These participatory practices affirm the local community and its cohesion through participation in the American fairy tale and the American musical.

Knowledge of *The Wizard of Oz* and theater culture is important cultural and social capital at these performances. Adults educate kids about Oz and the rituals of theater, and, if necessary, parents explain the story before the show begins. The director at a matinee attended by many children gave a speech before the show explaining that Oz was a special story that most people know. This was accompanied by a lecture about respectful theater etiquette, using the high reputation of the American fairy tale to bolster the sanctification of the theater space. This may have had the effect of stifling participation, as I found both the performers and the audience a bit stiff. By contrast, the director of a production of *The Wiz* encouraged the audience to help create theater magic by giving the cast lots of "energy" during the show.

At one high school performance, I was seated next to a little girl of perhaps three, whose uninhibited participation seemed to give outward expression to what many surely feel on the inside while seeing *The Wizard of Oz* or any musical. She had a stuffed dog with her, who might have been Toto (and was very like the stuffed Toto being used on stage). Before the show, a woman in the row in front of us asked her, "Are you ready for *The Wizard of Oz*? Are you gonna sing with them?" When the show started the girl did, in fact, sing along, if quietly and imperfectly. She seemed to know the story and to be doing some of the choreography in her seat. She might have known the movie or had an older sibling in the show and had witnessed some rehearsals. When Glinda announced, "The Wicked old Witch at last is dead," she spread her arms wide and cheered along with the Munchkins. When the Munchkins' number ended she screamed "Oh no!" in anticipation of the Witch's appearance, to the delight of the audience (and the chagrin, I suspect, of her accompanying father). Like Dorothy in her performative journey through Oz, she claimed her right to participate in the American fairy tale.

Kids appreciate the performances of their peers, which imply that anyone can aspire to participate in Oz, the musical, and their utopian promises. During postshow meet-and-greets, younger kids from the audience, many aspiring to be in the school musical in the future, get to meet the older actors in costume while also playing out the fantasy of meeting the Cowardly Lion or Dorothy. At a semiprofessional production of *The Wizard of Oz* that featured child Munchkins, a boy of perhaps eight or nine seated in my row told me how he was excited to have met the boy, about his age, who was playing the Munchkin Mayor. The personal contact that is possible with these live musicals in the community makes their performances, at least in this aspect, accessible. The songs seem created just for young people to exercise their right to participate, whether in MGM's chirpiness, *The Wiz*'s deep feeling and groovy rhythms, or either show's powerful expressions of youthful agency.

Dreaming the Dream and Getting the Part: Playing Dorothy

Dorothy is a coveted role in musical theater. Playing Dorothy is tantamount to being in theater, playing Oz, acting American, or being a star. Recognizing the importance of the role, actor Amy Poehler has called *The Wizard of Oz* "*Hamlet* for girls."[17] It's a "dream role." Dorothy gets to sing "Over the Rainbow" in the MGM version or "Home" in *The Wiz*, and the opportunity to sing either of these songs is reason enough to desire the part. Because playing Dorothy is equivalent to becoming a performer, Oz musicals make regular girls into stars (as the role arguably did for Garland). Unknown young actors cast in major productions of *The Wizard of Oz* and *The Wiz* embody this common dream in their "extraordinary ordinariness."[18] When Danielle Wade won the 2010 BBC reality television show *Over the Rainbow*, a contest to choose an ideal Dorothy for Andrew Lloyd Webber's West End production of *The Wizard of Oz*, she was portrayed as following her dream of becoming a singing actress while finishing high school.[19] Eighteen-year-old Shanice Williams was similarly positioned as the every-girl getting her big break when she was chosen to star in the NBC live broadcast of *The Wiz* in 2015.[20] In this respect she followed in the footsteps of Stephanie Mills, who was characterized in 1975 as a Brooklyn girl with working-class parents from North Carolina (her father was a construction worker), who didn't have the advantage of voice and acting lessons like other girls auditioning for the Broadway production of *The Wiz*.[21]

Differences in embodiment and voice matter in the performance of this defining role of American girlhood and what possibilities it offers to performers and audiences. Amelia, a trans woman, told me, "Of course I loved Dorothy, because I wanted to be Dorothy. Everybody wanted to be Dorothy. I think it transcended gender. I wanted to be the kid that had something special happen." And yet, it's undoubtedly the case often that a girl of color or a girl with the "wrong" body type is passed over for a White Dorothy, for the MGM version, or a certain type for *The Wiz*. Jackie wanted to play Dorothy in *The Wiz* specifically so that she could sing "Home," but as a self-described 20-year-old in a 14-year-old's body, she was "too alto" for Dorothy and too nice for the Evillene, so she was cast as Aunt Em. Where the imagination exists for it, though, Dorothy can be played by a person of any race, gender, or ability, and because she is written as an every-girl in both the MGM version and *The Wiz*, there is also room for her to be played kids who perform her as demure, brash, innocent, jaded, sweet, or confident. Dorothy can have as many accents as American childhood can offer.

A variety of vocal gestures are available to young singers in the performance of Dorothy's familiar songs. Many girls sing "Over the Rainbow" squarely in the chest register or a chest-dominant mix, sweetly, as the young Judy Garland did. Others belt it powerfully or sing in light, sighing tones in the head register. The iconic yearning octave on "Somewhere" requires many girls to sing across the voice's natural break. In these performances, girls' voices are rupturous, as described by musicologist Diane Pecknold, upsetting normative notions of docile femininity. They combine what musicologist Jacqueline Warwick identifies as the "loud" and "sweet" qualities that imply differing or changing modes of girl singers' innocence and agency.[22] Thus, even a single performance in the role can be multivocal, suggesting a multiplicity of identities and abilities that can fit the role.

Boys can be Dorothys too, of course, and in any gender, Dorothy can be queer. Boys' performances of Dorothy may often take place in private, given the risks and limitations on such performances in public. In his childhood, singer Rufus Wainwright who publicly identifies with, and as, Judy Garland, would wear an apron and play Dorothy on good days, the Wicked Witch on bad days. Regarding this play as part of growing up gay, he remarks, "I always wanted to be Dorothy from *The Wizard of Oz*. It's kind of a giveaway."[23] Singer and Broadway actor Todrick Hall's *Straight Outta Oz* repeats Dorothy's journey with Black and queer resonances to chart the emotional journey of his life and career. In 2001, I joined the Gay Men's Chorus of Washington, DC, mainly so I could be in their all-male production of *The Wizard of Oz*. Friends kept suggesting I should audition for Dorothy, but knowing my limits, I stayed in the chorus and was one of the Lullabye League Munchkins.

The lead role was reconceived as "Donny" in Kansas who became Dorothy in drag in Oz in an acknowledgment of many gay men's identification with Dorothy and the gay myth of going to Oz as a metaphor for finding one's community. For some, being able to play Dorothy at home or on the community theater stage could be an opportunity to perform their identity, or aspects of it, that are not otherwise expressible. The fairy tale and the musical justify putting on the gingham dress and the sparkling shoes in front of an audience.

In school musicals, the role of Toto expands the possibilities for performance across the human-animal line and challenges assumptions about who can participate in the musical, whether singing or not. Toto can be played by an actual dog, a stuffed animal, or a human child in a costume, highlighting interspecies relations and agency. If Toto is a stuffed animal in Kansas, he may emerge from the house with Dorothy in Oz as a child in costume evoking the pantomime tradition of the extravaganza. Whereas the Lion has the powers of both speech and song, Toto's vocalizations may constitute barking, or spoken lines might be added for him, making him a more recognizably equal member of the group. He may even sing along in group numbers as the characters travel on the road. But even a silent Toto in effective makeup can movingly mirror Dorothy's emotions with facial expressions. A practical reason for casting a child as Toto is to give every child a role, but doing so also provokes questions about what kind of agency the character has. With the implication of human-like agency, Toto's intentions read differently than in the movie. When he chases a cat, causing Dorothy to miss her ride in the Wizard's balloon, it seems like a natural impulse for a live dog, but a child in a dog costume can show a human range of mischievousness and guilty feelings about it. It's a characteristic of school and community theater that their creative or necessary casting choices may significantly transform the musical and its participants.

Playing the Parts and Transforming the Fairy Tale

Casting and performances in school shows are inherently transformative, as child actors play roles for which they are often usefully misfit by age, height, gender, and disability, reimagining the roles that make up the American fairy tale and expanding the imagination about who participates in the American musical. Male roles are often played by girls, possibly because of less involvement by boys in the theater. On the other hand, the Wicked Witch may be played by a boy (this of course also says something about the kind of femininity embodied by the Witch). Dorothy may be taller than Aunt Em while Uncle Henry may be swallowed up by a costume that is too large for him, influencing our perception of the relative power of adults and children. For maximum participation, the various roles played by Frank Morgan in the film may be given to multiple actors, and the farmhands may not be played by the same actors as Dorothy's three friends in Oz. The picket-fence Americana of the MGM film can be replicated or revised in these performances as they enact changing implications of gender, race, class, and local values in the performance of the American fairy tale.

Young performers transform the roles by combining the gestures of Oz, musicals, and other repertoires. An actor of any race or ethnicity can step into the "unmarked" roles of the MGM version, at least where local standards or "nontraditional" casting permit. The ability to have a Black Scarecrow, an Asian American Wicked Witch, or an Arab American Cowardly Lion provides opportunities for young actors of color while reflecting the diversity of the local community. Theater scholar Donatella Galella has shown that multiracial casting may provoke different responses. Some audience members may separate the role and the actor, seeing the character as White though played by an actor of color, or they may take a "colorblind" posture, pretending that race doesn't exist, or they may see a racial transformation of the character prompting new ways of thinking about the social dynamics of the script (and "America").[24] Stereotyping and unintended consequences are a risk if multiracial casting is done without racial consciousness. What does it mean for a Wicked Witch to be Black, given the history of the Other in Oz and musicals? It can be done, but with awareness and acknowledgment of how it resonates contextually. Conversely, what is the effect of a White Witch terrorizing a Black Dorothy?[25] A Black girl can play Dorothy as easily in the MGM musical as in *The Wiz*, transforming the role productively, but the racial and cultural specificity of *The Wiz* makes the casting of White actors problematic, resulting in erasure or appropriation. Multiracial casting in *The Wiz* introduces still more complexity. The possibility of continually recasting the musicals in school and community performances has the general effect of opening up participation and representation, but the outcomes of casting matter in their particularity and contexts.

The Munchkins are a highlight of a school production, and their playfulness reminds us that Oz belongs in the first and most essential instance to kids and their make-believe practices. While in "adult" productions of

The Wizard of Oz, they may be played by kids, in a high school or middle school show, they are often played by students from younger grades. In either case, the beloved spectacle of kids playing grownups in the theater elides with the idea of playing dress-up at home by trying on parents' shoes and clothing. Costumes may be elaborate or minimal as long as they are adorable. Colorful stockings and painted-on or paper moustaches will do nicely. A top hat is suitable for the Munchkin Mayor, a white lab coat for the Coroner. The Lollipop Guild kids are ideally even smaller and cuter than the other Munchkins. The infantilizing choreography and costumes designed for the little people who played Munchkins in the MGM film are equally suitable for sentimentalizing the kids who play them on stage. The songs and dances script participation in an onstage community, complete with the Mayor, the Coroner, soldiers, and other essential people in your hometown. At the same time, singing "Ding! Dong! The Witch Is Dead" is an expression of impertinence, and the dress-up play in the scene may be a way of parodying adults and their occupations.

We know that divas are the stars of the musical theater and its American fairy tale, and any person cast as one, in the theater or in informal play, gets to play the role of she who runs the show, whether as Glinda giving Dorothy her instructions and presiding over the people of Oz or as the Wicked Witch of the West who provides the drama by continually threatening to bring everything down. Glinda has inspired the identification of many an aspiring good witch. She gets to help Dorothy, be beautiful, and be a community caretaker, all while singing sweetly and waving her wand gracefully. She is a paragon of femininity. Amelia, relating her childhood as a transgender girl, remembered,

> When I was—I'm guessing—may have been nine—and one of our neighbors was a wonderful Polish seamstress who worked in [the city, which] seemed a world away, [and made] fancy girls' dresses. I wanted to be Glinda for Halloween. I guess they just had a lot of sparkly tulle at the time. I had a wand, and it was the first time I ever dressed as a girl.

To her delight, the seamstress and her mother said, "'Look how darling! What a wonderful girl!' . . . I was a witch. But I was a good one. With Glitter. Probably my first time in glitter. Wasn't my last." Given Amelia's aforementioned attempts to sing songs from the movie, it's easy to imagine her lightly tripping in her Glinda costume, singing fragments of the Munchkinland sequence. The gestures of the musical that were integral to her Oz play could well have entered into this act of dress-up, which for her as a transgender girl was not just pretending to be somebody she wasn't but rather coming closer to her truth.

The Wicked Witch is an equally desirable role, even though it's often a nonsinging one, that allows a young performer to act out power through character's vocal and bodily excess. Hannah was "desperate to be Dorothy" in middle school. Her performance of "Over the Rainbow" was the best in auditions, but the director believed she was the only person who could convincingly play the Wicked Witch. Hannah was disappointed at first because she wouldn't get to sing, but instead she found performative power in practicing Margaret Hamilton's voice and cackle, making it her job to scare little kids in the audience. She had always been "a good girl," so it was a transformative experience for her to be wicked. One Witch I saw screamed and rolled her eyes with total abandon. In another school production, the Witch was played in the cross-dressing pantomime tradition that goes back to the extravaganza by a tall boy with growling nasality, and camp enunciation of his lines and gestures.[26] Playing the Wicked Witch, then, allows kids to perform other aspects of themselves.

The Wicked Witch tacitly, and sometimes explicitly, presents herself as a person who has power as a performer. In the RSC stage version of the MGM *Wizard*, when Dorothy demands of the Witch, "How can anyone be so nasty, mean, and cruel?" the Witch responds with a theater joke, "Lots and lots of practice!"[27] As written, the Witch's performative powers are already formidable, but in the school or community musical, where talent is exploited wherever it can be found, she may have the chance to expand her range. Sometimes, she is given a solo in "The Jitterbug," a song cut from the MGM film but reinstated in the stage version, in which she sends a bug to make Dorothy and her friends dance into a mania. And of course *Wicked* gives her a whole bunch of songs, and although that show is not legally available for community performances (which occasionally happen anyway), many fans sing Elphaba's songs in their voice lessons, in auditions, and at home or on social media. Not only have Elphaba's songs likely been used by aspiring Witches (and Dorothys) in auditions for *The Wizard of Oz* or *The Wiz*, but I'll bet my ruby slippers that, in a school show somewhere, materials from *Wicked* have been interpolated into those shows to give the Wicked Witch something to sing. This problem is already solved, of course, in *The Wiz*, where a young person cast in the role of Evillene has a special opportunity to bring the house down with "No Bad News."

Accidents are a hazard in the school musical as they are on any stage. Here, the playful participation and collaboration between actors and audience assists with the recovery. In one school show I saw, the Wicked Witch's entrance in Munchkinland was delayed. Younger students playing munchkins lay scattered on the stage in awkward silence. At length, Dorothy stammered something about the Witch, and Glinda responded, "I thought she was here. Do any of you Munchkins know where she could be?" in the tone of a teacher addressing her students. The Munchkins looked uncertain. One or two shrugged. The audience laughed. Finally, the Witch appeared, and the performance continued. The familiarity of the script allowed a little bit of playful improvisation that could be treated as a wink between the actors and the audience rather than a dramatic failure. Everyone knew the Witch was coming, and it was only a matter of playing along till she arrived. Audiences' and performer's playful relationship to the Oz repertoire eases the recovery from mistakes, which even divas can make.

Actors playing Dorothy and her friends as they travel on the yellow brick road draw on performance models available to them, creating novel performances of the stock characters of the American fairy tale. Through the gestures of the musical, they create personal and locally specific transformations of the American fairy tale. Community performances may be much more daring than professional ones in their willingness to use creative casting (depending of course on the community and certain gatekeepers like the director), which further expands the range of participation. A Scarecrow may model their performance on the loose movement and transatlantic accent of Ray Bolger or, like a Black girl I saw in one show, incorporate aspects of Michael Jackson's performance in *The Wiz* into "If a Only Had Brain," bringing *The Wiz*'s commentary on *The Wizard of Oz* right into a performance of the MGM musical. A Dorothy in a wheelchair may be accompanied by her real-life service dog playing Toto, changing the nature of both roles.[28] The coordination of the dance down the yellow brick road, likely with one of the other characters pushing the wheelchair, offers an image of different bodies working together with a common purpose. In such a scenario, the actor's or character's visible disability may be incidental to the narrative or may be sentimentalized as "inspiring" by members of the audience. The complexities of such performances offer the possibilities of both expanded participation and reinscription of dominant attitudes. Diverse casting can never erase legacies of racial exclusion and colonialism built into the Oz and musical theater repertoires. Yet, for the moment of performance, there's a glimmer of hope that the American fairy tale can be inclusive, with performers staking a new claim on the best Oz and musicals have to offer.

The relative safety and cover of theatrical performance makes some daring explorations of identity possible. In Lahr's tradition, kids play the Lion with a range of available gestures. When the Lion is played by a girl, the already protean character is further transformed through vocal drag. With virtuosity, girls mix Lahr's New York accent with more contemporary urban youth affects, so that accents associated with geographical and class differences may alternate with dramatic, Shakespearean and English accents, in the tradition of lampooning high society. A Cowardly Lion played by a girl may alternate belting and *bel canto* with the ease of *Wicked*'s Glinda. One girl I saw imitated Lahr's operatic baritone and then flipped ostentatiously into her head voice for the "the sparrow would take wing," exploiting the voice's break and subverting normatively gendered vocal practices. Similarly, the Wiz is a protean role that can be played in any number of ways, in part because of the queerness of De Shields's characterization. Perhaps following the precedent of Queen Latifah's performance of the character in *The Wiz Live!*, one school production I saw cast a girl in that already queer and gender-fluid role.

The Lion's virtuoso comedy and his queer vulnerability can be both liberating and precarious for the young performer, who must demonstrate courage in playing the role before an audience of peers and adults from the community. In a middle-school production of *The Wiz* with mostly Black leads in a multiracial cast, a boy presenting as White played the Lion in fearlessly queer fashion, tossing his mane, and swinging his tail through his musical numbers. The audience loved it. As people took out their camera phones to capture the performance, I felt some admixture of the old feeling of queerness played for laughs and a general feeling of support for gender-variant expression—at least in this likely socially liberal community in the suburbs of a large city. While the Lion inspires many queer people to accept themselves, others feel shame and discomfort or see him as a stereotype—indeed it is one that dates back at least to the minstrel show.[29] For theater kids, likely already marginalized in the school community and its standards of masculinity, having to say lines like "It's sad believe me missy, when you're born to be a sissy," and "I got a permanent just for the occasion" in front of the school and community could be risky. The risks inherent in boys playing the Lion might help to account for what seems to be the common practice of casting girls in the role.

These unapologetically playful and theatrical performances are served well by the reflexively theatrical scripts, which display a consciously American sense of performance. In the RSC *Wizard of Oz*, when Dorothy and her friends ask the Guardian of the Gate how he knows there's a Wizard if no one has ever seen him, he stammers, "Because, because, because, because, because" in reference to the lyrics of "We're Off to See the Wizard," evoking the tendency of people to quote the movie in everyday life. Reflexive bits like this help to set up the encounter with the humbug Wizard and his revealed performances.

It's only fair to acknowledge some of the limitations of the school musical and the failures of theater that necessitate repeat performances and their renewed possibilities. The sometimes makeshift aesthetics and accident-proneness of the school musical are fodder for gentle poking fun in Jeff Kenney's *Diary of a Wimpy Kid*, which also reminds us that not everybody wants to be in the school musical or finds in the musical a mode of expression that suits them. Indeed, musicals make many people downright uncomfortable, and there are of course some gender dynamics involved here, too. Greg Heffley, a middle-schooler, reluctantly auditions for his school's production of *The Wizard of Oz*. He narrates, "A lot of kids came wearing costumes for the parts they were trying out for. I've never seen the movie, so for me it was like walking into a freak show" (the ghost of Barnum still haunts Oz). He considers auditioning for the Witch, so he can be mean to Patty Ferrell, the girl playing Dorothy, who he hates, but he worries he'll get the good Witch instead. He finally signs up to be a tree because it's a nonsinging role and he can throw apples at Patty. In community theater fashion, however, the drama teacher writes a song for the trees. He tries to sing quietly during the audition but is singled out for his "lovely soprano." Ultimately, his attempts to avoid embarrassment wreck the show.[30] However, as we know, the failure of utopia assures us that another performance will be mounted.

As utopian performatives, school and community shows come with the promise of repetition and return. One production I saw ended with the company singing "Over the Rainbow" as a curtain call, as if fulfilling the desire for a final song in a show that doesn't formally have one. I suspect that many performances end in such a group rendition of the ultimate "I want" song. The last words of the song, the lyrical question "Why oh why can't I?," offer the tantalizing suggestion that we might return to Oz soon, and of course we do. After another school show, I overheard a younger boy who played the Munchkin Mayor declare that it had been the second-best day of his life.

When asked what the best day was, he said, "yesterday," referring to opening night. This had not been his first performance and wouldn't be the last, as Oz and its utopian dream can be counted on to return like a song.

The Backyard and Beyond

The return to Oz in utopian performance plays out on another scale in community events and immersive environments. Sing-alongs, festivals, and theme parks expand on the practices of home and backyard play in ways similar to community theater. Situated in specific places, they weave utopian performatives out of the materiality of the local and the imaginary of elsewhere, forging connections among home, town, community, nation, and Oz. Their failures of permanence justify their repetition as annual events. As the unfinished business of "America," their repetitions are complicated by the acknowledgment, or failure of acknowledgment, of the previous inhabitants of their places. Participants navigate these events through knowledge of Oz and musicals, whether they sing along or find other ways to participate, playing along earnestly, ironically, or campily.

Sing-along screenings of the MGM film exploit its quotability and singability in communal performance.[31] There has been an official touring version, and there are community sponsored events, like a fundraiser I attended for an HIV/AIDS organization in Austin, Texas, with friends from the Oz Club. Typically, audience members are given participation packets that include bubbles to blow or wands to wave when Glinda appears or kazoos to play along with famous motifs in the score, such as the Miss Gulch/Wicked Witch theme. These sing-alongs fully allow and encourage audiences to participate in the gestures of musical theater from their seats. Audiences experience the fun of singing along with the characters, often attending in costume (prizes are given for these) in the full embodiment of the American fairy tale as they break into song.

Sing-along events are possible because of common experiences of Oz but are also influenced by the specific communities and contexts in which they take place. The convergence of children's and queer culture is often acknowledged at these events, which may be attended by a mix of families and the LGBTQ community.[32] I recall attending an official touring sing-along that was hosted by a Wizard-like emcee who made a sly joke about "Friends of Dorothy." *Wiz* sing-alongs work along similar lines but are often organized for events or benefits explicitly connected with the Black community, where it is beloved. *Wicked* singalongs likely already happen informally, and official screenings are surely on the horizon, pending production of the films. Participation in sing-alongs is nominally inclusive, but depends on where the event is held, whether the venue is accessible, and who would even know about it depending on the neighborhood—just as Broadway musicals are differently accessible to different audiences. These experiences fulfill a desire to experience community while figuratively going to Oz.

The Land of Oz, North Carolina

More elaborate destinations and musical environments provide further opportunities to have Oz at "home" in this world. In the summer of 2011, I drove from Philadelphia to Beech Mountain, North Carolina, to attend the annual Oz Convention, which was being held at what remains of the Land of Oz Park. This Oz-themed attraction is the only true, successful Oz theme park there has ever been, and when it was fully operational in the 1970s, it was structured like a walk-through musical allowing visitors to participate in familiar performances of the American fairy tale. It's now open at certain times of the year and on special occasions. During our visit, we were led down the park's yellow brick road and treated to a scaled-down simulation of the original experience. Originally, visitors were carried to a mountaintop, where the park is located, in a ski-lift designed to look like the Wizard's hot air balloon. On arrival, they entered Dorothy's Kansas farmhouse and were led to the basement, where a tornado was simulated with projections. They emerged in the Land of Oz. Led by Dorothy, guests then journeyed down the road past stations where the Scarecrow, the Tin Man, the Cowardly Lion, and the Witch each performed to a prerecorded track with songs by Alec Wilder and Loonis McGlohon (Figure 5.1).

At the end of the road, visitors arrived in the Emerald City, which was literally an outdoor theater, the place where dreams come true. Here, the characters appeared together for the first time in the *Magic Moment* stage show, which included the song, "Did You Come to See the Wizard?" This song has the same 6/8 meter and short-long rhythmic setting as "We're Off to See the Wizard" (Figure 5.2; companion website 5.2), evoking the memory of the movie without violating copyright by quoting it directly. At the end of the show, Dorothy lip-synced to "Over the Rainbow," the only song that was

Figure 5.1. Promotional photo from the Land of Oz Park in Beech Mountain, North Carolina, 1970s. Land of Oz, NC.

Did you come to see the Wiz-ard?___ Did you come to see the Wiz-ard?

Figure 5.2. Music of "Did You Come to See the Wizard?" from the Land of Oz Park, Beech Mountain, North Carolina. Words and music by Loonis McGlohon and Alec Wilder.

licensed from MGM, and disappeared in a puff of smoke. Her double was then seen ascending in a balloon on her way home. The Wizard was not revealed as a humbug, and the shoes were not given magical power. The magic seemed to reside in the song alone, which, here in the place of dreams, was the vehicle for going home rather than the dream of Oz. In a place that brings Oz into the "real" world, the classic "I want" song ambiguously refers to both Oz and home.

The park was a bit of a family-run operation with something of a do-it-yourself style recalling home-based Oz play and the everyday magic of Oz musicals. The yellow brick road and other structures were simply built into the natural environment of the mountain, transforming it into Oz. A particularly gnarled tree with a face carved in it suggested the apple trees from the MGM film. The actors' lip-syncing resembled kids' scripted play with recordings of the MGM film or *The Wiz*. For special events, local children would appear in dress-up as Munchkins. Toto was a hand puppet carried by Dorothy. Describing the original experience, Oz scholar Dina Massachi notes that "Guests could imagine themselves as any character they wished to become, travel the magical land as themselves, or play several parts, limited only by their imagination."[33] Like a conventional musical, the park experience could be repeated and replayed after it was over. A vinyl record of music from the park could be purchased for listening or playing and singing along back at home.

This musical version of Oz was a nostalgic one in its time, as it is for visitors in the present—nostalgic for Oz, theater, Hollywood, childhood, and Americana. The first thing visitors encountered when entering the park was a Fountain of Youth. Although the park was technically based on the public domain book, it evoked the beloved MGM film where possible. One of the first sights visitors saw at the top of the mountain was a memorial sculpture of Judy Garland (who had just died when the park opened) holding Toto and inscribed with her "heart's desire" speech from the end of the film. The actress playing Dorothy wore red shoes, but they were not referred to as ruby slippers. Postcards and other promotional materials showed the characters in poses suggestive of scenes from the book or movie that were not necessarily portrayed in the park itself, using consumers' memory of the Oz repertoire to create a familiar impression of the experience. Broadway, Hollywood, and American entertainment were reflexively represented in this performance of the American fairy tale. For showbiz credibility, Ray Bolger and Debbie Reynolds attended the opening ceremony. Reynolds, a major collector of costumes and props from the MGM film, donated items to the park's small museum. While "returning to childhood," visitors could participate in the film and stage performances they'd grown up with.

After closing in 1980, the park fell into disrepair but remained a loved fixture of the local community. Special events began to be held in the park in the 1990s. When it opened for the Fourth of July in 1991, students in costume from a high school production of *The Wizard of Oz* greeted visitors. In recent years, the park has found new life as a pilgrimage site, reopening for limited times each year, where something lost can be regained through renewed performance. During Autumn in Oz, guests are led down the yellow brick road by actors in costume, now resembling the movie versions of the characters and singing "We're Off to See the Wizard" and other songs from the MGM film along the way. Weekends in June are "Journey with Dorothy," in which visitors are selected to play various characters and sing their songs as a professional Dorothy leads the tour.[34]

The park and its environments still script participation through the gestures of muscial theater. The simple act of walking down the yellow brick road through the Land of Oz might well compel one to break into song and dance. Inclusive participation is compromised, however, by the original design and location of the park in an isolated mountainous environment with many steps and uneven walkways. Because the park is only partially restored, it has something of a dystopian appearance, adding to its mystique of loss and rebirth as a living museum of the American fairy tale and its past, reanimated by the conventions of the American musical.

Oz-Stravaganza!, New York

The numerous annual community Oz festivals are often strongly local in their identities, even while drawing Oz fans from far away, making of their localities a place where home and Oz converge. Beginning in 1982, there was a major festival in Chesterton, Indiana, and several other festivals, principally in the Midwest, carry on the tradition, including the Midwest Oz Fest, Wizard of Oz Days, and Oztoberfest in Wamego Kansas, which is also home to the Oz Museum. The Midwestern settings of many of these festivals reflects the historical popularity of Oz in this region of the country.

Chittenango, New York, the birthplace of L. Frank Baum, has an annual Oz festival, in its current incarnation called Oz-Stravaganza! A small-town-America event, it also attracts Oz enthusiasts and celebrities, such as Gregory Maguire, André De Shields, and actors who played Munchkins in the MGM film. I attended in 2014, when the Oz Club held its annual convention in conjunction with the festival. Much as the living room or the backyard becomes the theater for Oz play at home, the whole town gets into performance for Oz-Stravaganza! Performance has been integral to participation in the festival since its origin in 1978, when kids dressed up and paraded around the public library.[35] An "Emerald City Idol" singing contest is held several weeks before the festival as a fundraiser. Kids put on an Oz play in a church, and the outdoor stage performances feature singers and musicians, including some who write original Oz songs.

Oz-Stravaganza! is a bit like having your hometown turn into an Oz musical. Genesee Street, which runs through the center of Chittenango figuratively becomes the yellow brick road when people sing and dance on it. A parade is the centerpiece of the Oz-Stravaganza! festivities, with community groups, local businesses, and people of all ages progressing along the route. The year I attended, a dance academy was doing the skip dance to "We're Off to See the Wizard," and a school marching band played "Ease on Down the Road" as they eased on down Genesee Street. First prize went to a trailer load of kindergarteners in funnel hats singing "If I Only Had a Heart." It seemed to me that anyone in costume was allowed to join the parade. The Munchkin actors were almost always present at Oz-Stravaganza! and other festivals until recently—Jerry Maren, the Lollipop kid, was the last to pass away in 2018. They regaled fans with stories about being in *The Wizard of Oz* and their experiences as little people working in the entertainment industry. They always obliged requests to break into their songs and dances from the movie, a behavior that was fully expected of them, as they appeared in recreations of their original costumes.

Dressing in costume, as usual, prompts singing and dancing. There are children and adults dressed as Scarecrows, Tin Men, and Lions, but most of all there are Dorothys. Little girls in Dorothy dresses and ruby slippers are everywhere, and if you didn't bring your own costume, vendors sell the dresses and ruby slippers. In a costume contest I observed at the Midwest OzFest in Tinley Park, Illinois, a professional Dorothy instructed the contestants to click their heels, this performance being integral to the role.

In Chittenango, there's always Oz, not just at festival time but throughout the year. The sidewalk along the main street is designed as a yellow brick road. It runs by the All Things Oz Museum, where one can view costumes and props from the MGM film and the stage version of *The Wiz*. Local businesses have Oz-inspired names like Dorothy's Pet Grooming, and the public library is decorated to resemble the Land of Oz. The continual presence of Oz in Chittenango gestures toward the ubiquity of Oz in America, with all its complications.

These environments stage Oz in the community, where the memory, or forgetting, of local history conceals and reveals contestations over place and nation. Most of the people at most of these events are White, but all land in America is Native land. An Aberdeen, South Dakota, festival was controversial because of Baum's genocide editorials.[36] In an interesting twist, the local Oneida Indian Nation is a sponsor of Chittenango's Oz-Stravaganza! and has opened an Oz-themed casino in the area to criticism from other Native Americans, especially Lakota Sioux.[37] These contestations are a reminder that one person's utopia may be another's loss of home.

Home Again/Oz Again

Home, Oz, and utopia are where we find them. My mind keeps returning to Amelia's story. At the end of our interview, I asked her if she had any final thing she wanted to say about Oz. Earlier in our conversation, she had talked about being at the Allegro, a legendary queer bar, where she remembered singing along with other patrons while *The Wizard of Oz* was on the TV. Her parting reflection sums up much of what there is to say about Oz and the musical.

> I was the little geeky bookish kid growing up in a White, blue collar, concrete ghetto version of Kansas. Instead of everything sepia and dusty, everything was concrete and dusty. . . . Things going from dreary to fabulous rang my bell. . . . Something . . . baffled me forever, when the film was over, the lights came on, and the magic was gone, and I had to go back to the concrete streets. My parents loved me and all that was fine. But I was baffled by why Dorothy would want to leave. I would much rather stay. I know the Witch died and I was kind of sad because there was a part of me that liked her. But I would want to be with big flowers and little babies sleeping in eggs, and Glinda in a bubble, and can't imagine ever wanting to leave Oz, but Dorothy was really happy about it, you know, with the little morality play at the end, "There's no place like home." And I left the theater thinking, "I don't know, I sort of think there's no place like Oz!" 'Cause there was more than one place like that home, but there was no place like Oz. Until I found my way to the Allegro, and then there was Oz again.

I identify with Amelia's story, different as it is in origin from my own in rural America. There weren't a lot of opportunities to be in musicals in the place where I came from. But singing was always an important form of expression for me. I was often too shy to talk, but I would sing. I sang at home, at school, in church, and at times and in places where you weren't supposed to.

I still do. It was my difference, and it was a fairly solitary one for a while. But then there was the Oz Club. And then there was college on a small campus where I found a community of musically and theatrically inclined people. I honestly remember another student saying, "I never met so many people who live like they're in a musical till I came here!" That was my next arrival in a place where I could perform as a more colorful and fully musical version of myself in rehearsal with new friends. Then I went to the big cities of the East Coast, where I learned a lot more about humbug and witchcraft and found home with the person who changes me for good. There's no end to this story. Like musicals and utopia, I'm still becoming.

Recently, the Oz Club's national convention returned to Chicago, where the World's Fair, with its White City and Midway Plaisance, representing the best and worst of "America," inspired a humbug to write a children's book and stage a hometown musical. It was also, you might recall, the location of many of the conventions I attended as a young person, a misfit from the farm making his big journey to the city of Oz. A highlight of this recent convention was an evening concert of Oz music. It began with a small group, myself included, singing "Did You Come to See the Wizard?" from the Land of Oz Park. It proceeded with performances of songs from the extravaganza, the MGM film, *The Wiz*, and *Wicked*. I had declined to be featured on the program as a performer this time, but I found myself persuaded nonetheless, near the end of the night, to sit down at the piano and accompany a friend on her songs. With some clumsy sight-reading on my part, we made our way through the extravaganza's "Poppy Song" and a couple of other numbers, ending with "Over the Rainbow," which became a group sing-along. Incomplete, imperfect, and becoming on the horizon, there's always Oz again.

Epilogue

What Have You Learned, Dorothy?

I hope to have offered here a case study of the American fairy tale and the American musical in which each serves as a partial guide to the other. I've left many paths unexplored, but I'm encouraged by the assurance that others will pursue paths I have missed. It is the American way to repeat these performances with differences.

A lot has happened since I started this book. We've had a leader who showed us the line between humbug and outright fraudulence. We've persevered through ongoing dangers and challenges that include a global pandemic, the international rise of authoritarianism, and environmental crises.

Oz remains a point of reference (one among many, to be sure) for American musicals and American life. When theaters began reopening after closing for the first phase of the COVID-19 pandemic, *Wicked* was the first touring production to resume performances. The subsequent resumption of Broadway performances of *Wicked*, along with those of *The Lion King* and *Hamilton*, was highly anticipated. *Wicked* was emblematic among the Broadway reopenings that indexed the endurance of American musical theater. Kristin Chenoweth made a special appearance before the show. Standing on stage in the Gershwin Theater she declared, "there's no place like home," to enthusiastic applause from theatergoers. When Glinda appeared in her opening number, with Ginna Claire Mason in the role, her famous diva's first line stopped the show: "It's good to see me isn't it?" At the long-delayed 74th Tony Awards a few days later, Audra McDonald noted that the ceremony was taking place in the Winter Garden theater, where *The Wiz* had won its multiple Tonys in 1975. That ceremony had offered the hope, she remarked, of better representation on Broadway, a hope that remains part of the unfinished show business of the American musical. In the same broadcast, Idina Menzel and Kristin Chenoweth sang "For Good" as part of a series of classic Broadway duets, further securing the importance of Oz in the

Oz and the Musical. Ryan Bunch, Oxford University Press. © Oxford University Press 2023.
DOI: 10.1093/oso/9780190843137.003.0007

Figure E.1. *The Wizard of Oz* parody of *Hamilton* album cover, created and shared by Dave Demoreski on the Facebook group "Wizard of Oz: The everything OZ Club," June 27, 2019, https://www.facebook.com/groups/163530767040319.

repertoire during an important event marking the return of Broadway "after" the pandemic.

Even *Hamilton*, the next iconic musical of the new century, which is also (even more explicitly) about politics, humbug, and the American dreams of young people and immigrants, can't escape the shadow of Oz as measure of its place in the America art form. A meme has circulated on social media consisting of the *Hamilton* logo, but with the silhouette of Alexander Hamilton replaced by that of *Margaret* Hamilton as the Wicked Witch of the West (Figure E.1). Versions of this image appear on merchandise, including mugs and a t-shirt on which the tagline, "*Hamilton*: An American Musical" became "Hamilton: An American Icon." This tribute to a classic diva can be read in multiple ways. It is perhaps a commentary on the centrality of women in musicals, reclaiming that centrality from a musical whose female characters arguably have marginal and constrained roles.[1] It might be nostalgic for the "good old days," when musicals, in some aspect, were not what they are today. Or it could be a commentary on the persona of Lin-Manuel Miranda, the *auteur* showman whose self-confidence enables his personal conflation with the hero of his own musical. Perhaps these readings reflect my personally ambivalent feelings about the musical that has displaced *Wicked* as all the rage on Broadway. Both on and off stage, *Hamilton* and Oz offer us images of American performers, Wizards, divas, and regular folks like ourselves who engage with Broadway shows, their creators, and their stars through social media.

There's always Oz again, but for whom and to what end? Implicit in my project is how the musical and the American fairy tale might guide us in the everyday practice of "America." As we go about acting as wizards, divas, Dorothys, and friends of Dorothy, our utopian performatives have consequences. The Wizard says, "I'm a very good man. I'm just a very bad Wizard." What are we? How do we know the difference between a harmless humbug and an outright con-artist? Who are we dancing with? Humbugs don't work alone. We own their successes and failures, their intentions and "accidents" when we cooperate with these figures or play these roles ourselves.

Our public figures put on a show, and we know it, and they know we know it. That's why there have always been political cartoons on the theme of *The Wizard of Oz*, comparing US presidents and other powerful people to the Wizard behind the curtain for their humbuggery or to Dorothy's friends for their brainlessness, heartlessness, and lack of courage.[2] This practice goes all the way back to a series of cartoons that appeared in *Harper's Weekly* in 1906, portraying William Randolph Hearst as Fred Stone's Scarecrow and labeling him the "Wizard of Ooze" (Figure E.2). In addition to predictable comparisons to the Wizard, a number of cartoons and editorials compared Donald Trump to Barnum, an entertainer rising to power by playing to common prejudices. Some commentators attempted to make a distinction between Barnumian humbug and a more nefarious form of fraudulence practiced by Trump, but the availability of the comparison suggests that humbugs and conmen might not always be distinguishable.[3] Both sides of the curtain are equally suspect in a world where a political figure's most avid followers maintain their devotion in acknowledgment of his open fraudulence, embracing the thing good humbug was supposed to protect us from. A conman is not an affront to our national innocence but an exposing of what we know, or refuse to. The contradictions of nostalgia and futurity—mistaking an imagined past

THE WIZARD OF OOZE

Figure E.2. William Randolph Hearst depicted as "The Wizard of Ooze" in one of a series of editorial cartoons in *Harper's Weekly* inspired by the musical extravaganza *The Wizard of Oz* (1902), 1906. Cal Poly, Kennedy Online Public Library, Hearst Caricatures Collection, https://digital.lib.calpoly.edu/rekl-28424.

for a better future—persist equally in calls to "Make America Great Again" and complaints that "this is not who we are," when it always has been. Are the scripts we have for acting American good enough? Oz and musicals in many ways support the status quo. Heteronormative marriage plots remain the backbone of musicals, and while Dorothy deposes the Wizard, he returns a beloved figure. Can we celebrate a nation of immigrants while acknowledging the dispossession of Native Americans? Can literary and theatrical forms forged in the best and worst of our history serve as the scripts, or is the repetition of the forms still so much repetition? Can a better musical or a better fairy tale make a better "America?" Playing Dorothy—doing good, exposing Wizards, and fighting wickedness—remains important, but so does Glinda's query, "Are you a good witch or a bad witch?" This is a question not of what we are but how we act. Are we liberators? Traitors? Colonizers? Our actions cannot be accidents, and our outcomes cannot simply be, as *Wicked*'s Wizard suggests, "which label is able to persist." What kinds of friendships and communities are we (per)forming? What exclusions?

Musicals use singing and dancing to argue that feelings matter in American life. The details of a fairy tale or a musical may never be perfect, and so we should always keep asking questions of them. When we do, musicals can be, I hope, sites for the performances of alternatives. Neither the musical nor the American fairy tale would be possible without those who have managed to turn them to their purposes and keep expanding their reach. As Jill Dolan concludes, "the pleasure of a utopian performative, even if it doesn't change the world, certainly changes the people who feel it."[4] We keep singing, dancing, marching, and acting up at home, in the street, and in the theater to change the world, and to change ourselves. Successes and failures, including those of Oz and musicals, ensure that we still need utopia and its feelings.

Notes

Introduction

1. With reservation, I use "America" and "American" to denote a US national imaginary, despite the inaccuracy and bias of the term in the context of the Americas. Like Oz, "America" is an imaginary place believed in by many people within and beyond the borders of the Unites States.
2. This shirt was designed by actor and t-shirt magnate Stanley DeSantis, whose movie-inspired designs frequently used themes from *The Wizard of Oz*. See David Kronke, "He'll Act for Free as Long as His Shirts Are on Your Back," *Los Angeles Times*, June 7, 1994, https://www.latimes.com/archives/la-xpm-1994-06-07-ca-1408-story.html, accessed September 12, 2020.
3. See, for examples, Randall E. Auxier and Phillip S. Seng, eds., *"The Wizard of Oz" and Philosophy: Wicked Wisdom of the West* (Chicago: Open Court, 20018); Robert Gilmore, *The Wizard of Quarks: A Fantasy of Particle Physics* (New York: Copernicus Books, 2001); Henry M. Littlefield, *"The Wizard of Oz*: Parable on Populism," *American Quarterly* 16, no. 1 (1964): 47–58; Christopher Vogler, *The Writer's Journey: Mythic Structure for Writers* (Studio City, CA: M. Wiese Productions, 1998).
4. On the ritual dynamics of theater, see Jill Dolan, *Utopia in Performance: Finding Hope at the Theater* (Ann Arbor: University of Michigan Press, 2005), 11, 14. On departure and return in children's literature, including Oz, see Perry Nodelman, *The Hidden Adult: Defining Children's Literature* (Baltimore: Johns Hopkins University Press, 2008), 59–68, 222–227; Beverly Lyon Clark, *Kiddie Lit: The Cultural Construction of Children's Literature in America* (Baltimore: Johns Hopkins University Press, 2003), 142–144.
5. On Oz as American and utopian, see Edward Wagenknecht, *Utopia Americana* (1929; reprint, Seattle: University of Washington Book Store, 1970), 17; Brian Attebery, *The Fantasy Tradition in American Literature: From Irving to LeGuin* (Bloomington: Indiana University Press, 1980); Paul Nathanson, *Over the Rainbow: "The Wizard of Oz" as a Secular Myth of America* (Albany: State University on New York Press, 1991); Neil Earl, *"The Wonderful Wizard of Oz" in American Popular Culture: Uneasy in Eden* (Lewiston, Queenston, and Lampeter: Edwin Mellen Press, 1993); Jack Zipes, *Fairy Tale as Myth/Myth as Fairy Tale* (Lexington: University Press of Kentucky, 1994), 119–138; Suzanne Rahn, *"The Wizard of Oz": Shaping an Imaginary World* (New York: Twayne Publishers, 1998), 8–9; Michael Patrick Hearn, ed., *The Annotated "Wizard of Oz": Centennial Edition* (New York: Norton, 2000), xii; Mark Evan Swartz, *Oz before the Rainbow: L. Frank Baum's "The Wonderful Wizard of Oz" on Stage and Screen to 1939* (Baltimore: Johns Hopkins University Press,

2000), 10; Alissa Burger, *"The Wizard of Oz" as American Myth: A Critical Study of Six Versions of the Story, 1900–2007* (Jefferson, NC: McFarland, 2012), 30–54; William R. Leach, *Land of Desire: Merchants, Power, and the Rise of a New American Culture* (New York: Knopf Doubleday, 2011). On the American musical, see Rick Altman, *The American Film Musical* (Bloomington: Indiana University Press, 1987); Jane Feuer, *The Hollywood Musical*, 2nd ed. (Bloomington: Indiana University Press, 1993); John Bush Jones, *Our Musicals, Ourselves: A Social History of the American Musical Theatre* (Waltham, MA: Brandeis University Press, 2003); Michael Kantor and Laurence Maslan, *Broadway: The American Musical* (New York: Bulfinch Press, 2004), x; Raymond Knapp, *The American Musical and the Formation of National Identity* (Princeton, NJ: Princeton University Press, 2005), 3; Thomas Hischak, *The Oxford Companion to the American Musical: Theatre Film and Television* (New York: Oxford University Press, 2008), xi–xiii; Stacy Wolf, *Changed for Good: A Feminist History of the Broadway Musical* (New York: Oxford University Press, 2011), 13. On the American creed of self-inventive performance in the musical, see Andrea Most, *Making Americans: Jews and the Broadway Musical* (Cambridge, MA: Harvard University Press, 2004), 2.

6. Gvendo2005, reply to beautywickedlover, "Lloyd Webber's *Wizard of Oz* coming to Broadway? What do you all think?" Broadway Message Board, *Broadway World*, post #3 (June 25, 2011, 11:41 AM) and post #18 (June 25, 2011, 3:43 PM), https://www. broadwayworld.com/board/readmessage.php?thread=1033837, accessed December 25, 2019.

7. Wagenknecht, *Utopia Americana*, 17, 30–37.

8. Knapp, *The American Musical and the Formation of National Identity*, 9.

9. Richard Dyer, "Entertainment and Utopia," in *Only Entertainment* (New York: Routledge, 2005), 19–35.

10. Dolan, *Utopia in Performance*, 5. My thinking is also influenced by queer utopianism, as articulated by José Esteban Muñoz in *Cruising Utopia: The Then and There of Queer Futurity* (New York: New York University Press, 2009).

11. On repertoires of performance, see Diana Taylor, *The Archive and the Repertoire: Performing Cultural Memory in the Americas* (Durham, NC: Duke University Press, 2003). Applying these ideas to Oz, see Burger, *"The Wizard of Oz" as American Myth*; and Robin Bernstein, *Racial Innocence: Performing American Childhood from Slavery to Civil Rights* (New York: New York University Press, 2011), 159–193.

12. For insightful discussions of utopia and belonging in American musicals, see Jake Johnson, *Mormons, Musical Theater, and Belonging in America* (Urbana: University of Illinois Press) and Jake Johnson, *Lying in the Middle: Musical Theater and Belief at the Heart of America* (Urbana: University of Illinois Press, 2021).

13. In the fourth Oz book, we learn that the Wizard worked for Bailum and Barney's Great Consolidated Shows; L. Frank Baum, *Dorothy and the Wizard in Oz* (Chicago: Reilly and Britton, 1908), 48.

14. On humbug, see Neil Harris, *The Art of P.T. Barnum* (Chicago: University of Chicago Press, 1981); and Michael Taussig, "Viscerality, Faith, and Skepticism: Another

Theory of Magic." *HAU: Journal of Ethnographic Theory* 6, no. 3 (December 31, 2016): 453–483.

15. L. Frank Baum, *The Wonderful Wizard of Oz* (Chicago: George M. Hill Company, 1900), 184.

16. Maria Tatar, "Why Fairy Tales Matter: The Performative and the Transformative," *Western Folklore* 69, no. 1 (2010): 56–57, 62–63.

17. Wolf, *Changed for Good*, 11, 18.

18. Raymond Knapp and Mitchell Morris make a similar analogy about the man behind the curtain in their discussion of camp. See Raymond Knapp and Mitchell Morris, "The Filmed Musical," in *The Oxford Handbook of the American Musical*, ed. Raymond Knapp, Mitchell Morris, and Stacy Wolf (New York: Oxford University Press, 2011), 150.

19. For discussion of further aspects of useful lying in American musical theater with implications for belonging and utopia, see Jake Johnson, *Lying in the Middle*.

20. On fairy tales and musicals, see Jill Terry Rudy, "Musicals," in *The Routledge Companion to Media and Fairy Tale Cultures*, ed. Pauline Greenhill, Jill Terry Rudy, Naomi Hamer, and Lauren Bosc (New York: Routledge, 2018), 556–564; Knapp, *The American Musical and the Performance of Personal Identity*, 121–125; Altman, *The American Film Musical*, 129–199.

21. Dominic Symonds and Millie Taylor, eds, *Gestures of Music Theater: The Performativity of Song and Dance* (New York: Oxford University Press, 2014), 2–3. See also Dolan, *Utopia in Performance*, 7, on utopian performances and Brecht's concept of *gestus* embodying social relations and Boal's theories of revolution in theater of the oppressed; as well as Bertolt Brecht, *Brecht on Theatre: The Development of an Aesthetic*, trans. and ed. John Willett (New York: Hill and Wang, 1964); Augusto Boal, *Theatre of the Oppressed* (New York: Theatre Communications Group, 1974). On songs in musicals being about themselves, see Scott McMillin, *The Musical as Drama: A Study of the Principles and Conventions behind Musical Shows from Kern to Sondheim* (Princeton, NJ: Princeton University Press, 2006), 110.

22. Bob Fosse divided musical theater songs into "I am" and "I want" songs. See Richard Kislan, *The Musical: A Look at the American Musical Theater* (New York: Applause, 1995), 228. Some have suggested a more specific type, the "I am becoming" song. " 'I Am Becoming' Song," *TV Tropes*, https://tvtropes.org/pmwiki/pmwiki.php/Main/IAmBecomingSong, accessed February 1, 2020.

23. Bradley Rogers, *The Song Is You: Musical Theatre and the Politics of Bursting into Song and Dance* (Iowa City: University of Iowa Press, 2020).

24. Bernstein, *Racial Innocence*, 4–8, on the cultural innocence of Whiteness; Knapp, *The American Musical and the Formation of National Identity*, 239, on the musical's children and American innocence.

25. In a similar vein, see Marah Gubar, "Who Watched *The Children's Pinafore*? Age Transvestism on the Nineteenth-Century Stage," *Victorian Studies* 54, no. 3 (2012): 410–426.

26. My understanding of performativity is in the lineage that can be traced from J.L. Austin's speech acts to Judith Butler's gender performativity. See John Langshaw

Austin, *How to Do Things with Words* (New York: Oxford University Press, 2011) and Judith Butler, Gender Trouble, 2nd ed. (New York: Routledge, 1999).

27. Amy Herzog, *Dreams of Difference, Songs of the Same: The Musical Moment in Film* (Minneapolis: University of Minnesota Press, 2010), 7.

28. *Royal Wedding* (Donen, 1951). Similarly, see Feuer, *The Hollywood Musical*, 3–6, on bricolage and engineering.

29. Bernstein, *Racial Innocence*, 71.

30. Leigh Burtill, "We're Off to See the Wizard—and We'll Do It with a *pas de basque* Balance!" *Fit Ballet*, http://fitballet.blogspot.com/2018/06/were-off-to-see-wizard-and-well-do-it.html, accessed August 28, 2020; Irishprincess, "Wizard of Oz Step," Adult Ballet Students forum, *Ballet Talk for Dancers* (January 23, 2008), https://dancers.invisionzone.com/topic/38528-wizard-of-oz-step/?tab=comments#comment-350267, accessed August 29, 2020.

31. Knapp, The American Musical and the Formation of National Identity, 12–13.

32. On the creation of a new character in song, see Most, *Making Americans*, 10; McMillin, *The Musical as Drama,* 21.

33. Henry Bial, *Acting Jewish: Negotiating Ethnicity on the American Stage and Screen* (Ann Arbor: University of Michigan Press, 2005), 16–19.

34. Most, Making Americans, 23.

35. Aljean Harmetz, *The Making of "The Wizard of Oz"* (New York: Alfred A. Knopf, 1977), 156; John Fricke, Jay Scarfone, and William Stillman, *"The Wizard of Oz": The Official 50th Anniversary Pictorial History* (New York: Warner Books, 1989), 84.

36. On childhood and musicals, see James Leve and Donelle Ruwe, *Children, Childhood, and Musical Theater* (New York: Routledge, 2020) and Samuel Baltimore, "'Do It Again': Comic Repetition, Participatory Reception and Gendered Identity on Musical Comedy's Margins," PhD diss., University of California, 2013. On children's theater for all ages, see Marah Gubar, "Entertaining Children of All Ages: Nineteenth-Century Popular Theater as Children's Theater," *American Quarterly* 66, no. 1 (March 24, 2014): 1–34.

37. For example, Altman's theory of the heteronormative dual-focus narrative is somewhat confounded by child-oriented musicals such as *The Wizard of Oz* and Disney films. Lloyd Whitesell identifies "children's mode" as an important affective code in the film musical, while Raymond Knapp and Steven Cohan both frequently approach childhood topics in their general works on musicals. See Lloyd Whitesell, *Wonderful Design: Glamour in the Hollywood Musical* (New York: Oxford University Press, 2018), Knapp, *The American Musical and the Performance of Personal Identity*, and Steven Cohan, ed., *The Sound of Musicals* (London: British Film Institute, 2010).

38. Most, *Making Americans,* 9. Most's assimilation effect is a counterpoint to Brecht's "alienation effect" (*Verfremdungseffekt*).

39. On these erasures and performance generally, see Teves, Stephanie Nohelani. "The Theorist and the Theorized: Indigenous Critiques of Performance Studies," *Drama Review* 62, no. 4 (2018): 131–140.

40. On "playing Indian" as a White American preoccupation, see Philip Joseph Deloria, *Playing Indian* (New Haven, CT: Yale University Press, 1998).

41. On the erasure of Fiyero's cultural otherness in the musical, see Steven Greenwood, "Say There's No Future: The Queer Potential of *Wicked*'s Fiyero," *Studies in Musical Theatre* 12, no. 3 (2018), 307–308.

42. On Baum and Gage, see Katharine M. Rogers, *L. Frank Baum: Creator of Oz: A Biography* (New York: St. Martin's Press, 2002), 28–33, 50–54.

43. On Cinderella patterns in the American musical, see Maya Cantu, *American Cinderellas on the Broadway Musical Stage: Imagining the Working Girl from Irene to Gypsy* (London: Palgrave Macmillan, 2015) on Cinderella as musical theater template.

44. Wolf, *Changed for Good*, 197–218.

45. On the queerness of childhood, see Kathryn Bond Stockton, *The Queer Child or Growing Sideways in the Twentieth Century* (Durham, NC: Duke University Press, 2009); on queerness in children's literature, see Tison Pugh, *Innocence, Heterosexuality, and the Queerness of Children's Literature* (New York: Routledge, 2010), 1–37.

46. David Savran, *A Queer Sort of Materialism: Recontextualizing American Theater* (Ann Arbor: University of Michigan Press, 2003), 3–55, 59.

47. D. A. Miller, *Place for Us [Essay on the Broadway Musical]* (Cambridge, MA, and London: Harvard University Press, 1998); John M. Clum, *Something for the Boys: Musical Theater and Gay Culture* (New York: St. Martin's Press, 1999); Stacy Wolf, *A Problem Like Maria: Gender and Sexuality in the American Musical* (Ann Arbor: University of Michigan Press, 2002), and *Changed for Good*; Knapp, *The American Musical and the Formation of National Identity*, 5, 12–15.

48. On Oz as queer and in queer mythologies, see Tison Pugh, "Are we cannibals, let me ask?: Or are we faithful friends?': Food, Interspecies Cannibalism, and the Limits of Utopia in L. Frank Baum's Oz Books," *The Lion and the Unicorn* 32, no. 3 (2008): 324–343; Ronald Zank, "Come Out, Come Out, Wherever You Are': How Tina Landau's 1969 Stages a Queer Reading of *The Wizard of Oz*," in *The Universe of Oz: Essays on Baum's Series and Its Progeny*, ed. Kevin K. Durand and Mary K. Leigh, 61–76 (Jefferson, NC: McFarland, 2010). Pugh, *Innocence*, 21–37; Dee Michel, *Friends of Dorothy: Why Gay Boys and Gay Men Love* The Wizard of Oz (N.p.: Dark Ink Press, 2018), Kindle edition, chapter 9, location 2676; Walter Frisch, *Arlen and Harburg's "Over the Rainbow"* (New York: Oxford University Press, 2017), 84–91; Hannah Robbins, "'Friends of Dorothy': Queerness in and beyond the MGM Film," in *Adapting "The Wizard of Oz": Musical Versions from Baum to MGM and Beyond*, ed. Danielle Birkett and Dominic McHugh (New York: Oxford University Press, 2019), 143–160. See also chapter 2 in this book.

49. Harry M. Benshoff and Sean Griffin, *Queer Images: A History of Gay and Lesbian Film in America* (Lanham, MD: Rowman and Littlefield, 2006), 68.

50. Wolf, *Changed for Good*, 197–218.

51. Teresa Grant, Ignacio Ramos Gay, and Claudia Alonso Recarte, "Introduction: Real Animals on the Stage," *Studies in Theatre and Performance* 38, no. 2 (2018): 103–112.

52. As Raymond Knapp notes, musicals would seem to privilege the "sound"ness of normate bodies that can sing and dance conventionally, but musicals are full of disabled characters who, like immigrants, have to be dealt with in the utopian politics of the musical. Raymond Knapp, "'Waitin' for the Light to Shine': Musicals

and Disability," in *The Oxford Handbook of Music and Disability Studies*, ed. Blake Howe, Stephanie Jensen-Moulton, Neil Lerner, and Joseph Straus (New York: Oxford University Press, 2016), 815.On American persons versus things, see Bill Brown, "Reification, Reanimation, and the American Uncanny," *Critical Inquiry* 32, no. 2 (2006): 175–207; Bernstein, *Racial Innocence*, 17.

53. On disability narratives, freakery, and related issues raised here, see Rosemarie Garland-Thomson, "The Cultural Logic of Euthanasia: 'Sad Fancyings' in Herman Melville's 'Bartleby,'" *American Literature* 76, no. 4 (2004): 781; David Mitchell and Sharon Snyder, *Narrative Prosthesis: Disability and the Dependencies of Discourse* (Ann Arbor: University of Michigan Press, 2000). On these issues in Oz and musicals, see Joshua R. Eyler, "Disability and Prosthesis in L. Frank Baum's *The Wonderful Wizard of Oz*," *Children's Literature Association Quarterly* 38 (Fall 2013): 319–334; Jessica Sternfeld, "'Pitiful Creature of Darkness': The Subhuman and the Superhuman in *The Phantom of the Opera*," in *The Oxford Handbook of Music and Disability Studies*, ed. Blake Howe, Stephanie Jensen-Moulton, Neil Lerner, and Joseph Straus (New York: Oxford University Press, 2016), 975, 801; Wolf, *Changed for Good*, 205; Ann M. Fox, "Scene in a New Light: Monstrous Mothers, Disabled Daughters, and the Performance of Feminism and Disability in *The Light in the Piazza* (2005) and *Next to Normal* (2008)," in Howe, Jensen-Moulton, Lerner, and Straus, *The Oxford Handbook of Music and Disability Studies*, 776.

54. Matthew Lockitt, "'Proposition': To Reconsider the Non-Singing Character and the Songless Moment," *Studies in Musical Theatre* 6, no. 2 (2012): 187–198, critiques the idea that not singing necessarily makes characters in musicals less good, sympathetic, and powerful.

55. Savran, *A Queer Sort of Materialism*.

56. Dolan, *Utopia in Performance*, 5.

57. On childhood and nostalgia, see Svetlana Boym, *The Future of Nostalgia* (New York: Basic Books, 2001), xii–xv, 3–18; on queer time in musicals, see Sarah Taylor Ellis, "'No Day but Today': Queer Temporality in *Rent*," *Studies in Musical Theatre* 5, no. 2 (2011): 195–207; queer temporality is explicated in Jack Halberstam, *In a Queer Time and Place: Transgender Bodies, Subcultural Lives* (New York: New York University Press, 2005), 2.

58. McMillin, *The Musical as Drama*, 6–10; on similarly relevant functions of time in utopian performatives, see Dolan, *Utopia in Performance*, 13–15.

59. Linda Hutcheon, *A Theory of Adaptation* (New York: Routledge, 2012), xv.

60. For different views on the implications of Oz, adaptation, seriality, and repetition, see Richard Flynn, "Imitation Oz: The Sequel as Commodity," *The Lion and the Unicorn* 20, no. 1 (1996): 121–131; Joel Chaston, "The 'Ozification' of American Children's Fantasy Films: *The Blue Bird, Alice in Wonderland*, and *Jumanji*," *Children's Literature Association Quarterly* 22, no. 1 (1997): 13–20; Frank Kelleter, "'Toto, I Think We're in Oz Again' (and Again and Again): Remakes and Popular Seriality," in *Film Remakes, Adaptations and Fan Productions*, ed. Kathleen Loock and Constantine Verevis (New York: Palgrave, 2012), 19–44; Laurie Langbauer, "Off to See the Wizard Again and Again," in *Seriality and Texts for Young People*, edited by Mavis Reimer,

Nyala Ali, Deanna England, and Melanie Dennis Unrau (London: Palgrave, 2014), 34–56; Meghan Meeusen, "The Difficulty in Deciphering the 'Dreams That You Dare to Dream': Adaptive Dissonance in *Wizard of Oz* Films," *Children's Literature Association Quarterly* 42, no 2 (2017): 184–204; Kate Newell, *Expanding Adaptation Networks: From Illustration to Novelization* (London: Palgrave, 2017), 1–23.

61. La Donna L. Forsgren, "*The Wiz* Redux; or, Why Queer Black Feminist Spectatorship and Politically Engaged Popular Entertainment Continue to Matter," *Theatre Survey* 60, no. 3 (2019): 326.

62. Bruce Kirle, *Unfinished Show Business: Broadway Musicals as Works-in-Progress* (Carbondale: Southern Illinois University Press, 2005).

63. Dolan, *Utopia in Performance*, 13.

64. Suzi Nash, "Micah Mahjoubian: Politics, Religion, and Technology," *Philadelphia Gay News*, March 3, 2011, https://epgn.com/2011/03/03/12143865-micah-mahjoubian-politics-religion-and-technology, accessed July 25, 2022.

65. By conducting interviews, I follow the lead of scholars who are adopting ethnographic methods in the study of musical theater, particularly beyond the Broadway stage. See Stacy Wolf, *Beyond Broadway: The Pleasure and Promise of Musical Theatre across America* (New York: Oxford University Press, 2019) and the contributors to Judah M. Cohen and Jake Johnson, eds., special issue on musical theater and ethnography, *Studies in Musical Theatre* 14, no. 1 (2020).

66. Dyer, "Entertainment and Utopia," 35.

67. Joseph Roach, *Cities of the Dead: Circum-Atlantic Performance* (New York: Columbia University Press, 1996), 2–3; Diana Taylor, *The Archive and the Repertoire: Performing Cultural Memory in the Americas* (Durham, NC: Duke University Press, 2003).

Chapter 1

1. L. Frank Baum, *The Wonderful Wizard of Oz* (Chicago: George M. Hill, 1900), 184, 186.

2. Neil Harris, *The Art of P.T. Barnum* (Chicago: University of Chicago Press, 1981), 5, 57–89; Kembrew McLeod, *Pranksters: Making Mischief in the Modern World* (New York: New York University Press, 2014), 19–20.

3. On Baum and Barnum, see Michael Patrick Hearn, ed. and introduction, *The Annotated Wizard of Oz: Centennial Edition* (New York: Norton, 2000), 260–262; Katherine M. Rogers, *L. Frank Baum: Creator of Oz* (New York: St. Martin's Press, 2002), 82–85.

4. William R. Leach, *Land of Desire: Merchants, Power, and the Rise of a New American Culture* (New York: Knopf Doubleday Publishing Group, 2011), Kindle Location 1421 (Chapter 2); McLeod, *Pranksters*, 70; Zeese Papanikolas, *Trickster in the Land of Dreams* (Lincoln: University of Nebraska Press, 1995), 102.

5. Rogers, *L. Frank Baum*, 83.

6. L. Frank Baum, *Aberdeen* (SD) *Saturday Pioneer*, February 8, 1890, quoted in Hearn, *The Annotated Wizard of Oz*, 260.

7. On Baum and the World's Columbian Exposition, see Hearn, *The Annotated Wizard of Oz*, 176; Rogers, *L. Frank Baum*, 45–47, 82; Michael O. Riley, "The Great City of Oz: L. Frank Baum at the 1893 World's Fair," *The Baum Bugle* 42, no. 3 (Winter 1998): 32–38; Leach, *Land of Desire*, Kindle location 1871 (chapter 3). On the fair and its influence on musical theater, see David C. Paul, "Race and the Legacy of the World's Columbian Exposition in American Popular Theater from the Gilded Age to *Show Boat* (1927)," *American Music* 39, no. 3 (2021): 325–364.

8. Siobhan Somerville, *Queering the Color Line: Race and the Invention of Homosexuality in American Culture* (Durham, NC: Duke University Press, 2000).

9. Critics praised the book's commonplace fantasy. See, for example, "A New Book for Children," *New York Times*, September 8, 1900, BR12.

10. Hearn, *The Annotated Wizard of Oz*, 15; Rogers, *L. Frank Baum*, 93.

11. On dwarves and little people in literature and performance, see Lynne Vallone, *Big and Small: A Cultural History of Extraordinary Bodies* (New Haven, CT: Yale University Press, 2017).

12. Baum, *Wonderful Wizard*, 69–70.

13. However, he reveals in 1914's *Tik-Tok of Oz* that he *can* speak and has preferred not to.

14. On Toto, see Caryn Kunz Lesuma, "Domesticating Dorothy: Toto's Role in Constructing Childhood in *The Wizard of Oz* and Its Retellings," in *Childhood and Pethood in Literature and Culture: New Perspectives in Childhood Studies and Animal Studies*, edited by Anna Feuerstein and Carmen Nolte-Odhiambo (New York: Routledge, 2017), 124–137.

15. Baum, *Wonderful Wizard*, 189; on *The Wizard of Oz* as a prosthetic narrative, see Joshua Eyler, "Disability and Prosthesis in L. Frank Baum's *The Wonderful Wizard of Oz*," *Children's Literature Association Quarterly* 38 (Fall 2013), 319–334.

16. For examples, see Linda Rohrer Page, "Wearing the Red Shoes: Dorothy and the Power of the Female Imagination in *The Wizard of Oz*," *Journal of Popular Film and Television* 23, no. 4 (1996): 146–153; Noah Seaman and Barbara Seaman, "Munchkins, Ozophiles, and Feminists Too," *Ms.*, January 1974, 93; Joel D. Chaston, "If I Ever Go Looking for My Heart's Desire: 'Home' in Baum's 'Oz' Books, *The Lion and the Unicorn*, 18 (December 1994): 209–219; Hearn, *The Annotated Wizard of Oz*, 13; Alissa Burger, *"The Wizard of Oz" as American Myth: A Critical Study of Six Versions of the Story, 1900–2007* (Jefferson, NC: McFarland, 2012), 17–25, 55–91; Jack Zipes, *Fairy Tales and the Art of Subversion* (1983; New York: Routledge, 2012), 125–135; Katherine Rogers, "Liberation for Little Girls, *Saturday Review*, June 17, 1972, 72.

17. Rogers, *L. Frank Baum*, 28–33, 50–54; Angelica Shirley Carpenter, *Born Criminal: Matilda Joslyn Gage, Radical Suffragist* (Pierre: South Dakota Historical Society Press, 2018), 212; Dina Schiff Massachi, "Connecting Baum and Gilman: Matilda Gage and Her Influence on Oz and Herland," *Journal of American Culture* 41, no. 2 (2018): 203–214; Burger, *"The Wizard of Oz" as American Myth*, 161.

18. Matilda Joslyn Gage, *Woman, Church and State* (1893; Aberdeen, SD: Sky Carrier Press, 1998), 118–165; Marian Gibson, *Witchcraft Myths in American Culture* (New York: Routledge, 2007), 112–119; Angelica Shirley Carpenter, *Born Criminal: Matilda Joslyn Gage, Radical Suffragist* (Pierre: South Dakota Historical Society Press, 2018), 186–187.

19. Baum spoke of his objection to romantic love in children's books in "What Children Want" and in *The Advance*, July 22, 1909, reprinted in *The Baum Bugle*, 30 (Autumn 1986), 9.

20. Tison Pugh, *Innocence, Heterosexuality, and the Queerness of Children's Literature* (New York: Routledge, 2010), 1–19.

21. Kathryn Bond Stockton, *The Queer Child; or, Growing Sideways in the Twentieth Century* (Durham, NC: Duke University Press, 2009), 30–33.

22. Baum, *Wonderful Wizard*, 21.

23. Baum, *Wonderful Wizard*, 127.

24. L. Frank Baum, *Aberdeen* (SD) *Saturday Pioneer*, December 20, 1890, and January 3, 1891.

25. Baum, *Aberdeen* (SD) *Saturday Pioneer*, December 20, 1898.

26. Raymond Knapp, *The American Musical and the Formation of National Identity* (Princeton, NJ: Princeton University Press, 2005), 124–126.

27. Baum, *Wonderful Wizard*, 189.

28. Mark Evan Swartz, *Oz before the Rainbow: L. Frank Baum's "The Wizard of Oz" on Stage and Screen to 1939* (Baltimore: Johns Hopkins University Press, 2000), 36.

29. Here I'm influenced by Meredith Bak's concept of the ludic archive as a method for historical research in children's cultures; see "The Ludic Archive: The Work of Playing with Optical Toys," *Moving Image: The Journal of the Association of Moving Image Archivists* 16, no. 1 (2016): 1–16.

30. L. Frank Baum, *The Wizard of Oz*, playscript, 1903, Library of Congress copyright deposit, transcribed by Ann Fraistat, prepared for digital publication by Doug Reside, New York Public Library for the Performing Arts, https://www.nypl.org/blog/2011/12/13/musical-month-wizard-oz-1903, accessed September 2, 2020.

31. Recordings with lyrics and valuable historical notes by David Maxine are in *The Wizard of Oz: Vintage Recordings from the 1903 Broadway Musical*, Hungry Tiger Press 2003, CD.

32. On the carnivalesque character of the extravaganza and its influence on the Oz books, see Joel Chaston, "Baum, Bakhtin, and Broadway: A Centennial Look at the Carnival of Oz," *The Lion and the Unicorn* 25, no. 1 (February 1, 2001): 128–149.

33. On the extravaganza and *The Wizard of Oz*, see Swartz, *Oz before the Rainbow*, 35–36; and Jonas Westover, "'Starring Montgomery and Stone!': *The Wizard of Oz* Musical Extravaganza (1902) and the Birth of a Brand," in *Adapting the Wizard of Oz: Musical Versions from Baum to MGM and Beyond*, ed. Danielle Burkett and Dominic McHugh (New York: Oxford University Press, 2019), 11–14. Westover proposes that the show's loose structure positions it as a link between the nineteenth-century extravaganza and the musical revue, which became the disunified counterpart to the book musical in the twentieth century.

34. Swartz, *Oz before the Rainbow*, 103.

35. Bruce Kirle, *Unfinished Show Business: Broadway Musicals as Works-in-Progress* (Carbondale: Southern Illinois University Press, 2005).

36. On vestiges of minstrelsy in popular culture, see Nicholas Sammond, *Birth of an Industry: Blackface Minstrelsy and the Rise of American Animation* (Durham, NC: Duke University Press, 2015); On cross-talk as a legacy of minstrelsy, see Charles

Wolf, "'Cross-Talk': Language, Space, and the Burns and Allen Comedy Film Short," *Film History* 23, no. 3 (2011): 300.

37. Marah Gubar, "Entertaining Children of All Ages: Nineteenth-Century Popular Theater as Children's Theater," *American Quarterly* 66, no. 1 (2014): 1–34, and "Peter Pan as Children's Theatre: The Issue of Audience," in *The Oxford Handbook of Children's Literature*, edited by Julia Mickenberg and Lynne Vallone (New York: Oxford University Press, 2011), 475–496.

38. *Wizard of Oz* Clippings File (T-CLP), Billy Rose Theatre Collection, New York Public Library for the Performing Arts.

39. Armond Fields, *Fred Stone: Circus Performer and Musical Comedy Star* (Jefferson, NC: McFarland, 2002), 97.

40. *Wizard of Oz* Clippings File.

41. *New York Telegram*, January 21, 1903, *Wizard of Oz* Clippings File.

42. Swartz, *Oz before the Rainbow*, 58, 140.

43. Andrea Most, *Making Americans: Jews and the Broadway Musical* (Cambridge, MA: Harvard University Press, 2004), 1–11.

44. On Black Broadway musicals at this time, see Thomas L. Riis, *Just before Jazz: Black Musical Theater in New York, 1890–1915* (Washington, DC: Smithsonian Institution Press, 1989); Allen Woll, *Black Musical Theatre from Coontown to Dreamgirls* (Baton Rouge: Louisiana State University Press, 1989), 1–13.

45. Swartz, *Oz before the Rainbow*, 103–104.

46. Clipping marked "Weekly, Oct. 8, 1903," *Wizard of Oz* Clippings File.

47. Swartz, *Oz before the Rainbow*, 84.

48. On the effects of age transvestism on adult-child constructs, see Marah Gubar, "Who Watched the Children's *Pinafore*? Age Transvestism on the Nineteenth-Century Stage," *Victorian Studies* 54, no. 3 (2012): 410–426.

49. See, for example, Robin Ganev, "Milkmaids, Ploughmen, and Sex in Eighteenth-Century Britain, *Journal of the History of Sexuality* 16, no. 1 (2007): 40–67.

50. *Wizard of Oz* Clippings File.

51. On cross-dressed roles in the American theater, see Gillian Rodger, *Just One of the Boys: Female-to-Male Cross-Dressing on the American Variety Stage* (Champaign: University of Illinois Press, 2018).

52. Swartz, *Oz before the Rainbow*, 71.

53. Swartz, 71–73.

54. Swartz, 87.

55. Swartz, 92, 125–128.

56. Swartz, 97, 121, 124, 144–145, 147.

57. David Maxine, "Bang on My Chest if You Think I'm Perfect!" *The Wizard of Oz on Broadway*, October 23, 2019, https://www.vintagebroadway.com/2019/10/bang-on-my-chest-if-you-think-im-perfect.html, accessed August 15, 2022.

58. Westover, "'Starring Montgomery and Stone!,'" 15–16.

59. Swartz, *Oz before the Rainbow*, 77; Fields, *Fred Stone*, 97–98.

60. Robin Bernstein, *Racial Innocence: Performing American Childhood and Race from Slavery to Civil Rights* (New York: New York University Press, 2011), 168.

61. *Wizard of Oz* Clippings File. See Gubar, "Entertaining," 1–2, 24–27, on George Fox, working-class entertainment, and children's theater.

62. Sylvester Russell, "The Wizard of Oz," *The Freeman*, February 27, 1904.

63. Most, *Making Americans*, 25–26.

64. David Maxine has noted that there was a Black production of a "musical opera" of *The Wizard of Oz* directed by Gertrude Blanton and featuring students of Howard High School in Chattanooga, Tennessee, in 1922. Maxine speculates that this was a licensed amateur performance of the extravaganza. David Maxine, "The Black *Wizard of Oz*—Part Two," *The Wizard of Oz on Broadway*, February 23, 2022, https://www.vint agebroadway.com/2022/02/the-black-wizard-of-oz-part-two.html, accessed August 15, 2022.

65. Bernstein, *Racial Innocence*, 163.

66. Fields, *Fred Stone*, 274–275; Westover, " 'Starring Montgomery and Stone!,' " 21–23; Swartz, *Oz before the Rainbow*, 250; Jacqueline Warwick, "You Can't Win Child, but You Can't Get Out of the Game: Michael Jackson's Transition from Child Star to Superstar," *Popular Music and Society* 35 (2012): 252.

67. On the homoerotics of same-sex comedy duos, see Douglas Brode, "Stan Laurel and Oliver Hardy: Yin and Yang," in *Fools and Jesters in Literature, Art, and History: A Bio-Bibliographical Sourcebook*, ed. Vicki K. Janik (Westport, CT: Greenwood, 1998), 287; Lawrence J. Epstein *Mixed Nuts: America's Love Affair with Comedy Teams* (2004), 90. In children's literature, see Teya Rosenberg, "Arnold Lobel's *Frog and Toad Together* as a Primer for Critical Literacy," in *The Oxford Handbook of Children's Literature*, edited by Julia L. Mickenberg and Lynne Vallone (New York: Oxford University Press, 2011), 84–85.

68. Bernstein, *Racial Innocence*, 17; Bill Brown, "Reification, Reanimation, and the American Uncanny," *Critical Inquiry* 32, no. 2 (2006): 175–207.

69. *Wizard of Oz* Clippings File.

70. Unidentified clipping dated January 31, 1903, *Wizard of Oz* Clippings File.

71. Bernstein, *Racial Innocence*, 166, 184–193.

72. Fields, *Fred Stone*, 92–93; Swartz, *Oz before the Rainbow*, 115.

73. Swartz, 144.

74. Similarly, Bernstein, *Racial Innocence*, 149, describes black-and-whiteness in Raggedy Ann, a character inspired by Oz's Scarecrow, whose "flat, white mask of a face was a scrim that could, depending on the circumstance and the audience, reveal or screen out knowledge of race, history, and violence."

75. Philip Deloria, *Playing Indian* (New Haven, CT: Yale University Press, 1999).

76. Vallone, "The Place of Girls," 41.

77. Swartz, Oz before the Rainbow, 92.

78. Chaston, "Baum, Bakhtin, and Broadway," 128–149; Richard Flynn, "Imitation Oz: The Sequel as Commodity," *The Lion and the Unicorn* 20, no. 1 (1996): 121–131. On the more general uses of artifice in Baum's writing, see Paige Gray, *Cub Reporters: American Children's Literature and Journalism in the Golden Age* (Albany: State University of New York Press, 2019), 41–68.

79. L. Frank Baum, *The Marvelous Land of Oz* (Chicago: Reilly and Britton, 1904).

Chapter 2

1. Harold Meyerson and Ernie Harburg, *Who Put the Rainbow in "The Wizard of Oz"? Yip Harburg, Lyricist* (Ann Arbor: University of Michigan Press, 1993), 122–125.
2. Bradley Rogers, *The Song Is You: Musical Theatre and the Politics of Bursting into Song and Dance* (Iowa City: University of Iowa Press), 14–15.
3. There had been some spectacular failures in live-action fantasy, most notably, Norman Z. McLeod's *Alice in Wonderland* (1933). See Aljean Harmetz, *The Making of "The Wizard of Oz"* (New York: Alfred A. Knopf, 1977), 3; John Fricke, Jay Scarfone, and William Stillman, *The Wizard of Oz: The Official 50th Anniversary Pictorial History* (New York: Warner Books, 1989), 18, 45; Michael Patrick Hearn, "Introduction," in Noel Langley, Florence Ryerson, and Edgar Allan Woolf, *The Wizard of Oz: The Screenplay*, ed. Michael Patrick Hearn (New York: Delta, 1989), 5, 7.
4. Herman Mackiewicz, *The Wizard of Oz*, screenplay draft, March 12, 1938, 19–41, scenes 24–38, Box 1, Folder 1, Wizard of Oz mss., Lilly Library, Indiana University, Bloomington, Indiana. Additional script drafts can be found here and in the script collection of the Margaret Herrick Library, Academy of Motion Picture Arts and Sciences, Beverly Hills, CA. On the screenwriting process, see Harmetz, *The Making of "The Wizard of Oz,"* 25–59; Fricke, Scarfone, and Stillman, *The Wizard of Oz*, 26–30, 39–44; Hearn, "Introduction," 1–28; Jay Scarfone and William Stillman, *The Road to Oz: The Evolution, Creation, and Legacy of a Motion Picture Masterpiece* (Guilford, CT: Rowman and Littlefield, 2019), Kindle location 2596.
5. This was despite its historical associations with sophistication and sexuality. See Raymond Knapp, *The American Musical and the Performance of Personal Identity* (Princeton, NJ: Princeton University Press, 2006), 10, 121.
6. Rick Payne, "1939 Wizard of Oz Pressbook—The Snow White Pages," *Filmic Light Snow White Archive*, March 13, 2013, http://filmic-light.blogspot.com/2013/03/1939-wizard-of-oz-pressbook-snow-white.html, accessed August 11, 2019.
7. On double address in the children's or family film, see Noel Brown and Bruce Babington, *Family Films in Global Cinema: The World beyond Disney* (New York: IB Tauris, 2015), Kindle edition, introduction, location 313; on camp in the dual address to adults and children, see Knapp, *The American Musical and the Performance of Personal Identity*, 124.
8. Knapp, *The American Musical and the Performance of Personal Identity*, 132–133. Knapp's thorough coverage of *The Wizard of Oz* as a musical, 131–141, discusses at length the effects of doubleness in the characters.
9. On effects of the dream, see Annah E. MacKenzie, "From Screen to Shining Screen: *The Wizard of Oz* in the Age of Mechanical Reproduction," in *The Fantastic Made Visible: Essays on the Adaptation of Science Fiction and Fantasy from Page to Screen*, ed. Matthew Wilhelm Kapell and Ace G. Pilkington (Jefferson, NC: McFarland, 2015), 175–191.
10. Salman Rushdie, *The Wizard of Oz* (London: British Film Institute, 1992), 30.
11. For a psychoanalytic reading of Dorothy's dream, see Todd S. Gilman, "'Aunt Em: Hate You! Hate Kansas! Taking the Dog. Dorothy': Conscious and Unconscious

Desire in *The Wizard of Oz*," in *L. Frank Baum's World of Oz: A Classic Series at 100*, edited by Suzanne Rahn (Lanham MD: Scarecrow Press: 2003), 127–145.

12. Nelson B. Bell, "Prelude to the Coming of a Rare Achievement in Cinematography," *Washington Post*, August 20, 1939, AM3; *Variety*, August 10, 1939, 3.

13. Frank Nugent, "The Screen in Review: *The Wizard of Oz*, Produced by the Wizards of Hollywood, Works Its Magic on the Capitol's Screen," *New York Times*, August 18, 1939, 16.

14. On camp in particular serving this function, see Knapp, *The American Musical and the Formation of National Identity*; 13; Raymond Knapp and Mitchell Morris, "The Filmed Musical," in *The Oxford Handbook of the American Musical*, ed. Raymond Knapp, Mitchell Morris, and Stacy Wolf (New York: Oxford University Press, 2011), 146–150; Stephen Cohan, *Incongruous Entertainment: Camp, Cultural Value, and the MGM Musical* (Durham, NC: Duke University Press, 2005), 1–40.

15. On sound, the Hays Code, and family film, see *The Children's Film: Genre, Nation, and Narrative* (New York: Columbia University Press, 2017), Kindle edition, chapter 2, and his *The Hollywood Family Film: A History from Shirley Temple to Harry Potter* (New York: IB Tauris, 2017), Kindle edition, chapter 1, location 572.

16. Andrea Most, *Making Americans: Jews and the Broadway Musical* (Cambridge, MA: Harvard University Press, 2004), 12–31.

17. Knapp and Morris, "The Filmed Musical," 148. On Jewish and queer Hollywood, see Neal Gabler, *An Empire of Their Own: How the Jews Invented Hollywood* (New York: Anchor Books, 1989) and William J. Mann, *Behind the Screen: How Gays and Lesbians Shaped Hollywood, 1910–1969* (New York: Viking Press, 2001).

18. Cohan, *Incongruous Entertainment*, 47; Sean Griffin, *Free and Easy? A Defining History of the American Film Musical Genre* (Hoboken, NJ: Wiley, 2018), 142; Mann, *Behind the Screen*, 270.

19. According to Harmetz, *The Making of "The Wizard of Oz*," 46, Edgar Allan Woolf was described by MGM story editor Samuel Marx as a "wild, red-headed homosexual."

20. On Edens's involvement in the film, see Laura Lynn Broadhurst, "Arlen and Harburg and More, Oh My! The Cumulative Creation of the *Oz* Songs," in *Adapting "The Wizard of Oz": Musical Versions from Baum to MGM and Beyond*, ed. Danielle Birkett and Dominic McHugh (New York: Oxford University Press, 2019), 59–60.

21. On Jewish double coding, see Henry Bial, *Acting Jewish: Negotiating Ethnicity on the American Stage and Screen* (Ann Arbor: University of Michigan Press, 2005).

22. Michael Bronski, "Judy Garland and Others: Notes on Idolization and Derision," in *Lavender Culture*, ed. Karla Jay and Allen Young (New York: New York University Press, 1994), 201–212; Richard Dyer, *Heavenly Bodies*, 2nd ed. (New York: Routledge, 2004), 137–138; Charles Kaiser, *The Gay Metropolis: 1940–1996* (Boston, MA: Houghton Mifflin, 1997), 192–197; Dee Michel, *Friends of Dorothy: Why Gay Boys and Gay Men Love "The Wizard of Oz"* (Dark Ink Press, 2018), Kindle edition, chapter 9, location 2676; Walter Frisch, *Arlen and Harburg's "Over the Rainbow"* (New York: Oxford University Press, 2017), 84–91; Hannah Robbins, "'Friends of Dorothy': Queerness in and beyond the MGM Film," in Birkett and McHugh, *Adapting "The Wizard of Oz*," 143–160.

23. Edward Jablonski, *Harold Arlen: Rhythm, Rainbows, and Blues* (Boston, MA: Northeastern University Press, 1996; Jeffrey Paul Melnick, *A Right to Sing the Blues: African Americans, Jews, and American Popular Song* (Cambridge, MA: Harvard University Press, 1999), 50–52.

24. *Scholastic*, September 18, 1939, quoted in Fricke, Scarfone, and Stillman, *The Wizard of Oz*, 187; Nugent, "The Screen in Review," 16; Welford Beaton, *Hollywood Spectator*, 14, no. 10, September 2, 1939, 10, quoted in Fricke, Scarfone, and Stillman, 183.

25. Otis Ferguson, *New Republic*, September 20, 1939, quoted in Fricke, Scarfone, and Stillman, *The Wizard of Oz*, 187.

26. Christopher Finch, *Rainbow: The Stormy Life of Judy Garland* (London: Michael Joseph, 1975), 85.

27. On Garland's image and ambiguity, see Dyer, *Heavenly Bodies*, 163; Rushdie, *The Wizard of Oz*, 27; James A. Boon, "Showbiz as a Cross-Cultural System: Circus and Song, Garland and Geertz, Rushdie, Mordden . . . and More." *Cultural Anthropology* 15, no. 3 (2000): 424–456; Knapp, *The American Musical and the Performance of Personal Identity*, 132; Judith A. Peraino, *Listening to the Sirens: Musical Technologies of Queer Identity from Homer to Hedwig* (Berkeley: University of California Press, 2006), 122; Ciara Barrett, "'Just a Voice and Youth': Shirley Temple, Deanna Durbin, Judy Garland and the Rise of the Musical Child Star in the 1930s," in *Childhood and Celebrity*, ed. Jane O'Connor and John Mercer (New York: Routledge, 2017), 41–52.

28. Gayle Wald, "The Art of Yearning," afterword to *Voicing Girlhood in Popular Music*, ed. Jacqueline Warwick and Allison Adrian (New York: Routledge, 2016), 284.

29. For commentaries on "Over the Rainbow" and Garland's performance, see Knapp, *The American Musical and the Performance of Personal Identity*, 137–138; Rushdie, *The Wizard of Oz*, 23–26; Wald, "The Art of Yearning," 281–285; Frisch, *Arlen and Harburg's "Over the Rainbow."*

30. See Knapp and Morris, "The Filmed Musical," 145–146, on this transformation. On lyrical time and the omniscient orchestra in the musical, see Scott McMillin, *The Musical as Drama* (Princeton, NJ: Princeton University Press, 2006), 6–10, 31–33, 127.

31. See Wald, "The Art of Yearning," 281, on the crafting of emotion and Frisch, *Arlen and Harburg's "Over the Rainbow,"* 77–79, for a detailed analysis of the vocal performance.

32. Lloyd Whitesell describes the performance of "Over the Rainbow" as combining the "ordinary" and "glamour" style modes that encode the affects of the classical Hollywood musical. See. Lloyd Whitesell, *Wonderful Design: Glamour in the Hollywood Musical* (New York: Oxford University Press, 2018).

33. Rushdie, *The Wizard of Oz*, 23.

34. On the rainbow, see Meyerson and Harburg, *Who Put the Rainbow in "The Wizard of Oz"?*, 129.

35. Melnick, *A Right to Sing the Blues*, 16.

36. Michael Bronski, "Gay Men and Movies: Reel to Real," in *Gay Life: Leisure, Love and Living for the Contemporary Gay Male*, ed. Eric Rofes (Garden City, NY: Doubleday, 1986), 226–235.

37. Wald, "The Art of Yearning," 282; See also Frisch, *Arlen and Harburg's "Over the Rainbow,"* 108–123.

38. Caryn Kunz Lesuma, "Domesticating Dorothy: Toto's Role in Constructing Childhood in *The Wizard of Oz* and Its Retellings," in *Childhood and Pethood in Literature and Culture: New Perspectives in Childhood Studies and Animal Studies*, ed. Anna Feuerstein and Carmen Nolte-Odhiambo (New York: Routledge, 2017), 124–137. Rushdie, *The Wizard of Oz*, 17–18, acknowledges Toto's importance, grudgingly

39. Harmetz, *The Making of the Wizard of Oz*, 131–134; Fricke, Scarfone, and Stillman, *The Wizard of Oz*, 25; Scarfone and Stillman, *The Road to Oz*, location 1767; Willard Carroll, *I, Toto: The Autobiography of Terry, the Dog Who Was Toto* (New York: Abrams, 2001).

40. Richard Dyer, *Only Entertainment* (New York: Routledge, 2005), 22.

41. Cohan, *Incongruous Entertainment*, 3.

42. Rushdie, *The Wizard of Oz*, 30.

43. On silent film and musical nostalgia in MGM's Oz, see Nathan Platte, "Nostalgia, the Silent Cinema, and the Art of Quotation in Herbert Stothart's Score for *The Wizard of Oz* (1939)," *Journal of Film Music* 4, no. 1 (2011): 45–64.

44. Rushdie calls it "that camp classic of a line," *The Wizard of Oz*, 33.

45. Knapp, *The American Musical and the Performance of Personal Identity*, 67–70; Knapp and Morris, "The Filmed Musical," 143–145.

46. Knapp, *The American Musical and the Performance of Personal Identity*, 138–140; Platte, "Nostalgia." For more on the orchestral score and its effects, see Nathan Platte, "Underscore as Special Effect in *The Wizard of Oz*," in Birkett and McHugh, *Adapting "The Wizard of Oz*," 79–102; Fiona Ford, "Be It [N]ever So Humble? The Narrating Voice in the Underscore to *The Wizard of Oz*," in *Melodramatic Voices: Understanding Music Drama*, edited by Sarah Hibberd (New York: Taylor and Francis, 2011), 197–214; and Ronald Rodman, "'There's No Place Like Home': Tonal Closure and Design in *The Wizard of Oz*, *Indiana Theory Review* 19 (1998): 125–143.

47. This tune bears a striking resemblance to Schumann's "The Happy Farmer," associated with Kansas, as noted by Platte, "Nostalgia," 53–54.

48. Meyerson and Harburg, *Who Put the Rainbow in "The Wizard of Oz"?*, 15–17, 140.

49. Whitesell identifies the musical sequence in Munchkinland as a prime example of "children's mode" in the film musical. Whitesell, *Wonderful Design*.

50. Keri Watson, "'With a Smile and a Song': Representations of People with Dwarfism in 1930s Cinema," *Journal of Literary and Cultural Disability Studies* 14, no. 2 (2020): 137–153.

51. "'Little People' Dislike Name of 'Midgets': Many Odd Facts Are Revealed about Race by One of Them," *Washington Post*, August 27, 1939, A3.

52. On the Witch as Other, see Alissa Burger, *The Wizard of Oz as American Myth: A Critical Study of Six Versions of the Story, 1900–2007* (Jefferson, NC: McFarland, 2012), 108–111.

53. Rushdie, *The Wizard of Oz*, 43; Knapp, *The American Musical and the Performance of Personal Identity*, 133.

54. Rushdie, *The Wizard of Oz*, 43.

55. On Dorothy's "s-skip," see Rushdie, 44, 47.

56. Harmetz, *The Making of "The Wizard of Oz*," 159–160; Rushdie, *The Wizard of Oz*, 48–49.

57. Holly Van Leuven, *Ray Bloger: More Than a Scarecrow* (New York: Oxford University Press, 2019), 7–24; Armond Fields, *Fred Stone: Circus Performer and Musical Comedy Star* (Jefferson, NC: McFarland, 2002), 274–275.

58. Harmetz, *The Making of "The Wizard of Oz,"* 160; Meyerson and Harburg, *Who Put the Rainbow in "The Wizard of Oz"?*, 149–152.

59. Bruce Kirle, *Unfinished Show Business: Broadway Musicals as Works-in-Process* (Carbondale: Southern Illinois University Press, 2005), 42; On Jewishness and male effeminacy, see Daniel Boyarin, Daniel Itzkovitz, and Ann Pellegrini, eds., *Queer Theory and the Jewish Question* (New York: Columbia University Press, 2003), 2.

60. Fricke, Scarfone, and Stillman, *The Wizard of Oz*, 172–174, 183–187.

61. On haunting in the theater, see Marvin Carlson, *The Haunted Stage: The Theatre as Memory Machine* (Ann Arbor: University of Michigan Press, 2001).

62. On Temple and Oz, see Harmetz, *The Making of "The Wizard of Oz,"* 111–112; Fricke, Scarfone, and Stillman, *The Wizard of Oz*, 19–20; Scarfone and Stillman, *The Road to Oz*, Kindle location 1581.

63. Harmetz, *The Making of "The Wizard of Oz,"* 263–280, includes a whole chapter on accidents.

64. Rushdie, *The Wizard of Oz*, 45.

65. On Harburg's politics as a guide to the MGM film, see Francis MacDonnell, "'The Emerald City Was the New Deal': E.Y. Harburg and *The Wonderful Wizard of Oz,*" *Journal of American Culture* 13, no. 4 (1990): 71–75.

66. MacDonnell, 73.

67. Rushdie, *The Wizard of Oz*, 56.

68. Harmetz, *The Making of "The Wizard of Oz,"* 57.

69. Rushdie, *The Wizard of Oz*, 56–57; Linda Rohrer Page, "Wearing the Red Shoes: Dorothy and the Power of the Female Imagination in *The Wizard of Oz,*" *Journal of Popular Film and Television* 23, no. 4 (1996): 146–153.

70. Rushdie, *The Wizard of Oz*, 57.

71. Similarly, see Rushdie, *The Wizard of Oz*, 23.

72. Knapp, *The American Musical and the Performance of Personal Identity*, 135–136.

73. Fricke, Scarfone, and Stillman, *The Wizard of Oz*, 186.

74. Platte, "Nostalgia, the Silent Cinema, and the Art of Quotation," 56–58.

Chapter 3

1. On Black musical theater, and the place of *The Wiz* in its history, see Allen Woll, *Black Musical Theatre from Coontown to Dreamgirls* (Baton Rouge: Louisiana State University Press, 1989).

2. On the production and reception of *The Wiz*, see Stanley Green, *The World of Musical Comedy*, 4th ed. (New York: Da Capo Press, 1984), 366–367; Woll, *Black Musical Theatre*, 263–266; Stacy Wolf, *Changed for Good: A Feminist History of the Broadway Musical* (New York: Oxford University Press, 2011), 111–117; the Ken Harper Papers,

Billy Rose Theatre Collection, New York Public Library for the Performing Arts; *The Wiz* Collection, Schomburg Center for Research in Black Culture; and Jeremy Aufderheide's idiosyncratic but informative *How the Wiz Was* (Lulu.com, 2014).

3. Gilbert Moses, "Who Put the Fizz into *The Wiz*?," Theater Letters, *New York Times*, June 22, 1975, D5, *The Wiz* collection, Box 2, Folder 12, Green, *The World of Musical Comedy*, 367.

4. Ken Harper, "Is *The Wiz* Built on Rock?" *Christian Science Monitor*, November 14, 1978, 22; Original Broadway Cast, *The Wiz*, by Charlie Smalls, 1975, Atlantic, sound recording. On the rock musical, see Elizabeth L. Wollman, *The Theater Will Rock: A History of the Rock Musical, from Hair to Hedwig* (Ann Arbor: University of Michigan Press, 2009); Scott Warfield, "From *Hair* to *Rent*: Is 'Rock' a Four-Letter Word on Broadway?" in *The Cambridge Companion to the Musical*, ed. William A. Everett and Paul R. Laird (Cambridge: Cambridge University Press, 2002), 231–245.

5. W. E. B. Du Bois, *The Souls of Black Folk* (1903; New York: Dover, 1994).

6. Portia K. Maultsby, "Soul," in *African American Music: An Introduction*, ed. Mellonee V. Burnim and Portia K. Maultsby (New York: Routledge, 2006), 271–289.

7. Gregory S. Carr, "A Brand New Day on Broadway: The Genius of Geoffrey Holder's Artistry and His Intentional Evocation of the African Diaspora," *Theatre Symposium* 26 (2018): 118–126; Sam O'Connell, "*The Wiz* and the African Diaspora Musical: Rethinking the Research Questions in Black Musical Historiography," in *The Routledge Companion to African American Theatre and Performance*, ed. Kathy A. Perkins, Sandra L. Richards, Renee Alexander Craft, and Thomas DeFrantz (New York: Routledge, 2019).

8. Letter to Clive Richards, August 4, 1972, Harper Papers.

9. See for example Joseph Allen Boone, *The Homoerotics of Orientalism* (New York: Columbia University Press, 2014).

10. I'm grateful to Michael Feinstein for making me aware of Kerchner's contribution. See Rob Lester, "*The Wiz* and *Finding Neverland*: Inspired by Baum, Barrie and Believing," Sound Advice, *Talkin' Broadway*, n.d., 2016, https://talkinbroadway.com/sources/sound/january0816.html, accessed September 15, 2020; "Bio," *Larry Kerchner*, http://www.larrykerchner.com/bio.htm, accessed September 15, 2020.

11. La Donna L. Forsgren, "*The Wiz* Redux: or, Why Queer Black Feminist Spectatorship and Politically Engaged Popular Entertainment Continue to Matter," *Theatre Survey* 60, no. 3 (2019): 325–354; Wolf, *Changed for Good*, 111–117. See also Rhonda Williams, "*The Wiz*: American Culture at Its Best," in *The Universe of Oz: Essays on Baum's Series and Its Progeny*, edited by Kevin Durand and Mary K. Leigh (Jefferson, NC: McFarland, 2010), 191–199.

12. Harper Papers, box 11, folder 6; Ted Ross (the Cowardly Lion) had been in the cast of *Raisin* (1973) and appeared on *The Jeffersons* (one episode in 1978); André De Shields (the Wiz) starred in *Ain't Misbehavin'* (1978); Mabel King (Evillene) starred in *What's Happening!* (1976–1978), and appeared on *The Jeffersons* (one episode in 1984); and Clarice Taylor (Addaperle) appeared on *Sanford and Son* (one episode in 1974), on *Sesame Street* (1977–1989), and in a recurring role as the Anna Huxtable on *The Cosby Show* (1985–1992).

13. William B. Collins, "Brown Is White; His Wiz Is Black," *Philadelphia Inquirer*, September 17, 1978, 1-H, 13-H, *The Wiz* Collection, Box 1, Folder 7, Schomburg Center for Research in Black Culture.

14. Collins, "Brown Is White; His Wiz Is Black," 13-H.

15. Barbara Lewis, "Hinton Battle Doing and Feeling," *New York Amsterdam News*, 27, 1976, D-8.

16. Henry Louis Gates Jr., *The Signifying Monkey* (Oxford and New York: Oxford University Press, 1988), xxii; Claudia Mitchell-Kernan, "Signifying, Loud-Talking and Marking," in *Signifyin(g), Sanctifyin', and Slam Dunking: A Reader in African American Expressive Culture*, ed. Gena Dagel Caponi (Amherst: University of Massachusetts Press, 1999), 309–330. My analysis of *The Wiz* as signifying act is further influenced by Guthrie Ramsey's discussion of the gospel album *Handel's Messiah: A Soulful Celebration* in *Race Music: Black Cultures from Bebop to Hip-Hop* (Berkeley, Los Angeles, and London: University of California Press, 2003), 194. On signifying in Black music, see also Samuel A. Floyd Jr., *The Power of Black Music: Interpreting Its History from Africa to the United States* (New York and Oxford: Oxford University Press, 1995), 7.

17. Jack Kroll, "*Oz* with Soul," *Newsweek*, January 20, 1975, 82.

18. Clive Barnes, "Stage: The Wiz (of Oz): Black Musical Shows Vitality and Style," *New York Times*, 6 January 1975, 32.

19. Rex Reed, "The Wiz," *New York Daily News*, January 12, 1975, Leisure section, 6.

20. Green, *The World of Musical Comedy*, 366; Wolf, *Changed for Good*, 114.

21. Wolf, 114.

22. "Special Editorial Part II: Now, It's the Drama Critics," *New Amsterdam News*, January 11, 1975.

23. Woll, *Black Musical Theatre* 263–265; Wolf, *Changed for Good*, 114–115.

24. Jessica Harris, "Another View: The Wiz Is Great," *Amsterdam News*, January 25, 1975.

25. Bryant Rollins, "Does *The Wiz* Say Something Extra to Blacks?" *New York Times*, December 28, 1975.

26. On the role of racialized media discourses in these narratives, see Alfred L. Martin Jr., "Blackbusting Hollywood: Racialized Media Reception, Failure, and *The Wiz* as Black Blockbuster," *JCMS: Journal of Cinema and Media Studies* 60, no. 2 (Winter 2021): 56–79.

27. On the film's importance to Black audiences and political commentary in relation to blaxploitation film, see Destiny Salter, "'Doomed as Cartoons Forever': Subjection and Liberation in Sidney Lumet's *The Wiz*." *Studies in Musical Theatre* 15, no. 2 (2021): 133–149.

28. J. Randy Taraborrelli, *Diana Ross: A Biography* (New York: Citadel, 2014), 313; See also Neil Earle, The Wonderful Wizard of Oz *in American Popular Culture: Uneasy in Eden* (Lewiston, NY: Edwin Mellen Press, 1993), 165, on many of these issues, including *The Wiz*'s "1970s pop psychological uplift."

29. William F. Brown and Charlie Smalls, *The Wiz*, libretto (1974; revised and rewritten, New York: Samuel French, 1979), 9.

30. See Ernest Leogrande, "On the Road to a New Oz," *Daily News*, June 4, 1974, 51; Bob Weinstein, "*The Wiz* Has Its Own Whiz," *Rolling Stone*, January 2, 1975; Marian McEvoy, "The 'Wiz' Kid," *Women's Wear Daily*, January 15, 1975; Earl Wilson, "Samplings of the Fan Mail," *LA Herald Examiner*, April 1, 1975; Frederick D. Murphy, "Broadway's Hottest Musical Hit: *The Wiz*, *Black Stars*, June 1975, 65; Earl Wilson, "Where the Yellow Brick Road Led," *New York Post*, January 9, 1976; "It's People Who Count," *Sky*, January 26, 1976, n.p. After leaving the show in 1977, Mills acknowledged having been seventeen at the beginning of *The Wiz* in Ivan Webster, "Two from *The Wiz*: Ease on Down the Cabaret Circuit," *Encore Americana and Worldwide News*, December 4, 1978, 30, and Earl Wilson, "The *Wiz* Kid Has Grown Up," *New York Post*, January 27, 1979.

31. Kim Garfield, "Stephanie Mills: *The Wiz* Kid," *Sunday Tennessean*, Young World, August 17, 1975, 18.

32. On the historical association between whiteness and innocence, see Robin Bernstein, *Racial Innocence: Performing American Childhood and Race from Slavery to Civil Rights* (New York: New York University Press, 2011), 20.

33. Nikki Grimes, "Portrait: Stephanie Mills," unidentified publication, *The Wiz* Collection, Box 2, Folder 2, Schomburg Center for Research in Black Culture.

34. Forsgren, "*The Wiz* Redux," 332, 338.

35. Tommy J. Curry, "When *The Wiz* Goes Black, Does It Ever Go Back?," in "*The Wizard of Oz" and Philosophy: Wicked Wisdom of the West*, ed. Randall E. Auxier and Phillip S. Seng (Chicago: Open Court, 2008), 64, 68

36. Forsgren, "*The Wiz* Redux," 341.

37. Aimee Meredith Cox, *Shapeshifters: Black Girls and the Choreography of Citizenship* (Durham, NC: Duke University Press, 2015).

38. Dexter Thomas, "Why Everyone's Saying 'Black Girls Are Magic,'" *Los Angeles Times*, September 8, 2015, https://www.latimes.com/nation/nationnow/la-na-nn-everyo nes-saying-black-girls-are-magic-20150909-htmlstory.html, accessed September 15, 2020; Linda Chavers, "Here's My Problem with #BlackGirlMagic," *Elle*, January 13, 2016, https://www.elle.com/life-love/a33180/why-i-dont-love-blackgirlmagic/, accessed September 15, 2020.

39. On communal participation in the performance of Blackness, see Kimberly W. Benston, *Performing Blackness: Enactments of African-American Modernism* (New York: Routledge, 2013), 28–31.

40. Marian McEvoy, "The 'Wiz' Kid," *Women's Wear Daily*, Wednesday, January 15, 1975, 26; The Wiz Fan, "Home—*The Wiz* on Broadway 1975 LIVE," YouTube video, 3:30, June 12, 2015, https://www.youtube.com/watch?v=0woXX_GssaM, accessed September 6, 2020.

41. Jacqueline Warwick, "You Can't Win Child, but You Can't Get Out of the Game: Michael Jackson's Transition from Child Star to Superstar," *Popular Music and Society* 35 (2012): 252.

42. See also Stacy Wolf's analysis of "the 'cool,' relaxed hipness of Black vernacular in the music, lyrics, and choreography of "Ease on Down the Road" in *Changed for Good*, 116.

43. Forsgren, "*The Wiz* Redux," 333–334, 341–342. See also Jesse Scott, "The Black Interior: Reparations and African American Masculinity in *The Wiz*," in *Pimps, Wimps, Studs, and Gentlemen: Essays on Media Images of Masculinity*, edited by Elwood Watson (Jefferson, NC: McFarland, 2009), Kindle edition, chapter 4, location 1000.

44. Forsgren, "*The Wiz* Redux," 338–339, 346.

45. Forsgren, 338–339, describes this barring of entry as evoking both housing discrimination and racist and sexist gatekeeping practices that came with the mainstreaming of disco.

46. Collins, "Brown Is White; His Wiz Is Black," 13-H.

47. An early script draft describes his makeup as Kabuki, just before he appears as a transvestite who, in a gag thankfully omitted, makes unwelcome eyes at the Scarecrow. William F. Brown, "The Wiz of Oz" script sent to Mervyn LeRoy, Mervyn LeRoy Papers, Margaret Herrick Library, Academy of Motion Picture Arts and Sciences, Beverly Hills, CA.

48. Webster, "Two from *The Wiz*," 29.

49. Vito Russo, "New York's 'Wiz': Mr. De Shields Is from Mars," unidentified clipping, *The Wiz* Collection, Schomburg Center for Research in Black Culture.

50. Forsgren, "*The Wiz* Redux," 334–336.

51. Stacy Wolf, *A Problem Like Maria: Gender and Sexuality in the American Musical* (Ann Arbor: University of Michigan Press, 2002), 19–20; Forsgren, "*The Wiz* Redux," 338.

52. Brown and Smalls, *The Wiz*, libretto, 87.

53. Richard Pryor, however, could sing. Thanks to Sandra Kilman for pointing this out to me. See Chef Eric, "Richard Pryor Sings the Blues," *YouTube* video, 2:23, December, 21, 2012, https://www.youtube.com/watch?v=rUor_H7tGhQ&feature=youtu.be, accessed September 15, 2020.

54. Forsgren, "*The Wiz* Redux," 342.

55. Brown and Smalls, *The Wiz*, libretto, 89–90.

56. Noel Langley, Florence Ryerson, and Edgar Allan Woolf, *The Wizard of Oz: The Screenplay*, ed. Michael Patrick Hearn (New York: Delta, 1989), 128.

57. Meghann Meeusen, "The Difficulty in Deciphering the 'Dreams That You Dare to Dream': Adaptive Dissonance in *Wizard of Oz* Films," *Children's Literature Association Quarterly* 42, no. 2 (2017): 191–193.

58. Jeff Johnson, "Essay: *The Wiz* Is Pure Black Excellence," *NBC News*, December 3, 2015, https://www.nbcnews.com/news/nbcblk/essay-wiz-pure-black-excellence-n471586; Forsgren, "*The Wiz* Redux," 325; Curry, "When *The Wiz* Goes Black, Does It Ever Go Back?," 63.

59. For one example of White gay male fandom for *The Wiz*, see Patrick E. Horrigan, *Widescreen Dreams: Growing Up Gay at the Movies* (Madison: University of Wisconsin Press, 1999), 139–176.

60. Ryan Bunch, "'You Can't Stop the Tweet': Social Media and Networks of Participation in the Live Television Musical," in *iBroadway: Musical Theatre in the Digital Age*, ed. Jessica Hillman-McCord (New York: Palgrave Macmillan, 2017), 187–193; Forsgren, "*The Wiz* Redux," 344–350.

61. Forsgren, 330.

62. Bunch, "'You Can't Stop the Tweet,'"193; Forsgren, "*The Wiz* Redux," 344.

63. For another account of a production of *The Wiz* speaking to violence against Black people, but in a more conservative community, see Allison Gibbes, "How Do You Solve a Problem Like Institutional Racism? Producing *The Wiz* in Hostile Territory," *Theatre/Practice: The Online Journal of the Practice/Production Symposium of the Mid America Theatre Conference* 7 (2018), chrome-extension://efaidnbmnnnibpcajpcglcl efindmkaj/http://theatrepractice.us/pdfs/Gibbes_How%20Do%20You%20Solve%20 a%20Problem%20Like%20Institutional%20Racism.pdf, accessed May 16, 2022.

Chapter 4

1. Aljean Harmetz, *The Making of "The Wizard of Oz"* (New York: Alfred A. Knopf, 1977), 127–129, 178–181, 272–274; Jay Scarfone and William Stillman, *The Road to Oz: The Evolution, Creation, and Legacy of a Motion Picture Masterpiece* (Guilford, CT: Rowman and Littlefield, 2019), Kindle edition, location 4792.

2. On waters, see Robert K. Elder, *The Film That Changed My Life: 30 Directors on Their Epiphanies in the Dark* (Chicago: Chicago Review Press, 2011), 278–282.

3. David Cote, Joan Marcus, and Stephen Schwartz, *Wicked: The Grimmerie* (New York: Hyperion Books, 2004), 20–21; Carol de Giere, *Defying Gravity: The Creative Career of Stephen Schwartz from "Godspell" to "Wicked"* (New York: Hal Leonard, 2008), 273, 291); for more on *Wicked* the musical, see Paul R. Laird, *Wicked: A Musical Biography* (Lanham, MD: Scarecrow Press, 2011); and Kent Drummond, Susan Aronstein, and Terri L. Rittenburg, *The Road to "Wicked": The Marketing and Consumption of Oz from L. Frank Baum to Broadway* (New York: Palgrave Macmillan, 2008).

4. Jake Johnson, *Lying in the Middle: Musical Theater and Belief at the Heart of America* (Urbana: University of Illinois Press, 2021), Kindle edition, location 181. Alberto Mira observes a general ambivalence toward utopia in pop musicals of the postclassical era in film musicals, including a recognition that "some people's utopias arise out of somebody else's oppression," in *The Pop Musical: Sweat, Tears, and Tarnished Utopias* (New York: Columbia University Press, 2021), Kindle edition, location 414.

5. Anthony D'Alesandro, "Universal Releasing *Wicked* Musical in Two Parts," *Deadline*, April 26, 2022, https://deadline.com/2022/04/wicked-universal-two-part-release-1235010059/, accessed May 19, 2022.

6. Jessica Sternfeld, *The Megamusical* (Bloomington: Indiana University Press, 2006), 349.

7. Sternfeld, 1–7.

8. Stacy Wolf, *Changed for Good: A Feminist History of the Broadway Musical* (Oxford: Oxford University Press, 2011), 127–130.

9. Wolf, 200, 203; Alex Bádue provides a thorough discussion of the dramaturgical implications of sung-through musicals in *"Why Aren't They Talking? The Sung-through Musical from the 1980s to the 2010s* (Cambridge: Cambridge University Press, 2022).

10. On *Wicked*'s appeal to young women, see Wolf, *Changed for Good*, 219–236. On the young adult musical, see James Leve and Donelle Ruwe, eds., *Children, Childhood, and Musical Theatre* (New York: Routledge, 2020), 4, 8–9.

11. See Rachel Moseley, "Glamorous Witchcraft: Gender and Magic in Teen Film and Television," *Screen* 43, no. 4 (2002): 403–422 on witches and luminous aesthetics in popular culture. On the dominant Whiteness of many girls' stories, see Gayle Wald, "Clueless in the Neocolonial World Order," in *Sugar, Spice, and Everything Nice: Cinemas of Girlhood*, ed. Frances Gateward and Murray Pomerance (Detroit: Wayne State University Press, 2002), 103–123.

12. On the externalization of girls' stories in music, see Robynn Stilwell, "Listen to the Mockingjay: Voice, Identity, and Agency in *The Hunger Games* Trilogy," in *Voicing Girlhood in Popular Music: Performance, Authority, Authenticity*, edited by Jacqueline Warwick and Allison Adrian (New York: Routledge, 2016), 261–262, 267–268.

13. Cote, Marcus, and Schwartz, *Wicked*, 19–20.

14. Ben Brantley, "There's Trouble in Emerald City," *New York Times*, October 31, 2003, https://www.nytimes.com/2003/10/31/movies/theater-review-there-s-trouble-in-emerald-city.html, accessed January 14, 2020.

15. Cote, Marcus, and Schwartz, *Wicked*, 36; Wolf, *Changed for Good*, 204–205.

16. Michelle Dvoskin, "Audiences and Critics," in *The Oxford Handbook of the American Musical*, ed. Raymond Knapp, Mitchell Morris, and Stacy Wolf (New York: Oxford University Press, 2011), 374–376; Drummond, Aronstein, and Wittenburg, *The Road to "Wicked,"* 162.

17. John Lahr, "Bitches and Witches: Ulterior Motives in *Cat on a Hot Tin Roof* and *Wicked*," *New Yorker*, November 3, 2003 (print issue, November 10, 2003), https://www.newyorker.com/magazine/2003/11/10/bitches-and-witches, accessed February 15, 2020.

18. Brantley, "There's Trouble in Emerald City."

19. On the marginalization of girls' cultures, including music and musicals, see Wolf, *Changed for Good*, 221–222; Angela McRobbie, *Feminism and Youth Culture: From "Jackie" to "Just Seventeen"* (New York: Macmillan, 1990), 12.

20. Wolf, *Changed for Good*, 205.

21. Wolf, 197–218.

22. Jessica Sternfeld, "'Pitiful Creature of Darkness': The Subhuman and the Superhuman in *The Phantom of the Opera*," in *The Oxford Handbook of Music and Disability Studies*, ed. Blake Howe, Stephanie Jensen-Moulton, Neil Lerner, and Joseph Straus (New York: Oxford University Press, 2016), 795.

23. De Giere, *Defying Gravity*, 275.

24. "*Wicked* Celebrates 15 Years with New Show Clips," *Broadway.com*, October 25, 2018, https://www.broadway.com/videos/158938/wicked-celebrates-15-years-with-new-show-clips/, accessed September 8, 2020.

25. See Laird, *Wicked*, 129; and De Giere, *Defying Gravity*, 318–319, on Glinda's public *bel canto*.

26. Michael Phillips, "Brick Road Leads to Mediocre Musicals," *Chicago Tribune*, November 2, 2003, Section 7 (Arts and Entertainment), 17; on girl power, see Dawn Currie, Deirdre M. Kelly, and Shauna Pomerantz, *"Girl Power": Girls*

Reinventing Girlhood (New York: Peter Lang, 2009); and Mary Celeste Kearney, "Sparkle: Luminosity and Post-Girl Power Media," *Continuum* 29, no. 2 (2015): 263–273.

27. Kearney, "Sparkle: Luminosity and Post–Girl Power Media," 263–273.

28. Wolf, *Changed for Good*, 224.

29. Drummond, Aronstein and Wittenburg, *The Road to "Wicked,"* 172–174.

30. Michelle Boyd, "Alto on a Broomstick: Voicing the Witch in the Musical *Wicked*," *American Music* 28 (2010), no. 1: 99.

31. Idina Menzel News, Twitter post, June 10, 2018, 12:40 PM, https://twitter.com/idin amenzelnews/status/1005852300320165888

32. De Giere, *Defying Gravity*, 304–305; Laird, *Wicked*, 128.

33. Wolf, *Changed for Good*, 207.

34. Rebecca K. Hammonds shows how Elphaba's difference as a bookish heroine influences the dynamics of her relationships with her mentors and the particulars of her "I want" song in "(Un)Limited: The Influence of Mentorship and Father–Daughter Relationships on Elphaba's Heroine Journey in *Wicked*," *Theatre History Studies* 40 (2021): 157–171.

35. Wolf, *Changed for Good*, 197–198, 208–209.

36. Steven Greenwood, "'Say There's No Future': The Queer Potential of *Wicked*'s Fiyero," *Studies in Musical Theatre* 12, no. 3 (2018), 305–317.

37. Cote, Marcus, and Schwartz, *Wicked*, 78–79; De Giere, *Defying Gravity*, 309–310.

38. Jacqueline Warwick, *Girl Groups, Girl Culture: Popular Music and Identity in the 1960s* (New York: Routledge, 2007), 39–42.

39. Laird, *Wicked*, 199; Boyd, "Alto on a Broomstick, 107; Wolf, *Changed for Good,* 3, 212; Kelsey Blair, "Broomsticks and Barricades: Performance, Empowerment, and Feeling in *Wicked* and *Les Misérables*." *Studies in Musical Theatre* 10, no. 1 (2016), 55–67.

40. Stacy Wolf, *Changed for Good*, 3–4, identifies this as the moment when the show becomes Elphaba's, that is, when it belongs to the star.

41. See Wolf, 225–226, on girl fans' interpretations of this vocalization.

42. Wolf, 205; Ann M. Fox, "Scene in a New Light: Monstrous Mothers, Disabled Daughters, and the Performance of Feminism and Disability in *The Light in the Piazza* (2005) and *Next to Normal* (2008)," in Howe, Jensen-Moulton, Lerner, and Straus, *The Oxford Handbook of Music and Disability Studies,* 776.

43. Doris Raab, "From Book to Broadway: Elphaba's Gender Ambiguity and Her Journey into Heteronormativity in *Wicked*," *Studies in Musical Theatre*, 5, no. 3 (2011), 250–252.

44. Wolf, *Changed for Good*, 216; Greenwood, "'Say There's No Future,'" 309.

45. Wolf, *Changed for Good*, 212–213.

46. Greenwood, "'Say There's No Future,'" 310.

47. Wolf, *Changed for Good*, 201.

48. Laird, *Wicked*, 166–167, 203–204, identifies this tritone as a tribute to Bernstein's score for *West Side Story* (1957) as well as a musical evocation of moral ambivalence.

49. On women's culture and intimate publics, see Lauren Berlant, *The Female Complaint: The Unfinished Business of Sentimentality in American Culture* (Durham, NC: Duke University Press, 2008).

50. Wolf, *Changed for Good*, 222.

51. *Glee*, "New York," directed by Brad Falchuk, aired on May 24, 2011 on Fox.

52. On Menzel's personality and persona, see Cote, Marcus, and Schwartz, *Wicked*, 26–28.

53. See Brantley, "There's Trouble in Emerald City," for example.

54. Stephen Banfield, "Stage and Screen Entertainers in the Twentieth Century," in *The Cambridge Companion to Singing*, edited by John Potter (New York: Cambridge University Press, 2000), 67.

55. Donatella Galella, *America in the Round: Capital Race, and Nation at Washington DC's Arena Stage* (Iowa City: University of Iowa Press, 2019). See also Brandi Wilkins Catanese, *The Problem of the Color[blind]: Racial Transgression and the Politics of Black Performance* (Ann Arbor: University of Michigan Press, 2011). British actress Alexia Khadime played Elphaba in the West End production, June–November 2008 and May 2009–March 2010. She remains the only Black actress to play Elphaba full-time. Saycon Sengbloh was the Elphaba standby for many years beginning in 2005.

56. ElphabaGoodman and replies, "Black Glinda," Broadway Message Board, *Broadway World* (June 5, 2018, 9:59 PM), https://www.broadwayworld.com/board/readmessage.php?thread=1110038, accessed October 25, 2020.

57. Ruthie Fierberg, "Inside Brittney Johnson's Whirlwind Experience Going on as *Wicked*'s First Glinda of Color," *Playbill*, January 11, 2019, https://www.playbill.com/article/inside-brittney-johnsons-whirlwind-experience-going-on-as-wickeds-first-glinda-of-color, accessed October 25, 2020.

58. Ellise Shafer and Matt Donnelly, "Ariana Grande and Cynthia Erivo to Star in *Wicked* Musical for Universal," *Variety*, November 4, 2021, https://variety.com/2021/film/news/ariana-grande-cynthia-erivo-wicked-musical-universal-1235105480/, accessed May 19, 2022.

59. Wolf, *Changed for Good*, 13.

60. David Savran, "Trafficking in Transnational Brands: The New 'Broadway-Style' Musical," *Theatre Survey* 55, no. 3 (2014): 318–342.

61. Laura MacDonald and Myrte Halman, "Geen Grenzen Meer: An American Musical's Unlimited Border Crossing," *Theatre Research International* 39, no. 3 (2014): 198–216.

62. See Drummond, Aronstein, and Rittenburg, *The Road to Wicked*, 235–240, on "Behind the Emerald Curtain."

Chapter 5

1. *The Wizard of Oz: 50th Anniversary Edition*, VHS, directed by Victor Fleming (Culver City, CA: MGM/UA, 1989).

2. Alexander Doty, *Flaming Classics: Queering the Film Canon* (New York: Routledge, 2002), 54–55.

3. Peter Galvin, "A Wizard with Words," *The Advocate*, October 17, 1995, 56; quoted in Dee Michel, *Friends of Dorothy: Why Gay Men and Gay Boys Love "The Wizard of Oz"* (USA: Dark Ink Press, 2018), chapter 4, Kindle location 1216.

4. On the television broadcasts, see Annah E. MacKenzie, "From Screen to Shining Screen: *The Wizard of Oz* in the Age of Mechanical Reproduction," in *The Fantastic Made Visible: Essays on the Adaptation of Science Fiction and Fantasy from Page to Screen*, ed. Matthew Wilhelm Kapell and Ace G. Pilkington (Jefferson, NC: McFarland, 2015), 181–183, 186, and 193. See also on the television broadcasts John Fricke, Jay Scarfone, and William Stillma, *The Wizard of Oz: The Official 50th Anniversary Pictorial History* (New York: Warner Books, 1989), 213–222; MacKenzie, "From Screen to Shining Screen," 175–191; Kent Drummond, Susan Aronstein, and Terri L. Rittenburg, *The Road to "Wicked": The Marketing and Consumption of Oz from L. Frank Baum to Broadway* (London: Palgrave, 2018), 105–112.

5. In this chapter, I use pseudonyms for people who agreed to be interviewed about their experiences.

6. Michel, *Friends of Dorothy*, chapter 4, Kindle location 1264.

7. Michel, chapter 4, location 1271.

8. Gregory Maguire, "Foreword" to Michel, *Friends of Dorothy*, Kindle edition, location 169.

9. Ingeborg Lunde Vestad, "To Play a Soundtrack: How Children Use Recorded Music in Their Everyday Lives," *Music Education Research 12*, no. 3 (2010): 243–255.

10. *The Wizard of Oz: Sing-Along Edition*, Blu-Ray and DVD, Warner Brothers, 1939, November 2, 2009, UK.

11. On the relationship between fairy tales and children's material culture, see Meredith Bak, "Material Culture (Fairy-Tale Things: Studying Fairy Tales From a Material Culture Perspective)," in *The Routledge Companion to Media and Fairy-Tale Cultures*, ed. Pauline Greenhill, Jill Terry Rudy, Naomi Hamer, and Lauren Bosc (New York: Routledge, 2018), 328–336.

12. Stacy Wolf, *Beyond Broadway: The Pleasure and Promise of Musical Theatre across America* (New York: Oxford University Press, 2019).

13. The results of the Educational Theater Association's annual Play Survey are published periodically in *Dramatics* magazine. A summary of these results since the 1960s is available at Elissa Nadworny, "The Most Popular High School Plays and Musicals," *NPR*, July 31, 2019, https://www.npr.org/sections/ed/2019/07/31/427138970/the-most-popular-high-school-plays-and-musicals, accessed December 15, 2019.

14. Idina Menzel News, Twitter post, June 10, 2018, 12:40 PM, https://twitter.com/idinamenzelnews/status/1005852300320165888; Aljean Harmetz, *The Making of "The Wizard of Oz"* (New York: Alfred A. Knopf, 1977), 124.

15. Kristin Bell, Twitter post, December 10, 2017, 6:23 PM, https://twitter.com/IMKristenBell/status/939999103546560512.

16. On the MUNY *Wizard*, see Dominic McHugh, "'We're Not in Kansas Anymore': Three Stage Adaptations of the MGM Film," in *Adapting "The Wizard of Oz": Musical Versions from Baum to MGM and Beyond*, ed. Danielle Birkett and Dominic McHugh, (New York: Oxford University Press, 2019), 161–182.

17. Amy Poehler, *Yes Please* (New York: HarperCollins, 2014), Kindle edition, location 182.

18. I borrow this phrase from Stacy Wolf's description of the *Wicked* divas in *Changed for Good: A Feminist History of the Broadway Musical* (New York: Oxford University Press, 2011), 220.

19. "Danielle Hope Wins *Over the Rainbow*," *The Telegraph*, May 22, 2010, https://www.telegraph.co.uk/culture/tvandradio/7754683/Danielle-Hope-wins-Over-the-Rainbow.html, accessed March 7, 2020; David Morgan, "Danielle Hope Reaches Semi-Final of BBC's *Over the Rainbow* Competition," *Knutsford Guardian*, May 12, 2010, https://www.knutsfordguardian.co.uk/news/8161077.danielle-hope-reaches-semi-final-of-bbcs-over-the-rainbow-competition/, accessed March 7, 2020.

20. Cynthia Littleton, "*The Wiz* Star Shanice Williams on her 'Amazing' Journey to Oz," *Variety*, November 19, 2015, http://variety.com/2015/tv/features/the-wiz-shanice-williams-1201644220/, accessed August 28, 2020.

21. Angela E. Smith, "If You Can Do Broadway—You Can Do Anything!" *Amsterdam News*, Saturday, January 24, 1976, D-20; Joyce Wadler, "Pint-Sized Star," *New York Post*, February 7, 1975, 27; Marian McEvoy, "The 'Wiz' Kid," *Women's Wear Daily*, January 15, 1975; Didier Delaunoy, "Stephanie Mills," *Soul*, July 7, 1975, 6. These and other articles on Mills are in the Schomburg Center for Research in Black Culture, *The Wiz* Collection, Box 2, Folder 2.

22. Diane Pecknold, "'These Stupid Little Sounds in Her Voice': Valuing and Vilifying the New Girl Voice," in *Voicing Girlhood in Popular Music: Performance, Authority, Authenticity*, ed. Jacqueline Warwick and Allison Adrian (New York: Routledge, 2016), 77–98; Jacqueline Warwick, "Urchins and Angels: Little Orphan Annie and Clichés of Child Singers," in *Gender, Age, and Musical Creativity*, ed. Catherine Haworth and Lisa Colton (New York: Taylor and Francis, 2016), 129–140.

23. "Rufus Wainwright, 23, Musician," Generation Q: The Arts, *The Advocate*, no. 739/740 (August 19, 1997), 36, quoted in Michel, *Friends of Dorothy*, Kindle Locations 3840–3841.

24. Donatella Galella, *America in the Round: Capital, Race, and Nation at Washington DC's Arena Stage* (Iowa City: University of Iowa Press, 2019), 200–201; See also Brandi W. Catanese, *The Problem of the Color[blind]: Racial Transgression and the Politics of Black Performance* (Ann Arbor: University of Michigan Press, 2011).

25. On keeping *The Wiz* all-Black for similar reasons, see Bob Weinstein, "*The Wiz* Has Its Own Whiz," *Rolling Stone*, January 2, 1975.

26. In pantomime tradition, the Wicked Witch was also played by a man in the production by the Royal Shakespeare Company. See McHugh, "'We're Not in Kansas Anymore,'" 165.

27. John Kane, *The Wizard of Oz* (New York: Tams-Witmark Music Library, 1987), 81, 116–17.

28. "Teen in Wheelchair and Service Dog Star as Dorothy and Toto in School's *Wizard of Oz* Production," *Inside Edition*, https://www.insideedition.com/teen-wheelchair-and-service-dog-star-dorothy-and-toto-schools-wizard-oz-production-52050#:~:text=In%20one%20New%20Jersey%20high,at%20Hasbrouck%20Heights%20High%20School, accessed October 9, 2020.

29. On gay discomfort with the Lion, see Michel, *Friends of Dorothy*, chapter 5, Kindle location 1789; Doty, *Flaming Classics*, 49–50.

30. Jeff Kenney, *Diary of a Wimpy Kid* (London: Puffin, 2008), 95–113.

31. Oz sing-alongs followed the vogue for sing-along screenings of *The Sound of Music* (1965) and participatory screenings of *The Rocky Horror Picture Show* (1975). On *Sound of Music* sing-alongs, see Samuel Baltimore, "'Do it Again': Comic Repetition, Participatory Reception and Gendered Identity on Musical Comedy's Margins," PhD dissertation, University of California, 2013, and "Camping Out: Queer Communities and Public Sing-Alongs," in *Music and Camp*, edited by Christopher Moore and Philip Purvis (Middletown, CT: Wesleyan University Press, 2018), 118–136.

32. Michel, *Friends of Dorothy*, chapter 10, Kindle location 3012.

33. Dina Schiff Massachi, "Somewhere on Top of a Mountain: A Real Journey to Oz," in *Storybook Worlds Made Real: Essays on the Places Inspired by Children's Narratives*, edited by Mark I. West and Kathy Merlock Jackson (Jefferson, NC: McFarland, 2022). Details about the park and its history are from Tim Hollis, *The Land of Oz* (Charleston, SC: Arcadia Publishing, 2016).

34. Land of Oz, North Carolina, https://www.landofoznc.com/, accessed September 10, 2020.

35. Dan Bacalzo, "Photo Flash: Andre De Shields, Gregory Maguire at Oz-Stravaganza," *TheaterMania*, June 13, 2012, https://www.theatermania.com/new-york-city-theater/news/photo-flash-andre-de-shields-gregory-maguire-at-oz_58250.html, accessed August 28, 2020; *Oz-Stravaganza!*, http://www.oz-stravaganza.com/, accessed August 28, 2020.

36. Allie Healy, "From the Archives: The Oz Author's Newspaper Editorials Urged Annihilation of Native Americans," *Syracuse.com*, February 8, 2015, updated March 22, 2019, https://www.syracuse.com/news/2015/02/from_the_archives_the_oz_authors_newspaper_editorials_urged_annihilation_of_nati.html.

37. *Oz-Stravaganza!* website; Ernestine Chasing Hawk, "Oneida Nation Honors Man Who Called for Genocide of Sioux Nation," *Native Times*, December 29, 2014, https://www.nativetimes.com/index.php/life/commentary/10957-oneida-nation-honors-man-who-called-for-genocide-of-sioux-nation, accessed September 17, 2020; Allie Healy, "Report: Oneida Indian Nation to Build 'Oz' Casino Despite CNY Author Baum's Hate Speech," *Syracuse.com*, February 8, 2015, https://www.syracuse.com/news/2015/02/report_oneida_indian_nation_to_build_oz_casino_despite_cny_author_baums_hate_spe.html, accessed September 17, 2020.

Epilogue

1. Stacy Wolf, "Hamilton's Women," in "*Hamilton* as Cultural Phenomenon," special issue, edited by Peter Kunze, *Studies in Musical Theatre* 12, no. 2 (2018): 167–180. Further critical engagements with *Hamilton* are in the same special issue; in Charles Hiroshi Garrett, ed., "*Hamilton* Forum," special issue, *American Music* 36, no. 4 (2018), and in Mary Jo Lodge and Paul R. Laird, eds., *Dueling Grounds: Revolution and Revelation in the Musical Hamilton* (New York: Oxford University Press, 2021).

2. *Harper's Weekly*, October 6, 1906, front cover, Hearst Caricatures Collection, California Polytechnic State University, San Luis Obispo, MS 069, Box 3, https://digital.lib.calpoly.edu/rekl-28424, accessed July 31, 2020.

3. Sean Trainor, "Donald Trump, the Greatest Show on Earth: He's the Second Coming of P.T. Barnum, Not the Next Reagan," *Salon*, September 18, 2015, https://www.salon.com/2015/09/18/donald_trump_the_greatest_show_on_earth_hes_the_second_coming_of_p_t_barnum_not_the_next_reagan/, accessed August 3, 2020; Jason Silverstein, "Donald Trump Embraces Comparisons to P.T. Barnum, Says America Needs a 'Cheerleader,'" *New York Daily News*, January 11, 2016, https://www.nydailynews.com/news/election/donald-trump-embraces-comparisons-p-t-barnum-article-1.2491619, accessed August 19, 2020; Thomas Bender, "No Humbug: Striking Similarities between Trump and P.T. Barnum," *Reuters*, April 3, 2016; https://www.reuters.com/article/idUS41170939820160403/, accessed August 19, 2020; Suzanne Lynch, "America Letter: Trump a Masterclass in Humbug," *Irish Times*, March 18, 2017, https://www.irishtimes.com/news/world/us/america-letter-trump-a-masterclass-in-humbug-1.3014883, accessed August 19, 2020; Jennifer Mercieca, "Hyperbole and Humbug in P.T. Barnum's World," *Baltimore Sun*, November 8, 2017, https://www.baltimoresun.com/opinion/op-ed/bs-ed-op-1109-barnum-hyperbole-20171108-story.html, accessed August 19, 2020; James Warren, "What Donald Trump and P.T. Barnum Have in Common," *Vanity Fair*, November 10, 2017, https://www.vanityfair.com/news/2017/11/what-donald-trump-and-pt-barnum-have-in-common, accessed August 19, 2020; Chris Gavaler and Nathaniel Goldberg, "Beyond Bullshit: Donald Trump's Philosophy of Language," *Philosophy Now*, n.d., 2017, https://philosophynow.org/issues/121/Beyond_Bullshit_Donald_Trumps_Philosophy_of_Language, accessed August 19, 2020; Stephen Mihm, "No, Trump Is Not P.T. Barnum," *New York Times*, December 19, 2017, https://www.nytimes.com/2017/12/19/opinion/trump-barnum.html, accessed August 19, 2020.

4. Jill Dolan, *Utopia in Performance: Finding Hope at the Theater* (Ann Arbor: University of Michigan Press, 20015), 19.

Bibliography

Altman, Rick. *The American Film Musical*. Bloomington: Indiana University Press, 1987.

Attebery, Brian. *The Fantasy Tradition in American Literature: From Irving to LeGuin*. Bloomington: Indiana University Press, 1980.

Austin, John Langshaw. *How to Do Things with Words*. New York: Oxford University Press, 2011.

Bádue, Alex. *Why Aren't They Talking? The Sung-through Musical from the 1980s to the 2010s*. Cambridge: Cambridge University Press, 2022.

Bak, Meredith A. "The Ludic Archive: The Work of Playing with Optical Toys." *Moving Image: The Journal of the Association of Moving Image Archivists* 16, no. 1 (2016): 1–16.

Bak, Meredith A. "Material Culture (Fairy-Tale Things: Studying Fairy Tales from a Material Culture Perspective.)" In *The Routledge Companion to Media and Fairy-Tale Cultures*, edited by Pauline Greenhill, Jill Terry Rudy, Naomi Hamer, and Lauren Bosc, 328–336. New York: Routledge, 2018.

Baltimore, Samuel. "'Do It Again': Comic Repetition, Participatory Reception and Gendered Identity on Musical Comedy's Margins." PhD diss., University of California, 2013.

Baum, Frank J., and Russel P. MacFall, *To Please a Child: A Biography of L. Frank Baum, Royal Historian of Oz*. Chicago: Reilly and Lee, 1961.

Baum, L. Frank. *The Wonderful Wizard of Oz*. Chicago: George M. Hill, 1900.

Benshoff, Harry M., and Sean Griffin. *Queer Images: A History of Gay and Lesbian Film in America*. Lanham, MD: Rowman and Littlefield, 2006.

Berlant, Lauren. *The Female Complaint: The Unfinished Business of Sentimentality in American Culture*. Durham, NC: Duke University Press, 2008.

Bernstein, Robin. *Racial Innocence: Performing American Childhood and Race from Slavery to Civil Rights*. New York: New York University Press, 2011.

Bernstein, Robin. "Toys Are Good for Us: Why We Should Embrace the Historical Integration of Children's Literature, Material Culture, and Play." *Children's Literature Association Quarterly* 38, no. 4 (2013): 458–463.

Bial, Henry. *Acting Jewish: Negotiating Ethnicity on the American Stage and Screen*. Ann Arbor: University of Michigan Press, 2005.

Birkett, Danielle, and Dominic McHugh, eds. *Adapting "The Wizard of Oz": From Baum to MGM and Beyond*. Oxford and New York: Oxford University Press, 2019.

Blair, Kelsey. "Broomsticks and Barricades: Performance, Empowerment, and Feeling in *Wicked* and *Les Misérables*." *Studies in Musical Theatre* 10, no. 1 (2016): 55–67.

Boon, James A. "Showbiz as a Cross-Cultural System: Circus and Song, Garland and Geertz, Rushdie, Mordden, . . . and More." *Cultural Anthropology* 15, no. 3 (2000): 424–456.

Boyd, Michelle "Alto on a Broomstick: Voicing the Witch in the Musical *Wicked*." *American Music* 28, no. 1 (2010): 97–118.

Boym, Svetlana. *The Future of Nostalgia*. New York: Basic Books, 2001.

Brown, Noel. *The Children's Film: Genre, Nation, and Narrative*. New York: Columbia University Press, 2017.

Brown, Noel. *The Hollywood Family Film: A History, from Shirley Temple to Harry Potter.* New York: IB Tauris, 2012.

Brown, Noel, and Bruce Babington. *Family Films in Global Cinema: The World beyond Disney.* New York: IB Tauris, 2015.

Brown, William F., and Charlie Smalls. *The Wiz.* Libretto. New York: Samuel French, 1979.

Bunch, Ryan. "Oz and the Musical: The American Art Form and the Reinvention of the American Fairy Tale." *Studies in Musical Theatre* 9 (2015): 53–69.

Bunch, Ryan. "'You Can't Stop the Tweet': Social Media and Networks of Participation in the Live Television Musical." In *iBroadway: Musical Theatre in the Digital Age*, edited by Jessica Hillman-McCord, 173–205. New York: Palgrave Macmillan, 2017.

Bunch, Ryan. "'Ease on Down the Road': Black Routes and the Soul of *The Wiz.*" In *Adapting "The Wizard of Oz": Musical Versions from Baum to MGM and Beyond*, edited by Danielle Birkett and Dominic McHugh, 183–204. New York: Oxford University Press, 2018.

Burger, Alissa. *"The Wizard of Oz" as American Myth: A Critical Study of Six Versions of the Story, 1900–2007.* Jefferson, NC: McFarland, 2012.

Butler, Judith. *Gender Trouble.* 2nd ed. New York: Routledge, 1999.

Cantu, Maya. *American Cinderellas on the Broadway Musical Stage: Imagining the Working Girl from "Irene" to "Gypsy."* London: Palgrave Macmillan, 2015.

Carlson, Marvin. *The Haunted Stage: The Theatre as Memory Machine.* Ann Arbor: University of Michigan Press, 2003.

Catanese, Brandi Wilkins. *The Problem of the Color[blind]: Racial Transgression and the Politics of Black Performance.* Ann Arbor: University of Michigan Press, 2011.

Chaston, Joel D. "The 'Ozification' of American Children's Fantasy Films: *The Blue Bird*, *Alice in Wonderland*, and *Jumanji.*" *Children's Literature Association Quarterly* 22, no. 1 (1997): 13–20.

Chaston, Joel D. "Baum, Bakhtin, and Broadway: A Centennial Look at the Carnival of Oz." *The Lion and the Unicorn* 25, no. 1 (February 1, 2001): 128–149.

Clum, John M. *Something for the Boys: Musical Theater and Gay Culture.* New York: St. Martin's Press, 1999.

Cohan, Steven. *Incongruous Entertainment: Camp, Cultural Value, and the MGM Musical.* Durham, NC: Duke University Press, 2005.

Cohan, Steven., ed. *The Sound of Musicals.* New York: Palgrave Macmillan, 2010.

Cote, David, Joan Marcus, and Stephen Schwartz. *Wicked: The Grimmerie.* New York: Hyperion Books, 2005.

Cox, Aimee Meredith. *Shapeshifters: Black Girls and the Choreography of Citizenship.* Durham, NC: Duke University Press, 2015.

Craft, Elizabeth Titrington. "Becoming American Onstage: Broadway Narratives of Immigrant Experiences in the United States." PhD diss., Harvard University, 2014.

Culver, Stuart. "What Manikins Want: *The Wonderful Wizard of Oz* and *The Art of Decorating Dry Goods Windows*" *Representations* 21 (Winter 1988): 97–116.

Curry, Tommy J. "When *The Wiz* Goes Black, Does It Ever Go Back?" In *"The Wizard of Oz" and Philosophy: Wicked Wisdom of the West*, edited by Randall E. Auxier and Phillip S. Seng, 63–78. Chicago: Open Court, 2008.

De Giere, Carol. *Defying Gravity: The Creative Career of Stephen Schwartz from "Godspell" to "Wicked."* New York: Hal Leonard, 2008.

Deloria, Philip Joseph. *Playing Indian.* New Haven, CT: Yale University Press, 1998.

Dolan, Jill. *Utopia in Performance: Finding Hope at the Theater.* Ann Arbor: University of Michigan Press, 2010.

Drummond, Kent, Susan Aronstein, and Terri L. Rittenburg. *The Road to "Wicked": The Marketing and Consumption of Oz from L. Frank Baum to Broadway*. New York: Palgrave Macmillan, 2008.

Du Bois, W. E. B. *The Souls of Black Folk*. 1903. Reprint, New York: Dover, 1994.

Dvoskin, Michelle. "Audiences and Critics." In *The Oxford Handbook of the American Musical*, edited by Raymond Knapp, Mitchell Morris, and Stacy Wolf, 374–376. New York: Oxford University Press, 2011.

Dyer, Richard. *Heavenly Bodies: Film Stars and Society*. New York: Routledge, 2013.

Dyer, Richard. *Only Entertainment*. New York: Routledge, 2005.

Earle, Neil. *"The Wonderful Wizard of Oz" in American Popular Culture: Uneasy in Eden*. Lewiston: Edwin Mellen Press, 1993.

Ellis, Sarah Taylor. "'No Day But Today': Queer Temporality in *Rent*." *Studies in Musical Theatre* 5, no. 2 (2011): 195–207.

Eyler, Joshua R. "Disability and Prosthesis in L. Frank Baum's *The Wonderful Wizard of Oz*." *Children's Literature Association Quarterly* 38 (Fall 2013): 319–334.

Feuer, Jane. *The Hollywood Musical*. Bloomington: Indiana University Press, 1993.

Fields, Armond. *Fred Stone: Circus Performer and Musical Comedy Star*. Jefferson, NC: McFarland, 2002.

Floyd, Samuel A., Jr. *The Power of Black Music: Interpreting Its History from Africa to the United States*. New York: Oxford University Press, 1996.

Flynn, Richard. "Imitation Oz: The Sequel as Commodity." *The Lion and the Unicorn* 20, no. 1 (1996): 121–131.

Ford, Fiona. "Be It [N]ever So Humble? The Narrating Voice in the Underscore to *The Wizard of Oz*." In *Melodramatic Voices: Understanding Music Drama*, edited by Sarah Hibberd, 197–214. New York: Taylor and Francis, 2011.

Forsgren, La Donna L. "*The Wiz* Redux; or, Why Queer Black Feminist Spectatorship and Politically Engaged Popular Entertainment Continue to Matter." *Theatre Survey* 60, no. 3 (2019): 325–354.

Fricke, John, Jay Scarfone, and William Stillman. *"The Wizard of Oz": The Official 50th Anniversary Pictorial History*. New York: Warner Books, 1989.

Frisch, Walter. *Arlen and Harburg's "Over the Rainbow."* New York: Oxford University Press, 2017.

Gabler, Neal. *An Empire of Their Own: How the Jews Invented Hollywood*. New York: Anchor Books, 1989.

Galella, Donatella. *America in the Round: Capital, Race, and Nation at Washington DC's Arena Stage*. Iowa City: University of Iowa Press, 2019.

Gates, Henry Louis. *The Signifying Monkey: A Theory of African-American Literary Criticism*, New York and Oxford: Oxford University Press, 1988.

Gibbes, Allison. "How Do You Solve a Problem Like Institutional Racism?: Producing *The Wiz* in Hostile Territory." *Theatre/Practice: The Online Journal of the Practice/Production Symposium of the Mid America Theatre Conference* 7 (2018), http://www.theatrepractice.us/volume7.html, accessed May 20, 2022.

Gibson, Marion. *Witchcraft Myths in American Culture*. New York: Routledge, 2007.

Gilman, Todd S. "'Aunt Em: Hate You! Hate Kansas! Taking the Dog. Dorothy': Conscious and Unconscious Desire in The Wizard of Oz." In *L. Frank Baum's World of Oz: A Classic Series at 100*, edited by Suzanne Rahn, 127–145. Lanham MD: Scarecrow Press: 2003.

Greenwood, Steven. "'Say There's No Future': The Queer Potential of *Wicked*'s Fiyero." *Studies in Musical Theatre* 12, no 3 (2008): 305–317.

Gordon, Robert, and Olaf Jubin. "'Telling the Tale': Adaptation as Interpretation." *Studies in Musical Theatre* 9, no. 1 (2015): 3–11.

Griffin, Sean. *Free and Easy? A Defining History of the American Film Musical Genre.* Hoboken, NJ: Wiley, 2018.

Gubar, Marah. "Entertaining Children of All Ages: Nineteenth-Century Popular Theater as Children's Theater." *American Quarterly* 66, no. 1 (March 24, 2014): 1–34.

Gubar, Marah. "The Hermeneutics of Recuperation: What a Kinship-Model Approach to Children's Agency Could Do for Children's Literature and Childhood Studies." *Jeunesse: Young People, Texts, Cultures* 8, no. 1 (August 31, 2016): 291–310.

Gubar, Marah. "*Peter Pan* as Children's Theatre: The Issue of Audience." In *The Oxford Handbook of Children's Literature*, edited by Julia Mickenberg and Lynne Vallone, 475–496. New York: Oxford University Press, 2011.

Gubar, Marah. "Who Watched *The Children's Pinafore*? Age Transvestism on the Nineteenth-Century Stage." *Victorian Studies* 54, no. 3 (2012): 410–426.

Hammonds, Rebecca K. "(Un)Limited: The Influence of Mentorship and Father–Daughter Relationships on Elphaba's Heroine Journey in *Wicked*." *Theatre History Studies* 40 (2021): 157–171.

Harmetz, Aljean. *The Making of "The Wizard of Oz."* New York: Alfred A. Knopf, 1977.

Harris, Neil. *Humbug: The Art of P. T. Barnum*. Chicago: University of Chicago Press, 1981.

Hearn, Michael Patrick. *The Annotated "Wizard of Oz": Centennial Edition*, New York and London: Norton, 2000.

Herzog, Amy. *Dreams of Difference, Songs of the Same: The Musical Moment in Film.* Minneapolis: University of Minnesota Press, 2010.

Hollis, Tim. *The Land of Oz.* Charleston, SC: Arcadia Publishing, 2016.

Hutcheon, Linda. *A Theory of Adaptation.* Routledge, 2012.

Johnson, Jake. *Mormons, Musical Theater, and Belonging in America.* Urbana: University of Illinois Press, 2019.

Johnson, Jake. *Lying in the Middle: Musical Theater and Belief at the Heart of America.* Urbana: University of Illinois Press, 2021.

Kearney, Mary Celeste. "Sparkle: Luminosity and Post–Girl Power Media." *Continuum* 29, no. 2 (2015): 263–273.

Kelleter, Frank. "'Toto, I Think We're in Oz Again' (and Again and Again): Remakes and Popular Seriality." In *Film Remakes, Adaptations and Fan Productions*, edited by Kathleen Loock and Constantine Verevis, 19–44. New York: Palgrave, 2012.

Kidd, Kenneth B. *Freud in Oz: At the Intersections of Psychoanalysis and Children's Literature.* Minneapolis: University of Minnesota Press, 2011.

Kirle, Bruce. *Unfinished Show Business: Broadway Musicals as Works-in-Process.* Carbondale: Southern Illinois University Press, 2005.

Knapp, Raymond. *The American Musical and the Formation of National Identity*, Princeton NJ: Princeton University Press, 2005.

Knapp, Raymond. *The American Musical and the Performance of Personal Identity.* Princeton, NJ: Princeton University Press, 2006.

Laird, Paul R. *"Wicked": A Musical Biography.* Lanham, MD: Scarecrow Press, 2011.

Langbauer, Laurie. "Off to See the Wizard Again and Again." In *Seriality and Texts for Young People: The Compulsion to Repeat*, edited by Mavis Reimer, Nyala Ali, Deanna England, and Melanie Dennis Unrau, 34–56. London: Palgrave Macmillan, 2014.

Langley, Noel, Florence Ryerson, and Edgar Allan Woolf. *"The Wizard of Oz": The Screenplay.* Edited by Michael Patrick Hearn. New York: Delta, 1989.

Leach, William R. *Land of Desire: Merchants, Power, and the Rise of a New American Culture*. New York: Knopf Doubleday Publishing Group, 2011.

Leigh, Mary K. "The 'Wonderful' Wizard of Oz and Other Lies: A Study of Inauthenticity in *Wicked: A New Musical*." In *The Universe of Oz: Essays on Baum's Series and Its Progeny*, edited by Kevin K. Durand and Mary K. Leigh, 147–157. Jefferson, NC, and London: McFarland, 2010.

Lesuma, Caryn Kunz. "Domesticating Dorothy: Toto's Role in Constructing Childhood in *The Wizard of Oz* and Its Retellings." In *Childhood and Pethood in Literature and Culture: New Perspectives in Childhood Studies and Animals Studies*, edited by Anna Feuerstein and Carmen Nolte-Odhiambo, 124–137. New York: Routledge, 2017.

Leve, James, and Donelle Ruwe, eds. *Children, Childhood, and Musical Theater*. New York: Routledge, 2020.

Lodge, Mary Jo, and Paul R. Laird, eds. *Dueling Grounds: Revolution and Revelation in the Musical "Hamilton."* New York: Oxford University Press, 2021.

MacDonald, Laura, and Myrte Halman. "Geen Grenzen Meer: An American Musical's Unlimited Border Crossing." *Theatre Research International* 39, no. 3 (2014): 198–216.

MacDonnell, Francis. "'The Emerald City Was the New Deal': EY Harburg and *The Wonderful Wizard of Oz*." *Journal of American Culture* 13, no. 4 (1990): 71–75.

MacKenzie, Annah E. "From Screen to Shining Screen: *The Wizard of Oz* in the Age of Mechanical Reproduction." In *The Fantastic Made Visible: Essays on the Adaptation of Science Fiction and Fantasy from Page to Screen*, edited by Matthew Wilhelm Kapell and Ace G. Pilkington, 175–191. Jefferson, NC: McFarland, 2015.

Maguire, Gregory. *Wicked: The Life and Times of the Wicked Witch of the West*. New York: Harper Collins, 1995.

Martin, Alfred L., Jr. "Blackbusting Hollywood: Racialized Media Reception, Failure, and *The Wiz* as Black Blockbuster." *JCMS: Journal of Cinema and Media Studies* 60, no. 2 (Winter 2021): 56–79.

Massachi, Dina Schiff. "Connecting Baum and Gilman: Matilda Gage and Her Influence on Oz and Herland." *Journal of American Culture* 41, no. 2 (2018): 203–214.

Massachi, Dina Schiff. "Somewhere on Top of a Mountain: A Real Journey to Oz." In *Storybook Worlds Made Real: Essays on the Places Inspired by Children's Narratives*, edited by Kathy Merlock Jackson and Mark I. West, 87–100. Jefferson, NC: McFarland, 2022.

Maultsby, Portia K. "Soul Music: Its Sociological and Political Significance in American Popular Culture." *Journal of Popular Culture* 17, no. 2 (1983): 51–60.

Maultsby, Portia K. "Soul." In *African American Music: An Introduction*, edited by Mellonee V. Burnim and Portia K. Maultsby, 271–289. New York: Routledge, 2006.

McMillin, Scott. *The Musical as Drama*. Princeton, NJ: Princeton University Press, 2006.

Meeusen, Meghann. "The Difficulty in Deciphering the 'Dreams That You Dare to Dream': Adaptive Dissonance in *Wizard of Oz* Films." *Children's Literature Association Quarterly* 42, no. 2 (2017): 185–204.

Melnick, Jeffrey Paul. *A Right to Sing the Blues: African Americans, Jews, and American Popular Song*. Cambridge, MA: Harvard University Press, 1999.

Meyerson, Harold, and Harburg, Ernie. *Who Put the Rainbow in "The Wizard of Oz"? Yip Harburg, Lyricist*. Ann Arbor: University of Michigan Press, 1993.

Michel, Dee. *Friends of Dorothy: Why Gay Boys and Gay Men Love "The Wizard of Oz."* N.p.: Dark Ink Press, 2018.

Mitchell-Kernan, Claudia. "Signifying, Loud-Talking and Marking." In *Signifyin(g), Sanctifyin', and Slam Dunking: A Reader in African American Expressive Culture*, edited by Gena Dagel Caponi, 309–330. Amherst: University of Massachusetts Press, 1999.

Miller, D. A. *Place for Us [Essay on the Broadway Musical]*. Cambridge, MA: Harvard University Press, 1998.

Mira, Alberto. *The Pop Musical: Sweat, Tears, and Tarnished Utopias*. New York: Columbia University Press, 2021.

Moseley, Rachel. "Glamorous Witchcraft: Gender and Magic in Teen Film and Television." *Screen* 43, no. 4 (2002): 403–422.

Most, Andrea. *Making Americans: Jews and the Broadway Musical*. Cambridge MA: Harvard University Press, 2004.

Nathanson, Paul. *Over the Rainbow: "The Wizard of Oz" as a Secular Myth of America*. Albany, NY: SUNY Press, 1991.

Neal, Mark Anthony. *Soul Babies: Black Popular Culture and the Post-Soul Aesthetic*. New York: Routledge, 2013.

Newell, Kate. *Expanding Adaptation Networks: From Illustration to Novelization*. London: Palgrave, 2017.

Nodelman, Perry. *The Hidden Adult: Defining Children's Literature*. Baltimore: Johns Hopkins University Press, 2008.

Oja, Carol J. "*West Side Story* and *The Music Man*: Whiteness, Immigration, and Race in the US during the Late 1950s." *Studies in Musical Theatre* 3, no. 1 (August 2009): 13–30.

O'Connell, Sam. "*The Wiz* and the African Diaspora Musical: Rethinking the Research Questions in Black Musical Historiography." In *The Routledge Companion to African American Theatre and Performance*, edited by Kathy A. Perkins, Sandra L. Richards, Renee Alexander Craft, and Thomas DeFrantz, 83–87. New York: Routledge, 2019.

Paige, Linda Rohrer. "Wearing the Red Shoes: Dorothy and the Power of the Female Imagination in *The Wizard of Oz*." *Journal of Popular Film and Television* 23, no. 4 (1996): 146–153.

Paul, David C. "Race and the Legacy of the World's Columbian Exposition in American Popular Theater from the Gilded Age to *Show Boat* (1927)." *American Music* 39, no. 3 (2021): 325–364.

Pecknold, Diane. "'These Stupid Little Sounds in Her Voice': Valuing and Vilifying the New Girl Voice." In *Voicing Girlhood in Popular Music: Performance, Authority, Authenticity*, edited by Jacqueline Warwick and Allison Adrian, 77–98. New York: Routledge, 2016.

Platte, Nathan. "Nostalgia, the Silent Cinema, and the Art of Quotation in Herbert Stothart's Score for *The Wizard of Oz* (1939)." *Journal of Film Music* 4, no. 1 (2011): 45–64.

Platte, Nathan. "Underscore as Special Effect in *The Wizard of Oz*." In *Adapting "The Wizard of Oz": From Baum to MGM and Beyond*, edited by Danielle Birkett and Dominic McHugh, 79–102. New York: Oxford University Press, 2019.

Poehler, Amy. *Yes Please*. New York: William Morrow, 2018. Kindle edition.

Pugh, Tison. *Innocence, Heterosexuality, and the Queerness of Children's Literature*. New York: Routledge, 2010.

Raab, Doris "From Book to Broadway: Elphaba's Gender Ambiguity and Her Journey into Heteronormativity in *Wicked*." *Studies in Musical Theatre* 5, no. 3 (2011), 245–256.

Rahn, Suzanne, ed. *L. Frank Baum's World of Oz: A Classic Series at 100*. Lanham, MD: Scarecrow Press, 2003.

Rahn, Suzanne. *"The Wizard of Oz": Shaping an Imaginary World*. New York: Twayne Publishers, 1998.

Ramsey, Guthrie P. *Race Music: Black Cultures from Bebop to Hip-Hop*. Berkeley: University of California Press, 2003.

Rebellato, Dan. *Theatre and Globalization*. New York: Palgrave Macmillan, 2009.

Riis, Thomas L. *Just before Jazz: Black Musical Theater in New York, 1890–1915*. Washington, DC: Smithsonian Institution Press, 1989.

Riley, Michael O. *Oz and Beyond: The Fantasy World of L. Frank Baum*. Lawrence: University Press of Kansas, 1998.

Roach, Joseph. *Cities of the Dead: Circum-Atlantic Performance*. New York: Columbia University Press, 1996.

Rodger, Gillian M. *Just One of the Boys: Female-to-Male Cross-Dressing on the American Variety Stage*. Champaign: University of Illinois Press, 2018.

Rodman, Ronald. "'There's No Place Like Home': Tonal Closure and Design in *The Wizard of Oz*." *Indiana Theory Review* 19 (1998): 125–143.

Rogers, Bradley. *The Song Is You: Musical Theatre and the Politics of Bursting into Song and Dance*. Iowa City: University of Iowa Press, 2020.

Rogers, Katharine M. *L. Frank Baum: Creator of Oz: A Biography*. New York: St. Martin's Press, 2002.

Rudy, Jill Terry. "Musicals." In *The Routledge Companion to Media and Fairy-Tale Cultures*. Edited by Pauline Greenhill, Jill Terry Rudy, Naomi Hamer, and Lauren Bosc, 556–564. New York: Routledge, 2018.

Rush, Adam. "Recycled Culture: The Significance of Intertextuality in Twenty-First Century Musical Theatre." PhD diss., University of Lincoln, 2017.

Rushdie, Salman. *The Wizard of Oz*. London: British Film Institute, 1992.

Salter, Destiny. "'Doomed as Cartoons Forever': Subjection and Liberation in Sidney Lumet's *The Wiz*." *Studies in Musical Theatre* 15, no 2 (2021): 133–148.

Sammond, Nicholas. *Birth of an Industry: Blackface Minstrelsy and the Rise of American Animation*. Durham, NC: Duke University Press, 2015.

Savran, David. *A Queer Sort of Materialism: Recontextualizing American Theater*. Ann Arbor: University of Michigan Press, 2003.

Scarfone, Jay, and William Stillman. *The Road to Oz: The Evolution, Creation, and Legacy of a Motion Picture Masterpiece*. Guilford, CT: Rowman and Littlefield, 2019.

Scott, Jesse. "The Black Interior: Reparations and African American Masculinity in *The Wiz*." In *Pimps, Wimps, Studs, Thugs, and Gentlemen: Essays on Media Images of Masculinity*, edited by Elwood Watson, Kindle edition, chapter 4, location 1000. Jefferson, NC: McFarland, 2009.

Smith, Victoria Ford. *Between Generations: Collaborative Authorship in the Golden Age of Children's Literature*. Jackson: University of Mississippi Press, 2017.

Somerville, Siobhan B. *Queering the Color Line: Race and the Invention of Homosexuality in American Culture*. Durham, NC: Duke University Press, 2000.

Sternfeld, Jessica. *The Megamusical*. Bloomington: Indiana University Press, 2006.

Stilwell, Robynn. "Listen to the Mockingjay: Voice, Identity, and Agency in *The Hunger Games* Trilogy." In *Voicing Girlhood in Popular Music: Performance, Authority, Authenticity*, edited by Jacqueline Warwick and Allison Adrian, 258–279. New York: Routledge, 2016.

Stockton, Kathryn Bond. *The Queer Child or Growing Sideways in the Twentieth Century*. Durham, NC: Duke University Press, 2009.

Stone, Fred. *Rolling Stone*. New York: McGraw-Hill, 1945.

Sutton-Smith, Brian. *The Ambiguity of Play*. Cambridge, MA: Harvard University Press, 2009.

Swartz, Mark Evan. *Oz before the Rainbow: L. Frank Baum's "The Wonderful Wizard of Oz" on Stage and Screen to 1939*. Baltimore and London: Johns Hopkins University Press, 2000.

Symonds, Dominic, and Millie Taylor. *Gestures of Music Theater: The Performativity of Song and Dance*. New York: Oxford University Press, 2014.

Tatar, Maria. "Why Fairy Tales Matter: The Performative and the Transformative." *Western Folklore* 69, no. 1 (2010): 55–64.

Taussig, Michael. "Viscerality, Faith, and Skepticism: Another Theory of Magic." *HAU: Journal of Ethnographic Theory* 6, no. 3 (December 31, 2016): 453–483.

Taylor, Diana. *The Archive and the Repertoire: Performing Cultural Memory in the Americas*. Durham, NC: Duke University Press, 2003.

Trites, Roberta Seelinger. *Disturbing the Universe: Power and Repression in Adolescent Literature*. Iowa City: University of Iowa Press, 1998.

Vallone, Lynne. *Big and Small: A Cultural History of Extraordinary Bodies*. New Haven, CT: Yale University Press, 2017.

Vallone, Lynne. "The Place of Girls in the Traditions of Minstrelsy and Recitation." *International Research in Children's Literature* 10, no. 1 (2017): 39–58.

Wagenknecht, Edward. *Utopia Americana*. Seattle, WA: Folcroft Press, 1929.

Wald, Gayle. "The Art of Yearning." In *Voicing Girlhood in Popular Music: Performance, Authority, Authenticity*, edited by Jacqueline Warwick and Allison Adrian, 281–285. New York: Routledge, 2016.

Warwick, Jacqueline. "Urchins and Angels: Little Orphan Annie and Clichés of Child Singers." In *Gender, Age and Musical Creativity*, edited by Catherine Haworth and Lisa Colton, 129–140. New York: Taylor and Francis, 2016.

Warwick, Jacqueline. "You Can't Win Child, but You Can't Get Out of the Game: Michael Jackson's Transition from Child Star to Superstar." *Popular Music and Society* 35 (2012), 241–259.

Watson, Keri. "'With a Smile and a Song': Representations of People with Dwarfism in 1930s Cinema." *Journal of Literary and Cultural Disability Studies* 14, no 2 (2020): 137–153.

Whitesell, Lloyd. *Wonderful Design: Glamour in the Hollywood Musical*. New York: Oxford University Press, 2018.

Whitfield, Sarah. *Reframing the Musical: Race, Culture and Identity*. London: Macmillan, 2019.

Williams, Rhonda "*The Wiz*: American Culture at Its Best." In *The Universe of Oz: Essays on Baum's Series and Its Progeny*, edited by Kevin Durand and Mary K. Leigh, 191–199. Jefferson, NC: McFarland, 2010.

Wolf, Stacy. *Beyond Broadway: The Pleasure and Promise of Musical Theatre across America*. New York: Oxford University Press, 2019.

Wolf, Stacy. *Changed for Good: A Feminist History of the Broadway Musical*. New York: Oxford University Press, 2011.

Wolf, Stacy. *A Problem like Maria: Gender and Sexuality in the American Musical*. Ann Arbor: University of Michigan Press, 2002.

Woll, Allen. *Black Musical Theatre from Coontown to Dreamgirls*. Baton Rouge: Louisiana State University Press, 1989.

Wollman, Elizabeth L. *The Theater Will Rock: A History of the Rock Musical, from "Hair" to "Hedwig."* Ann Arbor: University of Michigan Press, 2009.

Zank, Ronald. "'Come Out, Come Out, Wherever You Are': How Tina Landau's *1969* Stages a Queer Reading of *The Wizard of Oz*." In *The Universe of Oz: Essays on Baum's Series and Its Progeny*, edited by Kevin K. Durand and Mary K. Leigh, 61–76. Jefferson, NC: McFarland, 2010.

Zipes, Jack. *Fairy Tale as Myth/Myth as Fairy Tale*. Lexington: University Press of Kentucky, 1994.

Index

For the benefit of digital users, indexed terms that span two pages (e.g., 52–53) may, on occasion, appear on only one of those pages.
Figures are indicated by *f* following the page number.